MADE YOU LOOK

HOW TO USE BRAIN SCIENCE TO ATTRACT ATTENTION AND PERSUADE OTHERS

CARMEN SIMON, PHD

NEW YORK   CHICAGO   SAN FRANCISCO   ATHENS   LONDON
MADRID   MEXICO CITY   MILAN   NEW DELHI
SINGAPORE   SYDNEY   TORONTO

1 2 3 4 5 6 7 8 9   DSS   29 28 27 26 25 24

ISBN 978-1-265-12865-4
MHID   1-265-12865-0

e-ISBN 978-1-265-13160-9
e-MHID   1-265-13160-0

McGraw Hill books are available at special quantity discounts to use as premiums and sales promotions or for use in corporate training programs. To contact a representative, please visit the Contact Us pages at www.mhprofessional.com.

McGraw Hill is committed to making our products accessible to all learners. To learn more about the available support and accommodations we offer, please contact us at accessibility@mheducation.com. We also participate in the Access Text Network (www.accesstext.org), and ATN members may submit requests through ATN.

To you—for paying attention

CONTENTS

INTRODUCTION   3

Quadrant I
Automatic Triggers

CHAPTER 1
Priming the Brain for Attention   25

CHAPTER 2
Embodied Cognition
Setting the Mind in Motion   49

CHAPTER 3
The Right Amount of Wrong
Handling Provocative Content   69

Quadrant II
Guided Action

CHAPTER 4
The Psychology of Boredom
Engaging the Brain on a Level Beyond Flash   99

CHAPTER 5
**Give Them Something
to Think About**   119

CHAPTER 6
Mastering Metaphors   139

Quadrant III
Introspection

CHAPTER 7
Mind Wandering
Help Them See When They Are Not Looking   167

CHAPTER 8
What Happens Next?
The Neuroscience of Predicting the Future   189

CHAPTER 9
Transitions
Help Them See Your Message
When You Aren't There   205

Quadrant IV
Visual Search

CHAPTER 10
The Decision to Look
Mixing Business with Pleasure   233

CHAPTER 11
Harnessing Complexity   257

CHAPTER 12
**The Risks and Rewards of
Collective Attention**   281

CONCLUSION
**Become a Choreographer
of Attention**   301

CHECKLIST FOR CREATING CONTENT
THAT CAPTURES ATTENTION   313

ACKNOWLEDGMENTS   319

REFERENCES   321

INDEX   333

MADE YOU LOOK

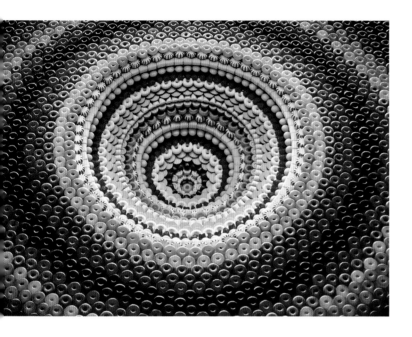

Sam Kaplan's photos make everyday items, like candy, gum, or salt, look monolithic, similar to grand sci-fi movie sets.

INTRODUCTION

Would you use your face cream as dressing on your salad and eat it? Insinuating that this is possible caught my attention when I came across Max Huber's story in a magazine. He was a real rocket scientist, and his story is one of the most intriguing tales in the history of cosmetics, involving not only moisturizer you can eat with dinner but also Huber's out-of-the-ordinary approach to beauty products. Max Huber is the aerospace physicist who crafted the legendary Le Mer moisturizing cream after he suffered extreme burns during an explosion in his lab and fully healed himself with his creation. He would recommend to anyone he met to use La Mer not just as a moisturizing cream for the face but also as a probiotic to mix with food and even as eye drops to soothe irritation. To craft his miracle potion, Huber did not rely on chemistry alone but also on physics.

After his death, when his daughter sold the brand, scientists tried to reproduce the zealously guarded formula but could not quite achieve the same potency. It was only when a scientist from the new team invoked a medium to channel Max (yes, a medium!) that they learned they had skipped two important steps: using light and sound energy to help with the fermentation process and seeding each batch with a culture from the previous batch, like yogurt. Many products La Mer makes today contain ingredients that can be traced back to Huber's original recipe from 1989. With the astonishing mix of science and the paranormal, it was hard for me not to pay attention to that article. Given the abundance of stimuli around you, what has attracted your attention lately and really made you look?

In my case, it was also Sam Kaplan's delightfully clever food photos. Kaplan is an artist who arranges cookies, candies, drinks, and common tools in elegant and hypnotizing geometric displays. Pyramids built out of ham sandwiches, deep pits of snack cakes, or gum sticks arranged with striking architectural symmetry are enveloped in atmospheric lighting. I was delighted when he gave me permission to include a few of his photos on this spread. Do they make you look a little closer?

Barry Rosenthal has also captured my attention. He collects thousands of pieces of trash in cities or at the beach, brings them to his studio, groups them according to color and type, and then photographs them. Shoe soles, plastic objects, glass bottles—arranged in aesthetically arresting ways—transformed into fine works of art. Take a look at his piece titled *Sealife*. It's hard not to stop and stay for a while.

What else draws attention? Moving from the static canvas to live models, it's hard not to look at Johannes Stötter's art. I was thrilled when he agreed to allow us to display one of his photographs on the book cover. He is a master at creating just the right amount of illusion that makes you look and rewards you when you do. Did you initially see both people in his creation?

Edible face cream, monolithic candy structures, aesthetically pleasing trash, live painted models—they all attract attention and make us look. Most recently, AI-generated images, such as "a real hippo sitting on a couch, smoking a cigarette," or "R2-D2 being baptized," and "a man kissing a blue deer," definitely attract attention. But you might ask: How do I compete with these when I try to draw attention to my *business* content? A corporate pitch deck about data analytics, governance issues, or cybersecurity may not have the same attention-grabbing power as the creations of a rocket scientist, gifted artist,

Barry Rosenthal makes us look and confront a paradox of modern life. Can we live together in a world crowded out by our own consumerism?

Persuasion is a function of how **attention-grabbing** you are.

or speedy AI that can remix images and text from millions of data inputs to create unusual outputs. We're here to bridge this significant gap in practical ways. And it's essential to solve the issue of attention to business content because attention paves the way to memory and decision-making, meaning that if your audiences pay attention and remember what you have to say, they are more likely to do what you say. A few years ago, I wrote a book called *Impossible to Ignore*, which addresses the importance of creating memorable content because memory fuels decision-making. This book is a prequel. One of the reasons people don't remember and don't decide to act is because they don't pay attention to begin with.

Before we look at practical guidelines for capturing attention, let's address some problems regarding attention because if we know the problems, then the solutions will be easier to understand and apply. And to solve any problem, we must first define what we're talking about. So, *what is attention?*

The concept might appear easy on the surface. However, the more we learn about the brain, the more we discover that attention is one of the most misleading and misused concepts in cognitive science. This is because we now know that attention is not one coherent set of cognitive or neural operations; there is no such thing as an "attention system" in the brain. We know this because multiple structures come together to account for several attention types, most of which are based on the selectivity that has evolved to enable us to achieve goals and avoid negative outcomes. With this spirit of selectivity in mind, consider these attention types:

- **Focused attention:** Selecting external events for further internal processing

- **Selective attention:** Focusing on *some* stimuli while ignoring others

- **Spatial attention:** Prioritizing the processing of events in the context of a particular location

- **Visual search:** Looking for a target event

- **Divided attention:** Performing multiple tasks at the same time

- **Feature integration:** Selectively integrating information belonging to one event within and across sensory modalities

- **Goal-centered attention:** Prioritizing one goal over others

- **Sustained attention:** Maintaining concentration over time (There is no short attention span for the healthy brain.)

A long (and not exhaustive) list like this might seem like good news because you may think that getting attention is easy when there are so many attention types. Unfortunately, this is not the case. At any given moment, our field of vision captures only a small area in focus. It would

The good news

Healthy people do not have a short attention span.

The bad news

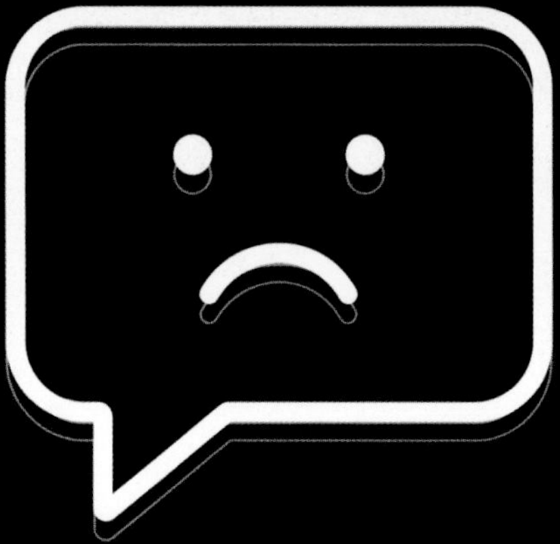

They may be looking at your competition.

not be efficient to pay attention to everything in our environment. Your audiences are not any different. They get only a glimpse of what you offer.

Use Brain Science When Determining How to Get Attention

As a cognitive neuroscientist focused on helping business professionals attract attention and persuade others, I frequently analyze the brain's reaction to corporate content, such as sales and marketing presentations, e-books, training materials, websites, corporate videos, and business apps. I use EEG (electroencephalogram) technology because of its high temporal resolution, meaning we can detect the brain's reaction to a stimulus, such as a Power-Point slide, precisely when it happens. We need this feature because cognitive and emotional or affective processes are fast and fleeting. Processing an idea can occur within tens to hundreds of milliseconds, and it may span a sequence that takes hundreds of milliseconds to a few seconds. You cannot capture what happens in these short time frames by asking people after the fact how they felt or what they thought.

Bypassing self-reports is also helpful because thoughts and emotions are often unconscious, difficult to describe, hard to remember, and in the case of negative experiences, such as tension or embarrassment, susceptible to social desirability, meaning that people might tell you what they think you want to hear. In behavioral research, this often leads to distorted or even invalid self-reports. Incidentally, I asked an AI tool what captures its attention, and it responded: "As an AI language model, I don't have personal preferences or emotions like humans do." Its answer correctly ties attention to preferences and emotions, and even though humans have them, they are often hard or impossible to express. Using neuroscience tools helps us overcome these drawbacks.

When we analyze EEG data, we create colorful brain maps that show brain activity during engagement (or lack thereof) with a specific stimulus. When content creators, such as sales, marketing, or training teams, are able to view an EEG topographic map of a customer who participated in their presentation, it serves as a powerful tool they can use in conjunction with other traditional techniques (e.g., training, big data analysis) to create and deliver attention-grabbing content.

In addition to EEG technology, I use tools such as ECG (electrocardiogram) electrodes, eye-tracking, and GSR (galvanic skin response) devices to detect what happens in the brain and body when people view business content. Unlike other methods of investigating the brain, such as PET or CAT scans or fMRI, this research uses no radiation, does not induce claustrophobic feelings, and can be done in convenient, comfortable, and, most importantly, realistic settings, such as offices and conference rooms.

This is a participant in one of my studies, watching a Zoom call while her EEG, ECG, GSR, and eye activity are recorded. Some people ask me: But isn't the person behaving differently because they are aware of these tools they are wearing? They are initially aware, but this awareness is short-lived, as people habituate quickly, and their focus goes to the tasks they need to complete. We aim to create content that is attention-grabbing, and the experiments are also fairly short. In the future, I am sure that these technologies will be even less intrusive, and research time can extend over an hour.

Biometric sensors

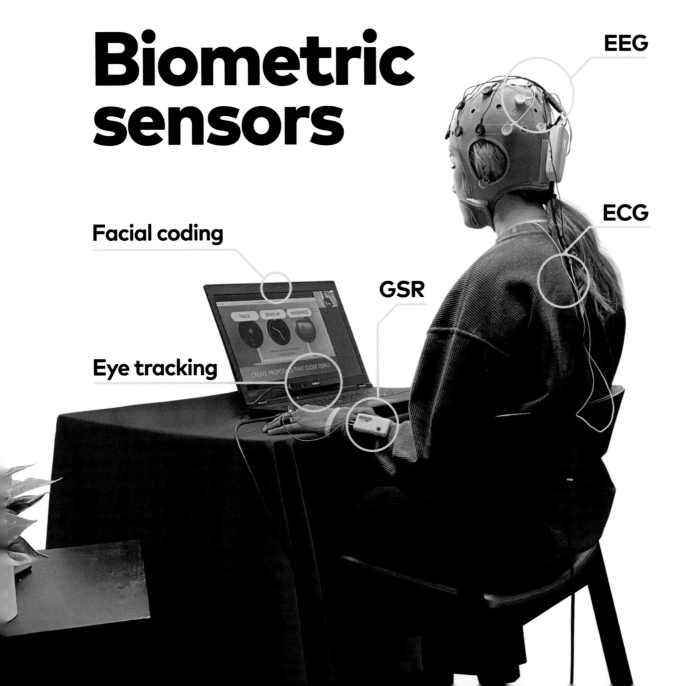

EEG

ECG

Facial coding

GSR

Eye tracking

The variables I study with these biometric tools have practical business consequences. For instance, in terms of cognitive variables, I analyze the following:

- **Attention:** Particularly the type of attention we defined earlier as the process of staying focused across time. This comes from the EEG signal. The eye tracker also gives us a measure of visual attention.

- **Motivation:** Let's define this as the desire to keep working to obtain something.

- **Approach/withdrawal:** This is based on the EEG signal and reveals the emotional response to positive or negative stimuli.

- **Working memory (cognitive workload):** The storing and manipulation of information in short-term memory until the completion of a cognitive task.

- **Fatigue:** A decrease in alertness that can impair efficiency, performance, and memory retrieval.

I also monitor affective variables, such as valence, which is an emotional state within a pleasure-displeasure continuum that ranges from positive to negative. Valence refers to whether people like or dislike what they view.

And I also record participants' arousal, which means their general level of alertness and wakefulness, ranging from calm to very intense.

Speaking of attention in specific, I am constantly humbled by how much the brain does *not* see in a business setting. For example, imagine you're sharing a series of slides with an audience. In many instances, I notice that when people view a presentation, especially in a virtual setting, they direct 10 to 12 percent of their attention to the presenter and about 60 percent to the slides. In a face-to-face environment, the presenter receives 11 to 21 percent of attention, and slides or other items in the environment receive 17 to 30 percent of attention. So, in both scenarios, 40 percent of the presentation—or even more—is never seen!

The screenshot on the next page was taken during a Zoom call simulated during one of my research projects; it shows a seller and his team sharing with a potential client the merits of their company's platform for managing customer success. The heat map at the top of the screenshot indicates through the more intense red spots that viewers are paying attention mainly to one of the speakers and are barely looking at the information on the slide. As a result, very few participants in the study could remember the four steps to customer success.

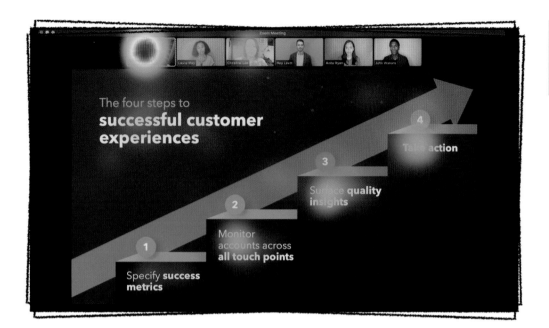

The four steps to
successful customer experiences

4 Take action

3 Surface **quality insights**

2 Monitor accounts across **all touch points**

1 Specify **success metrics**

This heat map is a reminder that people direct only a fraction of their attention to business content at any given moment.

Why Business Audiences Don't Pay Attention

When I conduct neuroscience experiments to discover what attracts people's attention and makes them look, I first ask participants to stare at a beige wall or screen for 30 seconds to take a baseline of their brain when they are not stimulated. Then they view a presentation, video, handout, or app, and I observe what happens in the brain when they should be stimulated. Calculating the difference between baseline and stimulus often reveals a rough reality: We often don't notice a statistically significant difference between the stimulus and baseline. This means that most business content you come across is not much better than staring at a beige wall.

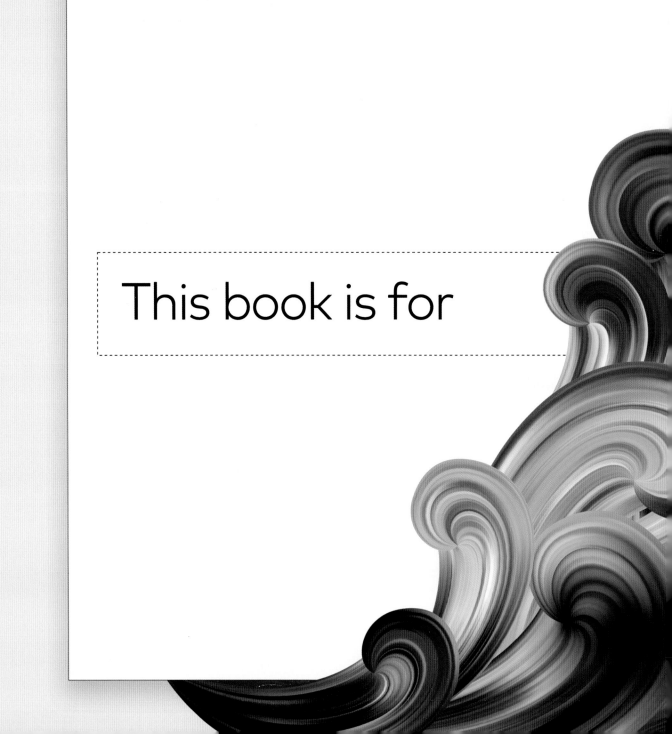

This book is for

those content creators who want to beat

the beige wall

When *content is not that stimulating*, there is another consequence. Take a look at this person who was participating in one of my studies. What you don't know about him is that he is asleep. Not intentionally. The experiment started strong, and he was attentive and engaged. But at some point, drowsiness set in. After hearing the presenter's voice for a while and seeing some pleasant pictures and motion, his brain started drifting away. I always study cognition in the wild, meaning we might set up a pop-up lab at a client's site or conference. This means that *people might be tired* from a night of networking or from a day of dealing with customers or coworkers. I mention this because sometimes you might offer stimulating content, but people are simply sleep-deprived.

Sometimes getting attention is hard because you're dealing with *pickier customers* who demand higher-quality content. They are used to seeing it in their personal lives. With movie franchises such as The Avengers, Star Wars, and Harry Potter grossing billions of dollars at the worldwide box office, and beautifully produced shows on streaming services, today's viewers are used to content that is faster, louder, and literally out of this world. Some business content creators can never compete with media moguls who have the budget and resources to capture and sustain attention.

Getting attention is also difficult because of *abundant choices*, which can also reinforce people's status quo bias. As I write this, I just received an ad presenting 16 options for boiled egg holders. There is one that looks like a flamingo, another like a bear, and another like a bunny. There is a dinosaur looking over his shoulder to make

This is a sleepy participant during one of my neuroscience experiments. He could easily be your client.

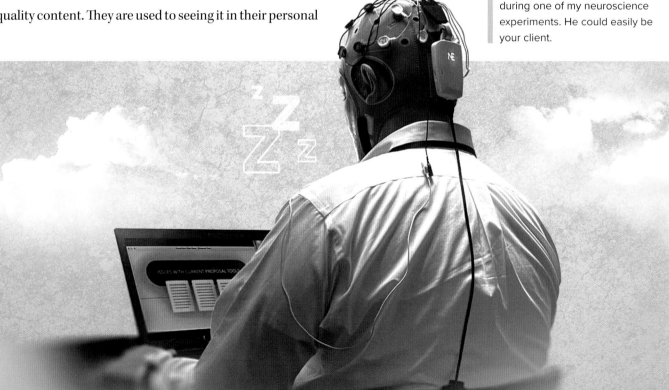

sure the egg is OK, and another is a squirrel eating a nut. I could also get a bearded man to hold the egg, a sheep, and the most obvious, a hen. It's easy to pay attention to the options at first, but after a while, the extra stimulation can lead to boredom and cause the viewer to look away.

Many content creators we work with in our neuroscience research share that it is *challenging to create something truly attention-grabbing*. You *think* you've captured something special. But when you put it all together, it's just striking how similar it looks to other content in the market. I often experience this feeling when I review a large inventory of slides we've created for customers over the years and realize that so many of them could be taken from one client's deck, placed in another's, and no one would know. At times, it's easy to give up and just find comfort in this similarity, sacrificing attention along the way.

Then there are times when you create the most amazing content, yet people don't pay attention because *the ego gets in the way*. CEOs or people in high positions feel they do not need to pay attention to their juniors because attention is often driven by self-gratification, and low-power sources may be perceived as unable to provide suitable rewards. High-power people live in a relatively reward-rich world where they often feel free from social consequences and others' judgments. As a result, they don't easily grant attention.

In addition, many people are designing communication as if they were addressing a perfect brain. We need some neuroscientific humility around this. The brain may be a wondrous thing with billions of neurons tied by a trillion connections, but it's not perfect. In fact, it has a limited vision system, and it often acts in messy, random ways.

So, if we pair an imperfect vision system with people being tired, picky, understimulated or overstimulated, and fueled by their egos, it's no wonder that so much content is missed. However, I am optimistic about addressing these attention problems and achieving a high ROA (return on attention). Here's how.

How Do We Solve the Problem of Attention?

Let's return to the definition of attention. Since there are multiple attention types, one way to avoid being overwhelmed when analyzing attention is to address it from the angle of two questions: *Where* is the brain looking? *Who* initiates the act of looking? The intersection of these variables forms a framework with four quadrants, which is also this book's structure. Knowing where the brain orients its attention (inward or outward) and whether it pays attention on its own or needs a push will offer you a set of practical guidelines you can apply right away to impact all the attention types listed earlier in the chapter.

The *upper-right quadrant* describes automatic triggers that you can use to influence someone's attention. A well-known technique to do this is by using physical properties of stimulation, such as colors, size, sound, or movement. In this quadrant, you will learn guidelines that are either not frequently talked about or techniques further substantiated by recent neuroscience research, offering new perspectives on how to prompt someone's brain to look externally and see your content.

The *lower-right quadrant* points out that one does not always need external stimulation to attract attention and generate engagement as long as there is someone to prompt you where to look internally. This eases the pressure for many communicators who may not have graphic design skills or access to resources to prompt external focus. For this quadrant, I offer practical guidelines on not just attracting attention but sustaining it and guiding the brain inward while providing a satisfying, engaging experience.

On the surface, the *lower-left quadrant* might suggest that communicators have little influence on an audience since people can look inward on their own accord. However, even in this stimulus-independent context, you will learn that it is still possible to influence others' attention and create persuasive content. This segment will also debunk the myth that the brain is inactive when not faced with external stimulation.

The *upper-left quadrant* is an area that communicators must take seriously because the brain constantly engages in outward visual searches on its own. The guidelines in this quadrant are formulated from the perspective of inviting the brain to find and pay attention to what is essential, even when content is complex, and even when people are influenced by others in how they search for what's important.

All the practical guidelines in this book are illustrated with examples from my work or work we've done for business clients. Since PowerPoint is a universal tool, many

External Focus

Visual Search

They orient their attention externally toward something they consider rewarding

Automatic Triggers

You capture their attention with physical properties of an external stimulus (size, color, shape, harmony)

Initiated by the Individual

Initiated by the Environment

Introspection

They orient their own attention internally toward something they consider rewarding

Guided Action

You guide them toward their internal thoughts and prompt them to focus on something rewarding

Internal Focus

examples are based on slides, but the principles apply to other media types as well. Where slides are involved, I included them in a few slide galleries. I've always envisioned the existence of a PowerPoint museum. And why not? There are museums about more bizarre and mundane things than slideware. You can visit the Museum of Ice Cream in New York City. A museum in Marietta, Ohio, invites you to explore the history of the funeral industry. In Massachusetts, you can go to the Museum of Bad Art. In Croatia, you can visit the Museum of Broken Relationships and see the ax a woman used to destroy her ex's furniture when she was jilted. I chose the PowerPoint gallery setup in a few instances because it's a way of exhibiting what works and what doesn't and because it's useful for all of you, modern communicators, to realize you're in charge of what goes into a document. *You*'re the curator of ideas and messages. *You* decide what stays and what goes to get attention.

Admittedly, implementing many of the guidelines in this book will require effort. There will be business content you create that will not capture attention. But that's OK. If you miss an occasion, try again. Your brain learns from what you do repeatedly. Small steps will lead to bigger steps later on. Your ability to grab attention will grow with practice over time.

Remember Barry Rosenthal, the trash-collecting artist? His collections take years to acquire before he attempts to create one photograph, which then takes about a month. His images, while aesthetically pleasing, make the viewer think of deeper issues. His messages attract attention by being multilayered—you can see trash and think "environmental impact," and then Barry reminds us that the trash he collects reveals the choices people make. Many of his collages speak deeply about people's addictions, such as alcohol, drugs, fast food, and smoking. I mention this because it is my hope that as you apply the techniques in this book, you will do more than attract attention: you will reward people for giving it to you, and one of the greatest rewards is deeper meaning and learning about ourselves.

External Focus

Automatic Triggers

You capture their attention
with physical properties
of an external stimulus
(size, color, shape, harmony)

**Initiated by
the Individual**

**Initiated by
the Environment**

Internal Focus

Automatic Triggers

In this quadrant, you will learn how to prompt the brain to pay attention by:

| Getting it in a ready state

| Combining perception and movement

| Offering just the right amount of wrong

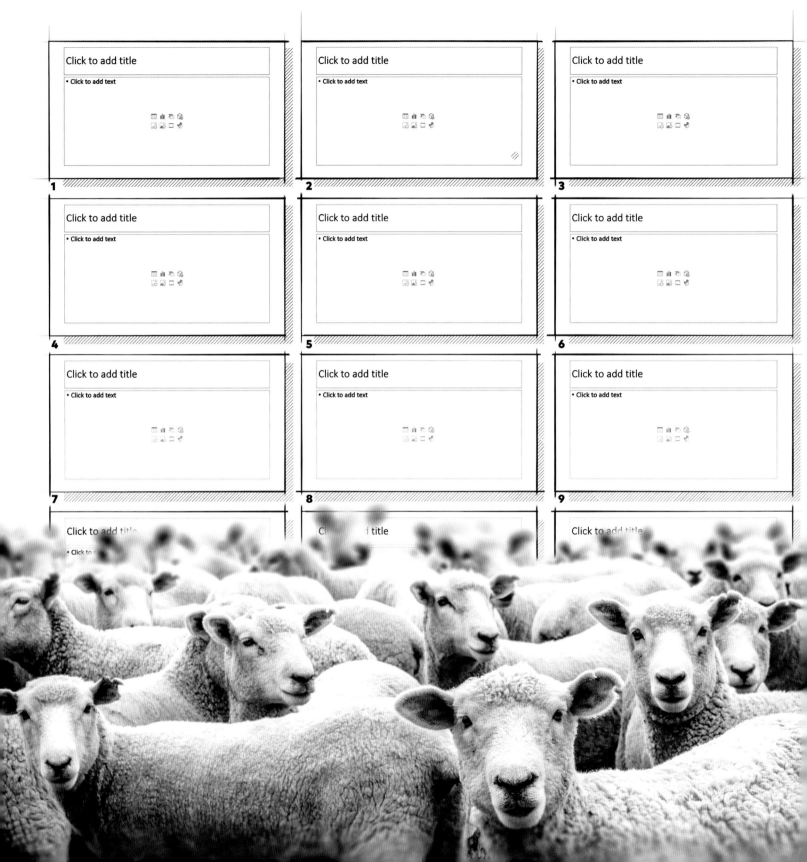

CHAPTER 1

Priming the Brain for Attention

Have you heard of Mark Lynas, the British author and green activist? You might know him for his work on environmental issues. He drew attention a few years back when he revealed his audacious attempt at kidnapping Dolly, the world's first cloned sheep. When Dolly was cloned, Lynas was so ideologically driven that he was willing to break the law to fight against biotechnology.

Mark's kidnapping plan failed because when he and his coconspirators broke into Dolly's shed at the Roslin Institute near Edinburgh, Scotland, they discovered that she was being kept with a lot of other sheep and they could not tell which one was Dolly. He realized at that moment that the Roslin scientists had outsmarted him by hiding Dolly in plain sight. He recalls in his writings: "As any half-competent shepherd can attest, all sheep look more or less the same. Cloned sheep, pretty much by definition, look even more the same."

The story caught my attention because this is what many business communicators do with some of their important messages: hide them in plain sight. The consequences for viewers are obvious: not knowing what to pay attention to and missing what's important.

One strategy to make something noticeable is to differentiate it in some way. After all, a black sheep would stand out among white sheep. But sometimes, the brain is not ready to detect differences. For instance, when people are tired, overwhelmed, distracted, or multitasking, it is possible for them to miss even what you think is significantly distinctive. You may have heard of the classic study in which multitasking students on campus did not notice a nearby clown riding a unicycle. And B2B content is not even as unusual as a clown on a unicycle. Therefore, before you consider attention-grabbing methods like distinctiveness, you must consider a more foundational technique: priming the brain so it is *ready* to pay attention.

Priming means that exposing the brain to one stimulus can influence its response to a subsequent stimulus. For example, if someone showed you the word "REASON" and later asked you to complete the stem REA _ _ _, you would be more likely to offer the solution REASON versus READER or REALITY.

Priming is essential in business content because it can lead to faster and easier understanding of a concept, as well as attention and engagement—all of which are desirable dimensions for business communicators. How do you use priming? Consider these steps, which will help you sequence your content strategically, regardless of format:

Step 1: Look at the components you plan to include in your content (e.g., slides in a presentation, segments in a video or podcast, paragraphs in an e-book, elements in a website, or screens in a mobile app).

Step 2: Identify points your audience must pay attention to. For instance, in a PowerPoint presentation, it might be important for the presenter that the audience pay attention to slides 4, 8, 12, and 18.

Step 3: Include a primer right *before* those important segments so the brain is *ready* to pay attention to what happens next.

I will identify several primer types in a moment. But overall, the advantage you gain from these steps is getting someone's brain in a more heightened state of awareness for what follows.

Priming elements put the brain in a heightened state of attention and engagement. In this example, the presenter wanted to bring attention to slides 4, 8, 12, and 18, so he used more intense slides *right before* those segments.

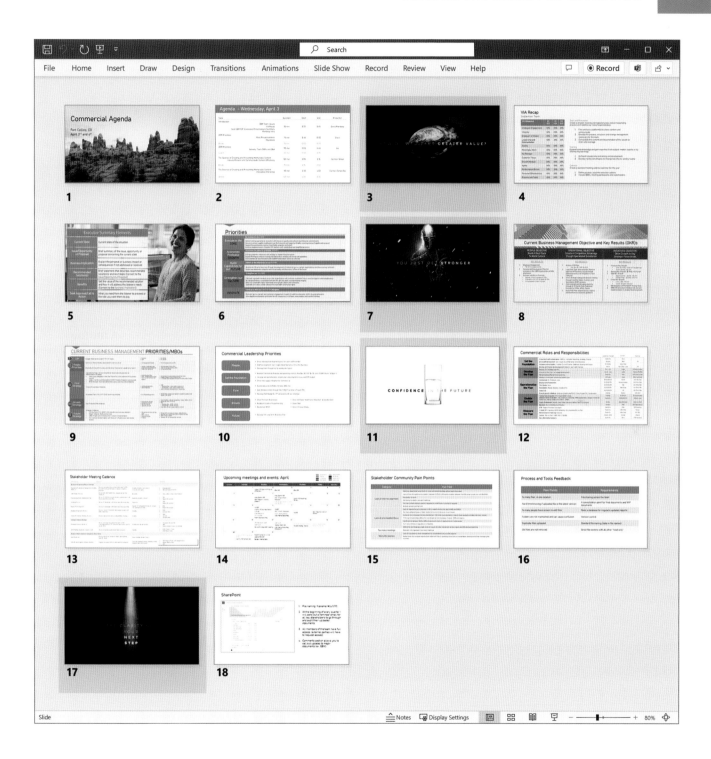

How Corporate Content Ignores Priming

As is often mentioned in jazz circles, there is no such thing as an inherently wrong note. Rather, the subsequent note can redeem or condemn the previous one. The same goes for business content. There is no such thing as a wrong slide or a wrong moment in a conversation; it's what follows that determines if something was wrong. And by "wrong," I mean not getting the attention it deserves. Imagine a typical technical presentation: slide after slide after slide with complex and dry information. None of those slides are bad on their own. But when you put them together, one after another, you get some bad—and often ignorable—content.

Even though priming is highly supported by scientific literature, business content falls short of implementing it. Here are some typical mistakes I notice in business content. Read them first, and then you will learn how you can fix them with proper priming:

- **Treating each component with equal importance.** Most corporate content I see includes components created with equal importance; no one segment serves as a critical point, and most segments look and feel like the next segment.

- **Creating content using the "copy and paste" technique.** When communicators are in a rush, they use existing resources, which saves them time. But this does not help with psychological effectiveness because when you copy and paste individual segments into another sequence, the logical links between them may be lost. If the PowerPoint deck you are referencing uses primers, others may not copy and paste them into a new deck because they may deem them unnecessary.

- **Outsourcing important messages to graphic designers.** Most business content includes a series of abstract conclusions. For instance, you might see messages like "Use streaming analytics to optimize your business processes," "AI unlocks human capabilities," or "Curate personalized experiences at scale." By nature, these are not easy to visualize, especially by a non-expert. If the concept itself is not easy to visualize, priming an abstract concept may be tougher yet, so priming techniques are not even considered.

- **Presenting bland ideas.** Sometimes communicators get the brain primed and pumped using a well-phrased concept or image, only to follow it with something bland and predictable. No matter how good a primer is, it will not rescue a bland idea.

The following two slides both attempt to visualize the concept of "business optimization with streaming analytics," meaning that if you're in an industry that uses IoT (Internet of Things) and monitors assets in real time, you can make or save money. The concept was important to the client to emphasize because it was linked to a solution they were selling. The left slide is superficial because it only visualizes an abstract conclusion ("optimize your business with real-time analytics") through an abstract image. No priming approach can rescue it because it's a bland idea wrapped in clichéd design. We see these types of slides often when subject matter experts don't spend enough time with a design team to outline how they've arrived at their abstract thoughts. The example on the right visualizes *how* they've reached that conclusion. In this case, the image shows data points from software monitoring an oil rig and displays real-time streaming data. The concrete example indicates how the advent of IoT enables a sensor to capture and send information to a database. For instance, if the temperature reading of any sensor reaches a specific number (e.g., 150ºC) in any 15-minute window, someone will be alerted.

This slide on business optimization would have appeared at the beginning of the presentation, most likely around slide 12 or so. But we must ask: What appears before it? If the concept is considered critical, then you must prime the brain to pay attention to it.

The slide to the left visualizes an abstract idea through an abstract design. The slide to the right makes you look more closely because it visualizes an abstract concept through a concrete design.

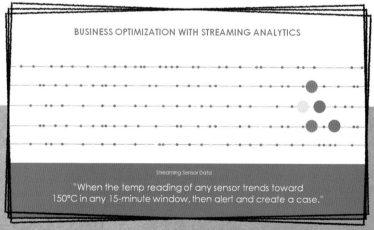

The Four Types of Priming

As you implement the steps we've identified earlier, here are four types of priming you can include in your content: perceptual, semantic, affective, and repetition.

 Perceptual Priming

Let's admit it: Business content, especially B2B content, is often bland. After all, concepts like governance, analytics, accounting, steel accessories, medical equipment, or supply chain processes, while important to society, are not inherently the most exciting topics to discuss. Let's call these topics "beige in a box." When presenting them, you might share charts and diagrams about complex technical architecture or perhaps some bullet points about abstract concepts you know your audience

will relate to and understand. All these segments are necessary, just like a pair of beige pants allows a red sweater to shine. But if beige is important, it will get lost if not primed properly. You will know what I mean when you step into the Beige in a Box Gallery.

One way to get the brain ready to pay attention even to "beige" content is to prime it with elements that impact perception, hence the phrase *perceptual priming*. What are such elements? Even if you're not a designer, it's easy to understand design techniques that influence perception, such as images, text, colors, and shapes often arranged in appealing compositions with high contrast. It is not the purpose of this book to delve deeply into design principles, but I do want to emphasize one perceptual technique that is underutilized in business but can be effective, especially as communication becomes increasingly virtual and digital: texture.

This is an example from one of my presentations where I used the slide on the left, which was more enticing to get the brain ready to pay attention to the slide on the right, which was more complex.

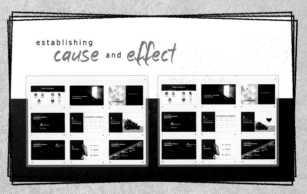

Business content

Full text page

Statistics slide

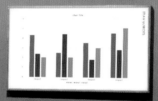

Brochure design   Brochure design   Brochure design

Brochure design   Brochure design   Brochure design

ACTUAL INFORMATION

beige in a box
gallery

Tempt the Brain with Texture

Look around you, and you will likely see something made of metal, glass, wood, leather, or plastic. The perceived visual and physical property of objects is called texture, and you're surrounded by it. Do you ever look at something and imagine what it would feel like to touch it, only to be surprised once you actually do? I was once in a pet café in Seoul, Korea, and had the opportunity to pet a raccoon. His fur looked fluffy and soft from a distance but felt course to the touch. On the flip side, our neighbor has a cat who sneaks into our place for treats and naps. When I first saw his gray fur, I thought it would feel rough, but it is so smooth that it makes me jealous. I wish my hair was as silky!

Evolutionarily speaking, it was important for the brain to develop the ability to detect texture and distinguish between animals, plants, foods, and fabrics. In modern times, texture is important because it can impact your audience's aesthetic evaluation and generate a response. In short, texture attracts attention.

How do our bodies interpret texture? To experience texture, we use our somatosensory system (sense of touch), which is controlled by three types of nerve receptors on our skin. These receptors work in combination with cells and enable us to feel different sensations. They also send signals to the nervous system, and the brain helps us respond. For example, nociceptors allow us to feel pain. Thermoreceptors enable us to detect temperature. And mechanoreceptors help us sense the change in surfaces or the degree of pressure on our skin, such as when we touch something rough or smooth or press the start button in the car.

Can you sense the texture in these business slides?

1

2

3

Imagined texture provides the same characteristics as *physical* texture. In the presentation example to the right, the third slide in the sequence is the one the client considered critical in terms of attention and memory. The content on that slide naturally renders itself into a list of points, as it displays priorities the company is adopting to respond to market trends. If other dull slides had preceded a naturally dull slide like the third one in the sequence, an audience might have found it harder to keep

The bland, yet important list on the third slide is primed with vivid designs and compositions.

paying attention. Priming the bulleted list of priorities in the third slide with two other slides that include vivid images and exciting compositions gets the brain in an attention-ready state. Can you sense the soft, shiny, velvety, wet texture in the previous two slides?

Texture is relatively easy to implement as long as you choose high-resolution images that are magnified to the point where the brain "feels" like it's there. With perceived texture, you can prime the brain in space or across time. Priming in space means pairing texture-filled elements with those that are not within the same "location," such as a slide or page. For example, in a session I was

delivering on connecting movement, environment, and cognition, I spoke about three scenarios that business professionals already use to invite audience movement: customer experience centers, demos, and technologies such as virtual reality (VR), augmented reality (AR), and extended reality (XR). The initial slide included images and text, but none exuded great texture to help the audience really "sense" the concepts I was talking about. So I created a version that included stronger texture, distributed over three slides (priming across time) to enable an audience to sense each one more strongly.

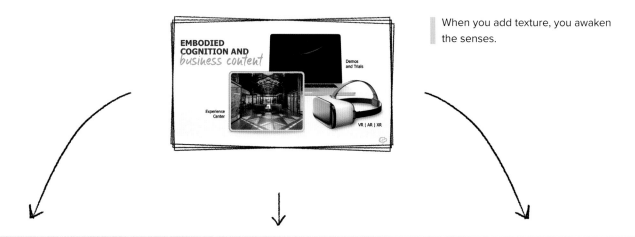

When you add texture, you awaken the senses.

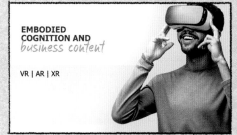

In this client example from a medical presentation, notice the vivid patient picture with a lot of sensory appeal, which gets the brain in an attentive state before displaying the slide with the chart.

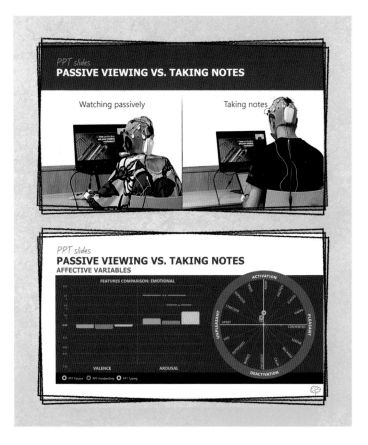

In my own presentations, I often use perceptual priming before chart slides. In this example, I first showed a vivid picture of participants wearing EEG caps in a neuroscience study I had conducted, and then shared the results in a typical chart format. The more vivid and intriguing slides put the brain in an attention-ready state.

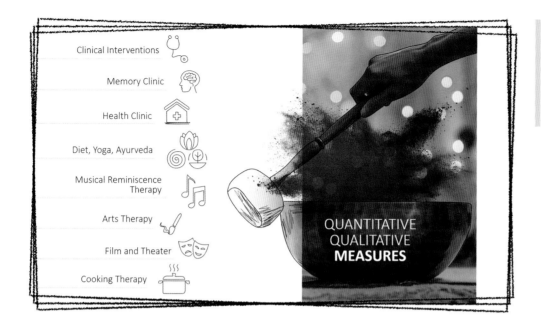

Clinical Interventions

Memory Clinic

Health Clinic

Diet, Yoga, Ayurveda

Musical Reminiscence Therapy

Arts Therapy

Film and Theater

Cooking Therapy

QUANTITATIVE
QUALITATIVE
MEASURES

The contrast between more and less intense texture mimics the experience of cognitive loss. This example is a reminder that if you toy with texture, even its absence can have meaning.

You can use texture and contrast to allude to more subtle ideas. In the presentation example above, the presenter spoke about the importance of creating an institution that provides care for people with dementia. The loss of texture portrayed by moving from the real photo to the hand-drawn illustrations symbolizes the loss of precision and builds the emotion for the need to regain it.

 **Semantic Priming**

If perceptual priming appeals to your audience's senses, conceptual or semantic priming appeals to their cognition, specifically to the *meaning* of the content you share. Semantic priming occurs if your audience recognizes a target stimulus more quickly when it is preceded by a related concept rather than an unrelated concept. For example, if I wanted you to understand the concept "plant" quickly and easily, I can help you do that if I precede it with the word "flower" than with the word "dentist." You could still somewhat get to "plant" from "dentist" by thinking of "implant," but it would take you slightly longer.

Semantic priming works because we store knowledge in our brains through associations. Related concepts such as plant and flower are linked to each other through a shorter path than *plant* and *dentist*. Thinking of one concept that leads to other associated concepts happens automatically and rapidly, in under 400 milliseconds. Why is it useful to appeal to quick associations in business content, especially when we talk about attention? When you make a concept easy and quick to understand, your audience has extra resources to allocate to other concepts.

Consider the following heat map from a study I conducted. During the study, participants were divided into two groups and then paired and asked to watch a sales presentation while wearing EEG, ECG, and eye-tracking devices. The presentation was a sales pitch for a software platform for corporate gift-giving, and because of this theme, we created slides that included concrete examples of corporate gifts. For instance, on one slide, you would see a coffee mug. On another, a gift box that is likely to contain a mug. On the software solution slide, we see another image of coffee mugs. With each visual example, we noted that participants' visual attention was progressively directed *away* from these elements, and focus traveled to other items on the slides. Yet the memory related to corporate gift-giving was accurate and unified among participants. Fifty-six percent of participants remembered the main message we wanted them to remember. The takeaway guideline: when you prime within the same semantic network (in this case, examples of corporate

When the visual theme is concrete and consistent, the brain does not have to exert much effort and can pay attention to additional elements. In this case, we used the coffee mug (either explicitly or implied in the gift box) to create conceptual consistency between the slides. In time, we see less attention to these visuals and more attention to other areas on the slide.

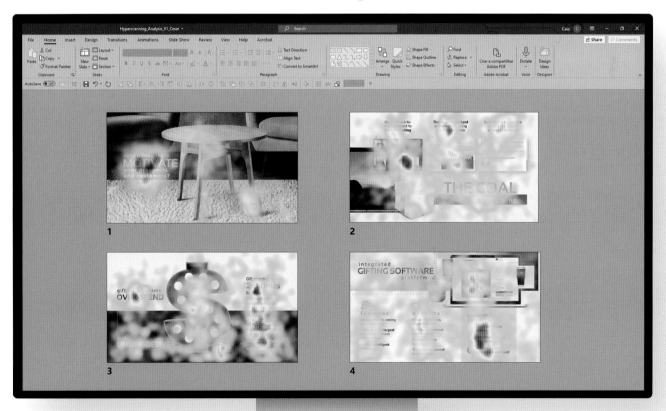

gifts, such as mugs), you can create enough mental space for the brain to focus elsewhere, which impacts not only attention but memory as well.

 Affective Priming

Imagine someone asked you to draw a traditional Asian building and did not prime your brain with any photos. You could go anywhere in your imagination and come up with any illustration you wish. Your rendition might look like the first examples in this collection, resembling traditional Chinese architecture. However, if someone primed you and showed you some crazy-looking, surrealist pictures first, igniting attention and emotion, you are likely to produce more creative drawings like the second set of examples. A neuroscience study was conducted on this very topic, and EEG scans during the primed condition showed the brain becoming active during the creative process. In contrast, in the non-primed condition, the brain was relaxed.

Not Primed

Priming the brain with stronger emotions leads to creativity. This is even easier to do in an age of AI tools that generate creative images, assuming creative prompts like "a medieval Egyptian using a computer" or "Leonardo in Metaverse."

Primed

Why would invoking emotions and priming for creativity matter in business contexts? Getting a client to see your solution embedded in their world often involves creativity on their part. A brain in a creative state is more open to possibilities and change.

What emotions can your content evoke to prime the brain and draw a reaction? First, consider the element of *surprise*. Let's define surprise in contrast to novelty because sometimes people use these terms interchangeably. Novelty is something you have not seen or experienced before. Surprise is something you have seen or experienced before but did not expect.

The brain seeks both for different reasons. Novelty gives us a buzz but requires extra effort. Surprise is unsettling because one of the brain's primary functions is to predict what happens next, and a surprise is a failure to predict. However, the difference between what the brain expects and what happens in real life is how the

This slide includes unexpected (but familiar) elements intended to prepare the brain for what comes after, which is typically more serious and complex content. The workout slide was combined with a story about CrossFit. This program has attracted a lot of members with almost evangelical zeal, especially at a time of loneliness and isolation. Referred to as the Church of CrossFit, the concept, slide, and story primed the brain to learn about the benefits of a membership service called Emblaze.

Offering the brain an unusual perspective puts it in a position of learning and therefore heightened attention.

brain learns. This is why surprises typically attract attention and help build memories. You can create surprise by sharing what is unusual, unreal, ridiculous, funny, or oddly vivid about your content. Notice how you recognize all the elements in the examples on this spread, but some are presented with a twist.

You can also use affective priming by *creating a Eureka moment*, an aha reaction, for your audience. Remember the gift-giving software presentation I mentioned earlier? The only difference between the two presentations included in the EEG study I conducted was the positioning of two multiple-choice questions that

Suspending reality, invoking humor, and appealing to the senses also invoke a sharper focus.

asked viewers whether they knew how much companies overspend on gift-giving campaigns and how much data related to gift-giving goes unmeasured. Group 1 viewed the presentation in which the two questions appeared toward the end after viewers learned some stats and insights about corporate gift-giving. Group 2 watched the same presentation, except that the questions appeared before the data and insights.

We analyzed the gamma frequency in participants' EEG signals in the temporal and parietal areas of the brain; this frequency is associated with a Eureka effect when it appears in these brain regions in certain proportions. We noted that Group 2, who watched the presentation where the questions appeared first, had a higher Eureka effect. The effect occurred during the first multiple-choice question. It was maintained throughout the whole experiment, whereas for Group 1, it appeared with lower intensity toward the end of the presentation. In addition, Group 2 also showed better synchronization for working memory tasks (which implies attention) and stronger motivation to act during the follow-up section of the presentation. Taken together, these results lead to the recommendation to prime the beginning of a presentation or a conversation with a few thought-provoking questions that create a Eureka effect and motivate the audience to act.

Group 2 viewed the presentation that included questions at the beginning and sustained a Eureka effect until its conclusion.

Group 1

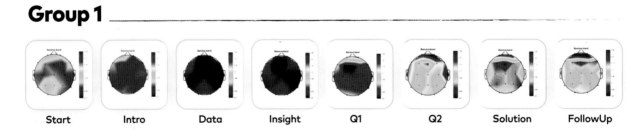

Start   Intro   Data   Insight   Q1   Q2   Solution   FollowUp

Group 2

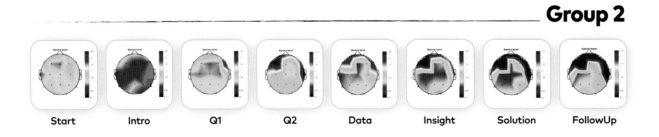

Start   Intro   Q1   Q2   Data   Insight   Solution   FollowUp

Since we're talking about priming with emotion, you might ask: What is better, negative or positive emotion?

In one experiment, scientists showed one group pictures of angry faces and another group pictures of happy faces. Then they asked both groups to evaluate whether they liked specific characters written in Chinese, even though they did not read Chinese. The group that was primed with happy faces liked the Chinese characters more than the group primed with angry faces, even though neither knew what the characters meant. Given this outcome, an important guideline emerges.

Priming your audience with positive pictures or words can activate subsequent positive emotions. This is important to know because it's customary for people to share a problem in persuasive contexts and then present a solution. This means you're priming the brain with something negative and expecting the solution to be perceived positively. This is not to say that you must exclude negative emotions, but if your typical flow includes something negative at first, consider neutralizing the negative by presenting a "wouldn't it be great if" segment, in which you share an ideal but neutral state that alludes to solving the problem. Then associate this ideal state with your solution. For example, after presenting several negative trends, instead of immediately describing your solution, prime the brain with, "It is a great time to be in business because technology is changing for the better. Wouldn't it be great if collaboration were simpler and more reliable? This is what our solution offers."

When you prime with positive affect, you're more likely to gain acceptance and recognition of the value you bring and invite cognitive flexibility, too. If you present to people who are more likely to focus on the details, they will be more inclined to see the bigger picture when you prime them positively. This is true the other way around: if you speak to people who naturally look at the bigger picture, affective priming will lead to stronger perceptual flexibility, enabling them to see more details.

 ## Repetition Priming

If you ever watch a Cirque du Soleil show, you are immediately captivated by the creative sets, colorful costumes, evocative music, and talented acrobats spinning in the air at dizzying speeds, all luring you into a dreamy world of fantasy. According to their website, the company started in 1984 with only 20 artists; now, they have over 1,300 talents of 55 nationalities performing in 250 cities worldwide. They have enchanted over 180 million people, many of whom have seen multiple shows. Their revenue grows even in declining economic times. How has Cirque du Soleil won its loyal audiences? Why do people go and see their shows over and over again?

Cirque du Soleil is successful in part because they have a tried-and-true formula that they *repeat* every show. Production directors and performers know how and what to repeat, so audiences pay attention to what counts, remember the thrill of the shows, and return many times over.

You, too, can use repetition to prime the brain to pay attention quickly and effortlessly. Neuroimaging studies of repetition priming have reliably demonstrated reduced neural activity during exposure to repeated stimuli. When you're exposed to something you've already seen, it takes you less processing power the second time around.

In this presentation for a client, we introduced a fun and positive element at the beginning of a sequence that would otherwise have been morose. The presentation was about company layoffs. In the introduction, you see the orange "picking itself up." The repeated orange element at the end refreshes attention toward a positive outlook.

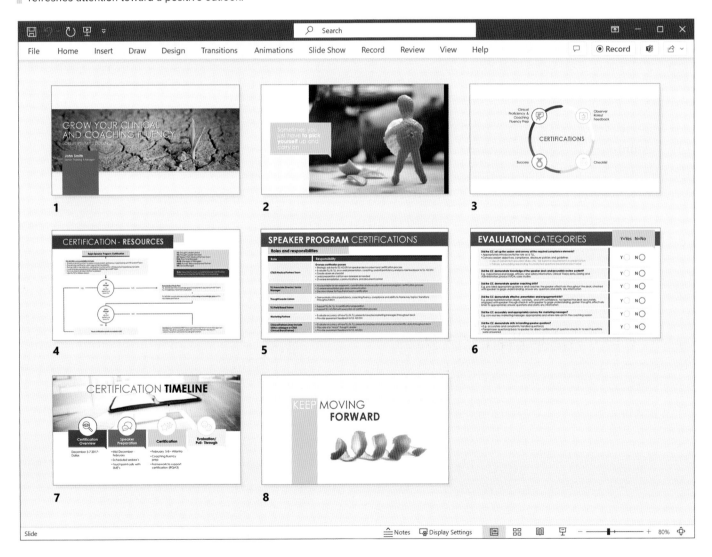

Your brain is more efficient. This works for visual and auditory stimulation, even if some intervening items are placed between the initial and subsequent presentations.

Despite the numerous benefits of repetition, I notice that business practitioners are reticent to repeat a message. I suspect this is because they are afraid of being perceived as:

1. Redundant and therefore boring

2. Remedial, looking down on the audience

3. Sharing unnecessary elements

To counteract these viewpoints, keep in mind that only *you* know you're repeating the same message. Your audience only realizes redundancy for simplistic messages repeated at intervals shorter than a minute. Most business content we come across, especially in B2B fields, is highly complex and takes a while to explain. For example, in a 20-minute presentation I tested, it took repeating the main message six times for an audience to remember a pattern we wanted them to remember. One of the experimental groups exposed to a message repeated 12 times had even more precise memories of the main message. And in another group that saw the main message repeated 24 times in 20 minutes, no one complained of too much repetition! This is because it takes a lot of exposure for someone to even notice the frequent repetition of an essential message in a complex presentation, and once they do, they understand it more quickly and easily.

You've heard the adage, "Tell them what you're going to tell them, then tell them, then tell them what you've told them." Known as the T3 principle, this adage has been popularized since Aristotle, embraced by Dale Carnegie, and quoted by millions of business presenters around the globe to the point where it has practically become a universally accepted law.

I'm sorry to report that it does not work. In a neuroscience study I conducted, I asked four groups to watch a five-minute sales presentation related to a software platform. Group A watched a presentation that mimicked a fluid conversation with no clear main message. Group B saw the same presentation, but this time, the introduction included an agenda slide, which clarified the main message. The presentation for Group C had an agenda slide and summary slide—the proverbial T3 construction—while the presentation for Group D repeated the main message four times.

The following chart indicates the cognitive variables for the entire presentation for all four groups. Group D was the most effective, showing a good balance between attention, working memory (which is a form of cognitive workload) and fatigue. The fluid presentation led to the highest fatigue (Group A), whereas the condition with the repeated main message led to the lowest fatigue (Group D). This difference between groups was found to be statistically significant, confirming other research that indicated that one of the benefits of repetition priming is less fatigue. Note that Group C has the lowest level of attention and highest level of cognitive workload, meaning that an agenda and summary slide were insufficient in sustaining attention and clarifying what was essential. You will learn more about the importance of repetition and challenging the T3 principle in the third quadrant of this book.

In this chapter, we have considered priming techniques that enable you to use one stimulus to impact how the next stimulus is processed by your target audience. Next time you craft any business content, consider that all the components in your content are linked, whether they are slides in a deck, segments in a video, or paragraphs in copy. And each segment can influence how the next segment is perceived. So, select some points that are important to you that your clients should remember, and insert a strong primer right *before* those. As a result, you will get extra attention and engagement, which will impact not only memory but also decisions. In short, you will stop hiding your important messages in plain sight.

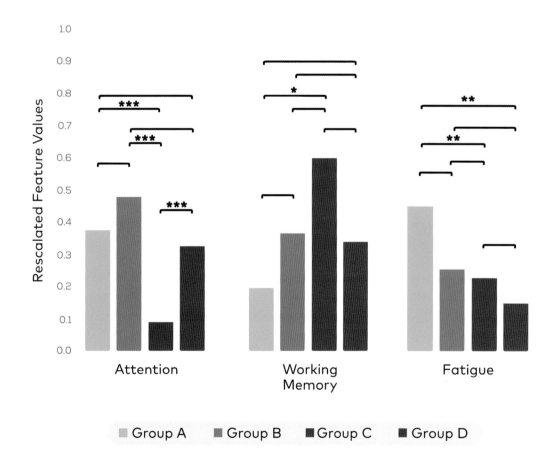

Bar plot of values for each group's three cognitive features: attention, working memory, and fatigue.

CHAPTER 2

Embodied Cognition

Setting the Mind in Motion

The only reason we have a brain is so we can move. This reliance on motion has evolutionary roots; in the ongoing battle for survival among predators and prey, the organisms with the ability to explore the environment had access to resources and could improve their biological fitness. So we are built to move, first and foremost. It's been argued that all other processes, such as thinking, attention, emotions, and consciousness, give us more refined ways of gathering inputs and generating appropriate outputs, such as knowing which way to move. The current view in cognitive science is that the brain, body, and environment contribute to how we think and make decisions. This perspective, called *embodied cognition*, has been gaining traction and has put the classic cognitivist view of how the brain works under pressure.

What did this classic cognitivist view claim? If you've watched the first Matrix movie, you may remember a scene in which Trinity, the heroine, needs to fly a helicopter to rescue her team, but when asked if she knows how, she says, "Not yet." Seconds later, though, a program is downloaded into her brain, and she can fly the helicopter like a pro. This scene portrays the classic view that cognitive science has held dear for many decades: comparing the brain with a computer. If you want to change how a computer behaves, you install a program—a set of instructions or "rules"—and get the appropriate output. If brains are like computers, then cognition is seen as the process that helps us represent the world by manipulating mental representations and rules. Learning a new activity, such as becoming a pilot, simply means internalizing a correct set of rules. This view seems sensible; we

Click to add title

Click to add subtitle

can all relate to following internalized instructions when cooking a meal, driving, or using proper grammar.

Newer and abundant research findings in cognitive science, psychology, neuroscience, linguistics, and computer science define cognition as the interaction between the brain, body, and environment. This interaction impacts perception and thinking, which subsequently impacts memory and comprehension. In short, cognition is based not just on the mind but also on the body—hence the term *embodied cognition*. There is ample evidence for this current view that links the mind and the body. For instance, reading comprehension improves when "acting out" messages and using movement to associate words with images and objects. Likewise, when we talk about language control, we find it associated with motor control (e.g., saying the word "kick" activates the motor cortex). Scientists also observe correlations between gestures and getting good at math and physics. For example, neuroimaging studies show that an abstract construct such as "frequency" activates postcentral and parietal brain regions that are also active when performing rhythmic movements. Studies have also linked interacting touch screens, such as kiosk environments, with a deeper understanding of the content on those screens.

Embodied cognition still accounts for mental representations. The brain engages in a bidirectional iterative process between sensorimotor input and conceptual knowledge. So we predict what sensory and bodily knowledge we will encounter, and then we refine those predictions using existing knowledge and feedback. With this view in mind, abstract concepts depend not only on the verbal system but are grounded in various modal systems, such as perception, action or events, emotion, and introspection.

Why Is Embodied Cognition Important in Business?

By interacting with the environment, we likely convey information or content directly to the centers for cognition through bodily routes, which forms a foundation for a better understanding of abstract concepts. It is also possible that by involving the body and the environment, we lighten our cognitive load, freeing up our brains to do their work better and faster. When the body and environment are involved, we are likely encoding information through different modalities and getting a more direct grip on what's relevant. Consider the illustration on this spread. I was inspired to recommend to our designers to create it because I remembered surrealist painter Paul Klee, who described drawings as "taking a line for a walk." I thought the same could apply to making business content come to life, so why not take a slide out for a walk? This way, it could interact with the environment and capture information that may appeal more to our senses than speaking only in abstracts.

Unfortunately, most business content relies on presenting value propositions through disembodied concepts, such as an array of slides or pages in an e-book, without engaging sensorimotor systems or understanding how the body influences the internalization of these concepts. It is not helpful that many inventions of modern society are tempting us to slow down and not use the body: The internet, social media, and television invite us to sit. We no longer have to get food—we click a button for meal delivery. We don't have to meet friends, family, and customers face-to-face—we do so online. When we sit, we're conserving energy by cutting brain capacity. When we move, the mind is set in motion again. Figuring out ways to involve the body and the environment in a persuasive context is challenging but not impossible.

Disembodied concepts included in abstract charts and diagrams are not likely to attract attention and turn into memory and action. Abstract concepts are OK (the brain still needs them), but it's better when you combine them with other methods, such as inviting people to experience ideas themselves, or, at a minimum, attaching the concepts to some implied movement. Imagine that the data in one of the charts helps with forward movement for a company. Maybe the numbers in the diagrams show how an organization can transport more people, perform better surgeries, or contribute to someone's exploration of the world.

When you set the body in motion, the brain follows. And the opposite is true: when the body movement slows down, the brain does too.

So how do we set business professionals in motion? Let's consider two ways: Invite your audience to physically engage in movement or offer them the perception of motion. In this chapter, we will explore both.

Engage Them in Physical Movement

There are various ways to create an interplay between the brain, the body, and the environment in a business context. For example, companies that offer physical products invite prospects and customers to an Experience Center or ship them samples, enabling direct physical contact with the products. Companies that operate in the digital space offer demos and trials, allowing prospects or existing customers to maneuver online tools. If you're a virtual worker presenting to an audience remotely, look for ways to invite them to experience your ideas by moving their bodies, even if it's nothing more than accessing a website on their own instead of sharing your screen.

Technologies such as VR (virtual reality), AR (augmented reality), and XR (extended reality) have also become popular, affording customers visceral experiences in business settings. Of course, these tools impose a cost, but if your content lends itself well to these technologies, these are very effective ways to involve your audience's brain, body, and environment.

If you're offering training to your audiences, there are ample opportunities to invite movement. For example,

in many virtual training sessions I teach, I often ask participants to take a picture with their phone of something in their environment to emphasize an important learning point. The collage of pictures represents entries for an assignment related to the importance of authentic emotion in building memories. The prompt was "Walk anywhere in your environment and capture a picture that

symbolizes the essence of being human." While some submit touching photos from an existing gallery, others do move around to capture a special moment.

Inviting an audience to take notes is a relatively easy and low-cost way to involve the brain and body and subsequently improve attention, memory, and motivation. Abundant research findings indicate that people who take notes by hand encode information better by activating multiple brain regions and having embodied experiences with the words. Handwriting activates both visual and motor regions of the brain, involving movement of the fingers, hands, wrists, arms, eyes, head, and back. Handwriting happens in real time. We see each letter forming stroke by stroke and observe the final handwritten

letter. This visual feedback informs subsequent motor control. This loop produces more meaningful stimuli, which translates into higher-quality external storage. When people handwrite, they are likely to be selective in what they put on paper, meaning that they synthesize and summarize information, which helps comprehension and retention. Overall, the literature suggests that taking notes by hand improves how people pay attention to and encode content, which results in better long-term memory. The pen is also mightier than the keyboard, as research findings indicate that memory performance in handwritten tests is better than in typed notes.

Handwriting may seem simple and intuitive, but it is challenging to a neuroscientist because movement and neuroscience tools don't often go hand in hand. For example, in our EEG experiments, one of the essential requests for participants is *not* to move because movement interferes with the quality of the signals recorded through the electrodes on the scalp; the more movement, the more noise we might record, and we cannot always differentiate what is muscular movement from what is cognitive processing. However, the algorithms that help us remove movement artifacts are improving, so we've invited more business participants to take notes during EEG studies.

Current business communication practices include two pervasive means of presenting complex content during a live sales presentation, whether delivered face-to-face or virtually: sharing slides and drawing on a whiteboard. Knowing that physical interaction with the world influences cognition, we set up a neuroscience study during which we invited business professionals to interact with the environment by taking notes while watching either a PowerPoint presentation or a whiteboard presentation. With this experiment, I aimed to study how the inclusion of different types of body movement impacts attention, memory, arousal (how alert the brain is), valence (how much the brain likes the experience), and motivation to act on the content.

In one study, we included 125 participants and asked them to watch a sales presentation about a marketing platform. This presentation was created in two formats: PowerPoint slides and whiteboard, and was delivered as a simulated Zoom call. Two groups watched one of these presentations passively. Two other groups watched the PowerPoint presentation and were asked to take handwritten notes or type notes, respectively. Finally, a fifth group watched the whiteboard presentation and was asked to draw along with the presenter. The voiceover was the same for all five groups.

We recorded EEG, ECG, and GSR signals. We collected eye-tracking data and combined these signals to compute variables such as valence, arousal, motivation, attention, working memory, and fatigue. Participants also answered a 48-hour memory test. Before the study, we asked about participants' preferences for taking

invite an audience
to take notes

notes during business presentations when they meet with a vendor for the first time. We found no match between their stated preference for notetaking and how much they liked the presentation they viewed. We observed that some people who stated they always preferred to take notes liked the passive presentation, while others who claimed not to prefer notes liked taking them after all.

All groups of participants taking notes during the study showed better results in the memory tests than participants in the passive condition. However, since participants did not use their notes before the long-term memory test because we did not allow them to keep them, those effects can only be attributed to actively engaging in the presentation through the writing process.

Participants in the typing condition who were watching the PowerPoint slides showed significantly higher levels of arousal than the rest of the groups. On the other hand, participants in the PowerPoint handwriting condition showed larger motivation values and lower cognitive workload. Participants who were asked to draw along with the presenter who was using a whiteboard showed significantly larger values of motivation than participants who consumed the whiteboard presentation passively. They also showed higher attention levels, lower fatigue, lower working memory levels, better memory accuracy, and better overall comprehension compared to the latter group.

We also computed an ISC (intersubject correlation) score, which allows us to monitor how well people's brains synchronize during an experimental condition. Synchronization is essential because it is linked to better collaboration and shared understanding. Participants in the passive whiteboard condition showed significantly larger levels of synchronization than the rest of the groups. However, participants in the handwriting and the whiteboard draw-along condition also showed higher synchronization levels than participants in the typing or the PowerPoint passive condition. This might be due to writing inducing synchronization.

Given these results, if you can choose the delivery medium and your content lends itself to this format, avoid slides and deliver a presentation on a whiteboard instead. Even if participants watch the whiteboard passively, they will likely experience significantly better brain synchronization by engaging their mirror neurons and creating embodied representations of the content.

If you deliver a whiteboard presentation, ask participants to draw along, as that significantly increases their motivation and memory without sacrificing visual attention to the presentation.

If you cannot use a whiteboard, ask your audience to take handwritten notes during your PowerPoint presentation. This activity will improve their motivation to act, reduce their working memory and cognitive workload, improve memory accuracy, enhance overall

Here is an example from the neuroscience study. The slide on the left is from the PowerPoint presentation, and the image on the right shows the presenter as he's drawing the same concepts on a whiteboard. When customers were watching the presenter move, their brains synchronized better compared to those watching PowerPoint slides. Brain synchronization is desirable because it's associated with shared attention and better collaboration, which are important in a business context. Decisions are hardly ever individual in a corporation, so the more people pay attention to the same things, the more likely that they will collaborate well on a solution.

comprehension, and enable them to recall a more significant number of additional details without sacrificing visual attention to the presentation.

Offer the Perception of Movement

We've discussed the many merits of motion and know that motion captures attention, not just intuitively but also based on evidence. The evidence comes from evolutionary psychology and many cognitive neuroscience experiments indicating that rapid movement in the visual field attracts attention. Of the many different sources of information around us, *motion information seems to be the most salient*, powerful, and relied on by our brains.

Unfortunately, the vast majority of us are exposed to static business content—slides, for example—which can lead to boredom, drowsiness, and lack of attention; content that is ultimately forgettable. One way to fix static content is to draw inspiration from the movie industry. After all, they don't have it easy: They need to attract people's attention and sustain it for about 90 minutes, usually in the dark. One of the reasons you are likely to stay focused on a movie for a prolonged period of time is the short duration of shots, and the amount of movement in those shots—lots of movement. If you are considering similar techniques in your business content, you may wonder: How short is a shot, and how much movement should I include?

I asked the same questions in a neuroscience study within the context of a virtual sales pitch. Specifically, I wanted to observe the impact of movement on variables such as attention, valence, arousal, fatigue, and motivation to act on the information. The general conclusion was that a combination of animation (built in Power-Point) and annotation (created in real time by the presenter) positively impacted attention, working memory, motivation to act, and long-term memory. Participants also liked the presentation with the animations and annotations more; they were more relaxed and experienced less fatigue.

What Kind of Movement Can You Include in Business Content?

First, a description: Animation in our study was based on PowerPoint effects such as "fade in" and "appear" and on annotations that the speaker included by using the Pen function available in PowerPoint when you play a slide in slideshow mode. With the Pen, you can draw shapes, such as circles or lines, around elements of interest or write words. For example, in the presentation exemplified by this screenshot, the presenter drew circles, lines, arrows, and other marks in green as she spoke about different stages related to how the brain handles change.

In these examples, the presenter was annotating PowerPoint slides, delivered via Zoom, drawing different shapes to make people look at specific elements and help them understand some concepts more easily.

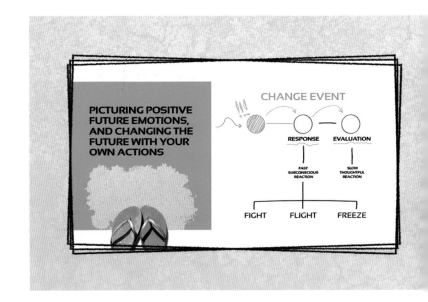

In our study, seven slides were delivered in approximately nine minutes, so a tangible metric with positive results was a slide switch every 94 seconds. Given this number, listen to a recording of a presentation you delivered or helped someone deliver lately that included slides. Was there a slide switch every minute and a half? If there wasn't, that means stimulation must come from other sources. For example, stories have "scene changes" built in and words that symbolize action and motion (e.g., "they moved the files from on-prem to the cloud"), so tell more stories.

Whether through structure or words, you can offer the *perception* of movement, but the guideline is clear: movement must happen if you want attention, memory, and persuasion.

Let's consider a slide switch equivalent to a shot change in a movie. We noted in our neuroscience experiment that the average shot length (or slide length) was 94 seconds. The average shot length for contemporary movies is 4.3 seconds. The contrast might be striking, but comparing a Hollywood movie with technical presentations is like comparing apples to oranges. However, you can draw inspiration from techniques that movies use to impact attention, emotion, engagement, memory, and motivation to keep watching.

A practical step is to keep in mind the *distribution* of shot length and the amount of movement in each shot across the entire narrative. After all, movies tell stories, and persuasive business presentations also try to tell stories to impact attention, memory, and motivation. Movie

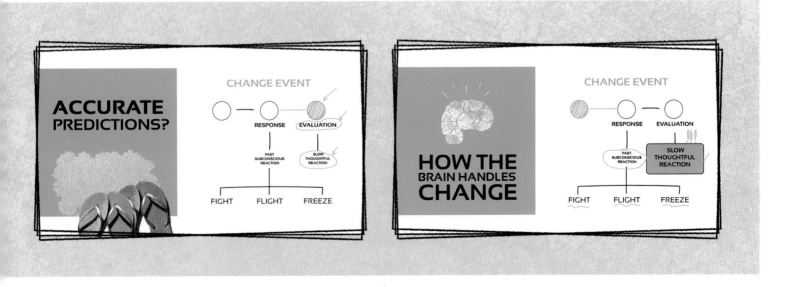

Let's consider the combination of animation and annotation as "movement" in a slide. If you're using slides for virtual business presentations, movement can come from several sources:

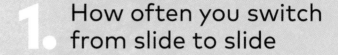

1. How often you switch from slide to slide

2. The amount of animation or annotation you add within each slide

3. The perception of movement you build in people's minds with words

4. Your physical movement if you share your video

5. The movement your audience may add if they share their video or if you're asking them to engage in any movement

directors and editors treat shot duration and movement differently depending on the *place* within the narrative. Let's look at how this works and how it can apply to business content.

Stories typically include these components:

- The exposition, which helps us understand the context

- The conflict, a clash of opposing forces or an obstacle that develops the plot

> The left chart indicates the *shot duration* in modern movies. The chart on the right shows slide duration in a business presentation. The data on the right shows only one example, but it's helpful to consider it because movies can serve as inspiration for attracting attention, and we can see how the business presentation can improve to mimic tested Hollywood formulas.

- The climax, the highest point of tension

- The denouement, the final resolution

Considering these story components, as you can see from the chart, the shot duration in modern movies is longer at the beginning (6–7 seconds), helping to ease the viewer into the setup. The shot duration becomes shorter as the plot develops (4–6 seconds), shorter yet during the climax (2–3 seconds), and longer again toward the end (6–7+ seconds). The following chart shows this plot for movies (left) and a business presentation (right) in terms of shot/slide presentation length.

Even though this is just a cursory comparison, we can observe a few things that can be improved in business content and give you tangible guidelines for your next Zoom call:

Hollywood
Movies

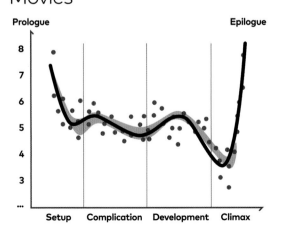

Technical
Presentations

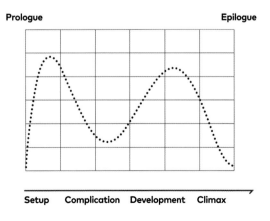

1. Try a longer slide duration during the introduction and setup of the context in the beginning compared to what you would consider the climax of your presentation. Return to the longer length in your conclusion.

2. Shorten slide length during the development portion of your story, using more frequent slide switches.

3. Keep the duration of the slides even shorter during the climax of the presentation.

> The left chart shows *movement* in modern movies. The chart on the right indicates movement in a business presentation. Even though this is the plot for one presentation, you can see how we can learn from tested movie patterns and vary the amount of movement at specific points in a flow.

In the neuroscience experiment I mentioned earlier, the fundamental differences came from how much movement was included in each slide. On average, every 8.7 seconds, something moved on a slide to positively impact attention, liking, engagement, and motivation.

In this comparison, we can observe certain patterns in modern movies: we see less motion in the exposition, more motion as the conflict arises, and less motion during the denouement. Looking at the business presentation example, you can see how we can learn to:

1. Include more motion in the introduction or story setup.

2. Decrease movement during complications (e.g., sharing industry trends).

3. Increase motion just slightly as the story develops.

Hollywood
Movies

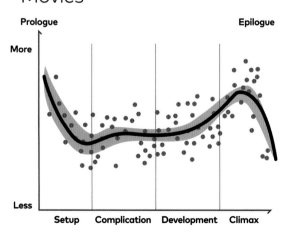

Technical
Presentations

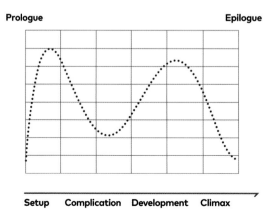

4. Add more movement during the climax.

5. Reduce motion in the conclusion.

In short, consider decreased slide durations and increased movement during the climax of your content, followed by their reversal in the epilogue. From a brain science perspective, longer duration shots and decreased motion place fewer demands on eye movement and attention, which enables you to end a presentation in a relaxed state for your audience, avoiding Zoom fatigue. This will suggest to your audience that it will be a cognitively pleasant experience the next time they meet with you.

Is *Some* Movement Better than None?

In our neuroscience study, I was surprised that participants who viewed the deck with PowerPoint animation only (versus animation and annotation) liked the presentation less and were more frustrated than those who viewed the deck with no animation at all. Our animation-only experimental condition contained four times less movement than animation and annotation. So, if you cannot offer frequent movement, it's better to display all the elements in a slide at once and speak about them (at least there is something to draw attention to) instead of teasing an audience with infrequent animation.

If nothing is moving on the slide and you're sharing your web camera (or if you're presenting face-to-face), your movement will attract attention, which means you're relying on your gestures and verbal message to attract and sustain attention. In another neuroscience study that included a persuasive pitch delivered via Zoom, we noted that when the slides did not contain too much information, 50 to 80 percent of the attention was directed at the presenter, who appeared in the upper right corner.

In this Zoom call, the heat maps (stronger red spots) indicate that the presenter attracted most of the attention when the slides were simple.

This indicates that if you have simple slides with no movement and not much visual stimulation, you must develop a solid verbal message and supplement it with gestures that impact the audience's motor cortex. I suspect that one of the reasons the whiteboard experimental group mentioned in one of the earlier studies did so well is because viewers could see more of the presenter's gestures and movement across the screen.

In virtual presentations, movement can become even more critical because your presenter area is about 18 times smaller when you share slides. In this case, do delivery skills even matter? This broad question was the basis of a neuroscience study I conducted at the beginning of 2022 when virtual presentations were at their peak. My specific focus was to investigate whether *sitting or standing* makes a difference in the effectiveness of a virtual sales presentation. I selected this particular question because anecdotally, some communication experts propose that standing while presenting makes you a more dynamic speaker, arguing that you can present with more movement and energy when you stand. The heart will pump faster, the voice will be more powerful, and the posture will inspire more confidence. The only benefit of sitting I could find, where communication is concerned, is in hospital contexts, where doctors who sit report being understood better by patients. This is likely because their eyes are at the same level. In our neuroscience experiment, participants who viewed a sales presentation via Zoom liked the sitting presenter more (as evidenced by their EEG and ECG signals) but built more precise memories while viewing the presentation delivered by the standing presenter.

Does movement help in an asynchronous situation when people can look at content on their own? I asked this question during a neuroscience study where I aimed to observe the impact of text versus video in an email format. How do you react to text-based emails versus video-based emails? The surprising finding was that the business brain starts in a negative state while in an inbox environment. However, after watching movement in an email that contained a video, the emotion switched to a more relaxed state. If you read the previous chapter on priming, you understand the importance of using one stimulus to impact another. Movement can serve as a strong perceptive primer.

The body is made to be in motion, and even the slightest movement can make a difference by boosting brain health, improving attention and memory, and inducing a happy state of mind. So dare to move away from pixels to movement and interact with physical objects. To do this well for your audiences, a great place to start is to think about your own way of moving and impacting cognition. What are some of your "moves"? What type of activity do you do when you feel your mind is clear and you have an optimistic outlook on life? Making time and space for movement is not an indulgence; it is a necessity. The more movement you create for yourself, the more you appreciate the importance of creating it for others.

The right
amount
OF WRONG

CHAPTER 3

The Right Amount of Wrong

Handling Provocative Content

Think of how your attention changes when you see a frozen moment in a dance routine, hear a gunshot in a quiet movie, or recall how Bobby Fischer sacrificed his queen and still won big.

Sometimes individuals and companies have dared to do just the right amount of wrong to stand out in some way, feel better, stick it to someone, or generally evolve. Doing something entirely right is often boring and can easily be ignored. Being completely wrong is often unethical and not profitable. This chapter is about playing with proportions in the provocative, so you enjoy the rewards of getting attention and staying on people's minds.

Let's define being provocative as startling an audience deliberately, rather than inadvertently, by breaking personal or social norms. Think of norm violations such as sexual references, profanity, vulgarity, or things that outrage the moral or physical senses, such as raw or sensitive words and images. Since we're talking about violating norm, we must understand how norms work. Humans are a social species, and when we interact in groups, we learn what is and what is not acceptable—in short, we build shared expectations or norms. And we often use these norms to evaluate objects, people, actions, and ideas.

Famously controversial campaigns have received much attention by violating norms. For example, the clothing brand F.C.U.K created a billboard ad that advised consumers to F.C.U.K. "all night long." Bad Frog Brewery used profanity in an ad showing a frog with its middle finger extended. In a PlayStation ad a few years

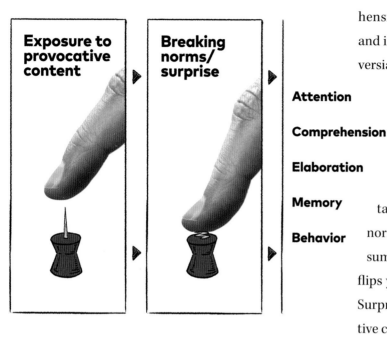

Attention

Comprehension

Elaboration

Memory

Behavior

hension and elaboration, enhance message retention, and influence behavior. For instance, shockingly controversial campaigns for condoms led to safer sex.

Why does provocative content work from a brain science point of view? When you initially see something provocative, you evaluate it or appraise it to determine if it breaks a personal or social norm. You know if it does because, as we established earlier, your brain has already created many norms against which you match the content you're consuming. For example, you don't typically see a frog that flips you off, so it catches you by surprise when you do. Surprise, or incongruity, is essential in viewing provocative content because it prompts you to focus longer. This observation is supported by a theory called *expectancy disconfirmation*, and research evidence in this area indicates that we process what is unexpected more and longer than what is expected. The extra cognitive processes impact how we understand the message (comprehension) and can also generate other thoughts (elaboration), all of which influence recall and behavior.

You don't have to be a cognitive scientist to know that provocative content gets attention. If you're a fan of the TV show *Schitt's Creek* and enjoyed Moira, you know that what provokes captivates. Moira may have had narcissistic bursts, but her sophisticated vocabulary, with multiple and rewarding layers of meaning, was worthy of extra attention.

ago, a chef wiped a steak around a toilet bowl rim and added rolled-up nose pickings as a garnish before serving. And there was an Adidas ad that featured a nude male soccer team.

Why Does Provocative Content Work?

Shocking stimuli have been included in communication for decades because scientific findings confirm they significantly increase attention, facilitate message compre-

Click to add title

- Click to add text

Provoke
with a
pivot point

Here is how Moira provoked an audience and grabbed attention:

- **Unexpected vocabulary.** Most people speak in standard colloquialisms. Moira uses antiquated, highbrow jargon to defy linguistic expectations. Some people would say, "I am busy with meetings." Moira is "bedeviled with meetings, etcetera." When referring to one of the singers in a choir, she calls her a "trained chanteuse." Most people would say to someone, "Let's talk." Moira's invitation is "Let's confabulate in the back room." Even when she laments her lost youth, she does so with poetic elegance: "The last traces of my juvenescence vanished into thin air."

- **Delivery.** She makes all these unusual pronouncements in an ambiguous accent, and she often emphasizes the wrong syllable, too.

- **Over-the-top aesthetics.** Moira is completely overdressed for her current lifestyle. She wears eccentric clothing and wigs, almost like armor, to shield herself from her new grim reality. Outrageous jewelry (which she also wears to bed), beading, ostrich feathers, and even a papal miter make her look like a walking piece of art. When she babysits, Moira dresses in a super shiny sequined silver mini dress that seems more fit for a New Year's Eve party. She pairs the dress with chunky heel booties and opaque black tights. With her ensembles, it would be difficult not to pay attention.

If Provocative Content Is So Effective, Why Don't We See More of It in Business?

Most business content aims to be efficient, comfortable, and pleasant. We often default to familiar designs intended to be linear and logical. In contrast, if you were provocative, you would aim to:

- Challenge the status quo
- Question a social or personal norm
- Propose something counterintuitive
- Expose assumptions
- Invite perspective-taking
- Trigger tension or a dilemma

Do your content assets accomplish any of this? It's possible to apply any of these techniques to any content you develop. Let's step into the No, but Yes Gallery to look at examples of how others have dared to be provocative.

If you look closely at each example, your attention is rewarded by provoking a reaction. The person wearing the "click to add title" slide as a skirt was in one of my presentations a while back when I was visualizing one of my dad's favorite quotes: a presentation should be like a mini skirt, he would remind me, short enough to be interesting and long enough to cover the subject.

the no, but yes gallery

Click to add title

Click to add text

Optimal Length

Your presentation should be like a skirt: **short enough** to be interesting, and **long enough** to cover the subject

HOW RISKY IS YOUR ◆ **NEXT MOVE** ?

Provocation: Legitimate Technique or Attention-Grabbing Gimmick?

Provocation may have a negative connotation because it may be linked to inciting others. However, there is a difference between provocative and inflammatory content, and that difference stems from intent. Inflammatory people seek a reaction. In addition, inflammatory comments usually oversimplify, while provocative content provides nuance and depth.

So when you use provocation, ask yourself: Am I doing it to incite emotion or to generate discussion and change perceptions for the good? With this question in mind, let's first look at several major *don'ts* for provocation:

- **Don't provoke with superficiality.** The wrong kind of provocations typically include statements that condense a situation or reach extreme conclusions based on broad generalizations. I remember philosopher, bestselling author, and TED speaker Alain de Botton prompting us to look at Othello, Oedipus, or Madame Bovary. Suppose their fates had been covered by tabloids. In which case—spoiler alert!—articles might be titled "Madame Bovary: Shopaholic Adulteress Swallows Arsenic After Credit Fraud," "Othello: Love-Crazed Immigrant Kills Senator's Daughter," or "Oedipus: Sex with Mum Was Blinding." In contrast, a reasonable provocation offers layers of interpretation. If you're going for brevity, consider saying, "There is more to the story," so the audience appreciates that you've considered layers and depth. Show them that you've been in the trenches.

- **Don't target only emotions.** Provocation is typically associated in business with the word "thought," as in, "Our organization is creating thought-provoking content." The way to tell if you're toying with the wrong amount of wrong is to create something that will generate a purely emotional reaction. Although a provocation will ignite reactions, it should be balanced with thoughtful debate.

- **Don't punch down.** We can learn a lesson from stand-up comedians, who remind us not to make jokes about the less privileged or marginalized. It is the same in business: don't go after the easy targets or the underrepresented, even if you're talking about the competition.

In short, don't create provocative content just to be controversial. But if you do have a point that goes beyond the norm, share it. And since provoking means disrupting or challenging the status quo, be prepared for it to invite adverse reactions. Unanimously positive responses would contradict the goal itself. So if your desire is to be accepted, provocative content is not for you. But if you don't like to sit silently, and if you can manage the potentially negative reactions and avoid the *don'ts* listed here, then you can use the practical techniques on how to share just the right amount of wrong.

Provoke with Design

When the norm in business is bland design (see the Beige in a Box Gallery in Chapter 1), you can provoke with unpredictable design. How do you create a provocative design when your tendencies might be nonprovocative?

In the examples below, I was speaking about dopamine behavior and submissive behavior in monkeys, linking the word "submissive" with the word "courtesy," which then is linked to "court" and "nobility." Showing monkeys as nobility was considered a provocative design.

Combining hand-drawn illustrations with real photography can also lead to provocative design. In the example on the next page, a client was contrasting two methods for software development: the cathedral versus the bazaar method. The cathedral method implies that software is carefully and quietly crafted by individuals within an isolated, primarily secret development team. The bazaar method indicates chaotic, open-source development and is miraculously coherent in the midst of the signal and the noise of the crowd. This method means you're using small tools, rapid prototyping, and evolutionary programming. You release the software early and often, delegate everything you can, and are open to the point of promiscuity. To visualize these ideas, we could easily have downloaded stock photos, but instead, we used hand-drawn illustrations to suggest that both methods involve human creation, which is free-flowing and not as rigid as a precise photo. The rest of the presentation also included hand-drawn illustrations to indicate a human touch.

The cathedral

The bazaar

Here are several other designs that combine hand-drawn illustrations with real images. The underlying theme for these examples is to indicate that reality can expand and that there are solutions to be explored at a broader scale. These invite an optimistic and innovative outlook by posing what-if scenarios.

Stimulate discussion and receive early feedback. In this metaphorical example of expanding on an existing solution, adding a sketch next to a completed drawing was intended to stimulate a debate about new directions and even present the audience with ideas to get feedback early in the development process. This also worked well because asking viewers to respond to a sketch prototype can reveal the motivation behind their choices.

Simulate reality. I used this slide in one of my presentations to share an experiment conducted in Australia, in which scientists wanted to demonstrate people's paucity of attention by asking: Who will notice money "growing" on trees? So they placed real money in trees near a well-trafficked alley in a park. The results were not promising for people's attention capabilities. I could not find pictures from the actual experiment, so I used an illustration with a few photos to simulate how it was carried out.

The mix of real photography and hand-drawn illustrations symbolizes the combination of machine precision and human creativity. It is provocative because custom design with hand-drawn illustrations is rare, especially when used in presenting technical content. This type of design might become more common with the advent of generative AI tools.

Trigger empathy. Combined with a real image, an illustration like the one above can engage a viewer's imagination and empathic response.

Explore a range of ideas. In the examples below, you can see how one might explore a range of new ideas, rather than finalizing or validating something that already exists.

Take the viewer on a journey. This vertical image is a screenshot from the website of a company I started in 2019 that used neuroscience to help corporations craft memorable messages. The hand illustrations, in contrast with the real photos, were intended to symbolize that memory is never perfect; it is always a reconstruction of reality, and some memories are more precise than others. The line guiding the eyes came as an inspiration from two sources: the proverbial phrase "memory lane" and a famous quote I mentioned in the previous chapter by surrealist painter Paul Klee, who described drawings as taking a line for a walk. As you consider provoking with design, ask: Can I extend a predictable image through some line drawings and take my audience's imagination for a walk? Can you use generative AI tools and prompt them to take a common idea and turn it into something unusual, given a specific context?

Another way to provoke with design, especially if you're appealing to audiences who do not have access to advanced graphic designers, is to reconsider using photographs with straight edges. Most business content is built by combining words with charts developed in another program (such as Microsoft Excel) or images downloaded from a personal or stock photo gallery; these images typically have straight edges. Anything you create that moves away from the straight edge and displays

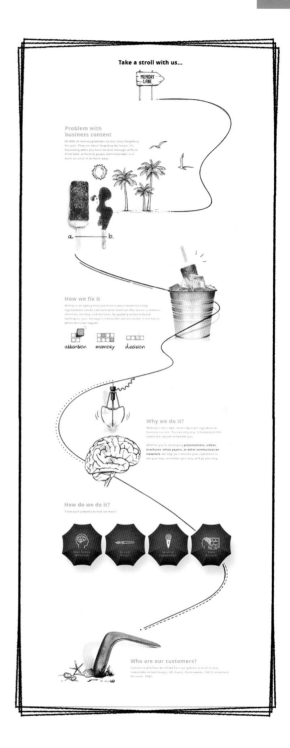

a more flowing, integrated design may be seen as outside the norm. In the following example, the first screenshot is something I initially created without applying any effects to an image I was using in a presentation to showcase some advantages of neuroscience studies. Note the different impact in the second screenshot when you wrap text around an image, eliminating the straight edges that are the hallmark of PowerPoint's templatized design.

Eliminate straight edges in the images you use for a more enticing design.

If you do use PowerPoint, resist the temptation to accept PowerPoint's "click to add text here" invitation. There's more you can do with design. Play!

Exaggeration Is Utterly, Extremely, Totally Underutilized

Do you ever watch fashion shows? Even if fashion is not your focus, a fashion show may have caught your eye on a screen in a store window display or elevator. And at some point, you may have asked, "Who in the world would wear that?" Fashion designers are strategic about these shows. While they opt for the unusual and eccentric *during* a show, not all items make it to the store after a show. A Gucci dress on the runaway is hardly the one at the store, where you're likely to see "safer," more wearable options. In a show, fashion designers have one goal only: to grab attention, which then creates buzz.

If you're in a content creation role and need to get approval from a client or an internal supervisor, try this technique: Offer a safe design and an unsafe one. You will be surprised how often people select less safe and more attention-grabbing options.

In the Exaggeration Gallery, you will see other examples that use hyperbole to make us look and command exploration. Reflecting on your content, seek opportunities to intentionally disregard accuracy to draw attention.

> Exaggeration helps you draw attention to an important point.

I use the exaggeration technique frequently in my own presentations. For example, in the above deck, I speak about the importance of inserting the right images to capture attention and impact memory. I share several eye-tracking data charts to indicate that picture choice is essential, even when communicating with experts. They are, after all, human too (also, potential decision makers!), and we should not treat expert audiences like robots by showing them communication that is devoid of interesting elements, such as images. Imagine the sequence above as an animated one, in which I show the robot and then click to reveal the human underneath. The exaggeration is intended to draw attention to the conclusion that experts are also human and appreciate cognitive ease.

In the examples to the right from a neuroscience study I conducted, we replaced a predictable image (of a woman looking at a computer screen) with a provocative one (of an iron bird in chains). We then generated a cognitive map using the EEG signal. Typically, in neuroscience experiments, you might see a heat map indicating visual attention. In this case, the cognitive map reflects cognitive load. The lighter load is designated by the blue color and the heavier load by the more intense yellow and orange. Note how much more cognitive processing happens on the page with the iron bird.

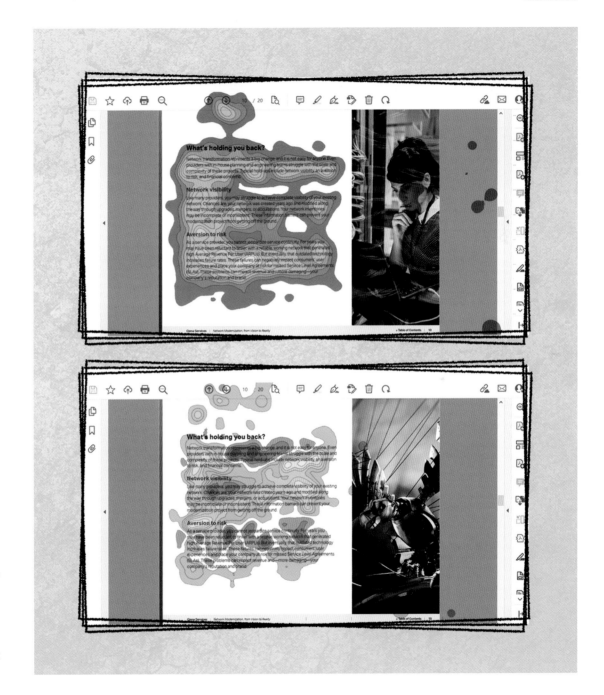

When the image is more daring (chained iron bird versus predictable businessperson looking at a computer screen), the brain processes the text more deeply.

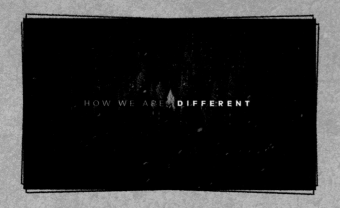

Visualizing conflicting ideas prompts attention and exploration of the design.

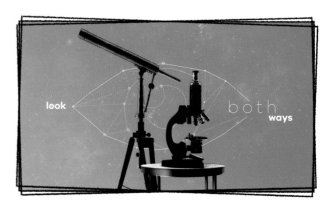

Sometimes a literal interpretation of a concept can invoke exaggeration and provoke attention. For instance, I remember a commercial presentation where the presenter stated, "We were in a tough spot, and our hands were really tied." The image showed a person in a trunk who literally had their hands tied. It was a heavy-duty image that appeared only for a few seconds. Many exaggerated images provoke strong emotions, so it's helpful not to dwell on them for too long, but instead make a convincing point quickly and move on.

Another way to provoke with design is by juxtaposing elements that emphasize a dilemma. Reflecting on your content, are there some contradictions you can reference? Humans are full of contradictions, ranging from the obvious (eating sweets while trying to lose weight) to the more profound (the more we know, the less we feel we know). What are the conflicting concerns in your field? What is mutually exclusive in your world? What is marked by indecision and doubt? Even though asking these questions and visualizing the answers may feel uncomfortable, there is a significant advantage: it invites the brain to pay attention, slow down and reflect, collect information, and improve decision-making.

This slide introduces one of my keynotes on whether sellers should just "be themselves" during customer conversations or whether it's more profitable to abide by expected norms.

When you're willing to provoke, consider *levels of provoking*. Notice in the following examples how the same question, "Is your business dying, surviving, or thriving?," is accompanied by various levels of provocative designs. Almost any field in life provides the opportunity for progression. I am reminded of this whenever I watch professional skiers competing at the Winter Olympics, doing moguls. Mogul courses are challenging and fast by default, and just when I think they can't get more challenging, a skier does a backflip.

The tendency I observe in business content is for business practitioners to give it all they've got early in a sequence, with nowhere else to go. How far you're willing to take your provocation levels depends on your courage and your audience's baseline of accepting your approach. While you're creating your content, ask yourself: What could be my next level of acceptable intensity? Always leave some room to go higher.

Always look for ways to amp up the intensity of your ideas and compositions. This progression demonstrates the increase in design intensity.

Information appeal

Fear appeal

Shock appeal

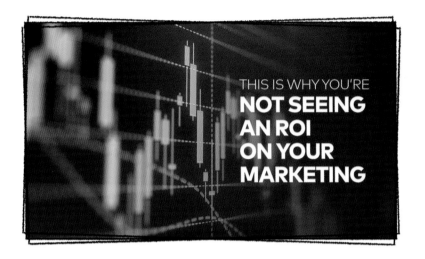

THIS IS WHY YOU'RE
**NOT SEEING
AN ROI
ON YOUR
MARKETING**

This is
how to
capture customers
before your
competition

this is what
makes you a *leader*

THESE TRENDS
WILL MAKE YOU
**THINK TWICE
ABOUT BUYER
PERSONAS**

Use Referencing
(Aka Well-Intended Clickbait)

Writers know how to get attention with a technique called forward referencing, which involves using generic and mysterious pronouns that create a curiosity gap. Contrast this with backward referencing, which means clear, unequivocal language. For example: Dan rode his bike. *He* bought *it*. When we see the pronoun, we understand it because it's related to a noun that's been mentioned before. Provocative headlines reverse this technique (hence the term *forward referencing*), typically with the word "this," which is prevalent in clickbait headlines: "*This* is what inequality looks like. *It* will shock you." You can only uncover what "it" is if you click.

Business practitioners can take advantage of the forward referencing technique as long as the content intrigues viewers without misrepresenting ideas, which is how you avoid being perceived as clickbait. For example, you can play with a range of phrases such as "this is why…," "this is what…," "this is the…," and "this is how…." The examples across the spread show how these phrases would prompt attention to the presenter, who ideally reveals the "mystery" with trustworthy data and stories.

As you can see in the clickbait collection, which includes slides from business presentations, there could be a good side to clickbait if you deliver on your mysterious promises in ethical ways.

Provoke with Perspective-Taking

Perspective-taking means you are creating words or designs that *invite interpretation* of an event, situation, behavior, person, or object. The essential nature of the person, object, or event your audience is looking at does not change—only their perception of them. This phenomenon can also be interpreted as framing: when you exchange an old frame for a new one, things could look different from the norm.

Jokes, for example, depend on reframing. The punchline is when one frame is substituted for another wildly incongruous or inappropriate frame.

Reframing can also help you provide your audiences with a sudden disturbance. Whether it's a behavior, object, situation, event, or anything else you want to focus on, consider these questions to determine new ways to frame a message:

- Meaning: Could it mean something entirely different?

- Context: Could it be useful somewhere else?

- Humor: Is there a funny side?

- Silver lining: Are there any opportunities that arise from this problem?

- Different points of view: What does it mean to other people?

- Opposite perspectives: What if we consider it backward?

- Transitivity: Can we interchange elements?

What does switching frames do to our brains? This can be explained through reappraisal: our emotional responses flow out of our appraisals of the world (our frames), and if you can shift those appraisals for an audience, you can shift their emotional responses.

There are several ways to prompt someone to switch perspectives. One easy method is to show something from an unusual vantage point, such as a bird's-eye view, extreme close-up, long distance, detached from space and time, or every possible angle.

Another way to switch perspectives is to imagine your consciousness leaving your body and stepping into other people, animals, or objects. With this technique, your imagination is the limit. You can take the perspective of a bike, a goat, a toaster, or a server room!

BEAUTY
IS IN THE
**EYE OF
THE END
USER**

YOU ARE RESPONSIBLE
FOR EACH STEP YOU TAKE

**WILDFIRES BURN
MORE THAN TREES**

The image in the top slide suggests that the computer board can "speak" and tout its positive impact on user experience. Perspective-taking is achieved in the middle slide by a zoomed-in shot viewed from underneath—not a viewpoint typically taken in displaying images. The effect works because it magnifies the importance of each step, which is the essence of the message. The bottom slide gives the porcupine a "voice," and the entire message becomes attention-grabbing by provoking empathy.

Role Reversal Gallery

FEAR IS NOT AN OPTION

PLANS, NOT PANIC.

nothing is off limit

Business content, which typically is aimed at fixing problems, can be attractive territory for switching perspectives because you can take others' viewpoints and extrapolate thoughts or emotions regarding business issues. For example, let's say you have a solution that promises to reduce employee turnover. When using provocation, you might ask how you can *increase* employee turnover. Then you might say, "Let's identify factors that contribute to this challenge, such as implementing a negative culture or overworking employees." And then you would add, "These are undesirable factors, which lead to our solution for reducing them, such as manageable workloads and creating a more positive work environment."

To switch perspectives and command attention, think of your content and ask these questions:

- Can we convert our benefit into a disadvantage?

- Can we briefly visualize the negative instead of the positive?

- Can we reverse roles? Change the viewpoints of the people involved?

- Can we switch cause and effect?

I love switching perspectives with animals. Step into the Role Reversal Gallery to see a collection of slides in which various animals and birds help us pay attention to a business message more quickly and easily.

A final thought on making your content provocative to compel attention: Make sure you link provocation, which should be temporary, with a more enduring approach, such as thought leadership. For example, actor Ken Jeong might be provocative with his role in the movie *Hangover* or his speeches in *The Masked Singer*, but he can be inspirational to any business professional or entrepreneur. Holding an actual medical degree, he knows that medicine and comedy can be compatible, and his advice includes enduring principles, such as "don't be afraid to admit you're scared, and don't be afraid to fail."

Practical Guidelines from Quadrant I: Automatic Triggers

1. Use perceptual, affective, semantic, and repetition priming to prepare the brain to pay attention to what is important.

2. If you prime the brain with negative images or text, neutralize the negative and then move on to positive priming before you present your solution so your buyer's brain is more likely to be in a state of cognitive flexibility.

3. Engage your audience with physical movement when your content permits, such as asking them to take notes or draw along with you, if you're using a whiteboard.

4. If you cannot involve your audiences physically, offer the perception of movement through animations, using words that symbolize movement, and sharing stories with action that "moves" across a timeline.

5. Use provocative content to attract attention and impact memory and decisions. You can create provocative content by challenging the status quo, proposing something counterintuitive, exposing assumptions, viewing an issue from an unexpected perspective, and offering exaggeration.

6. You can also provoke with design by creating materials that are not expected or popular in your field (such as custom, hand-drawn illustrations on top of stock photography or avoiding photos with straight edges).

7. Perspective-taking also impacts provocative content and can be achieved by asking whether you can change something in your content in terms of its meaning, context, humor, components (can you interchange elements), finding a silver lining, or even looking at it backward.

External Focus

**Initiated by
the Individual**

**Initiated by
the Environment**

Guided Action

You guide them toward
their internal thoughts
and prompt them to focus
on something rewarding

Internal Focus

Guided Action

In this quadrant, you will learn how to:

- Use external stimulation, such as variety, challenge, and choice, to guide attention internally and prevent the brain from getting bored

- Engage the brain by appealing to critical thinking

- Master metaphors to impact focus, understanding, and memory

Everyone gets bored at some point

CHAPTER 4

The Psychology of Boredom

Engaging the Brain on a Level Beyond Flash

Gordon MacKenzie, the former cartoonist and writer for Hallmark Cards, recalls a surprising time he got bored. He was skydiving. It wasn't always like that. Gordon had reached a point in his life where he sought more excitement and freedom, so he took skydiving lessons. The first few times he jumped, he was taken by the thrill of falling and the rush of seeing the neat patterns of tiny Kansas farms as he zoomed toward them. The intense rush of feeling alive got him so hooked that he committed to skydiving once a week for six months. On his last jump, during a 120-mile-an-hour free fall, as the wind raged through his jumpsuit, he thought, *I wonder what's for dinner.*

You would think that with all the external stimulation and abundant thrills around us, it would be hard for the brain to disengage, turn inward, and become bored. Our neuroscience research indicates, however, that boredom is ubiquitous and universal. Business communicators must tackle the issue because bored customers are disloyal and eventually become former customers. So, in this quadrant in general, and in this chapter specifically, let's look at the scientific underpinnings of boredom and practical guidelines on how to avoid it when you guide the brain internally.

What Is Engagement, and What Is Boredom?

Both engagement and boredom have presented a semantic issue for scientists because of the multitude of ways to define them. How would *you* define them?

Let's start with *engagement* because this is a desirable attribute. In our neuroscience experiments, we consider the brain engaged when we observe high arousal levels, motivation to keep looking, and visual attention (since you look at what you think of, therefore implying engagement). You may remember from the Introduction that in terms of affective variables, valence and arousal are considered two independent neurophysiological systems at the foundation of all other affective states. Varying degrees of valence and arousal influence emotions, which impact attention, memory, and decisions. Valence implies an emotional state within a pleasure-displeasure continuum that ranges from positive to negative. Arousal is a person's general level of alertness and wakefulness, ranging from calm to intense. In the following image, you can see the intersection of valence and arousal forming an emotional circumplex. This circumplex is not new; it's been around since the 1980s. What is new is the ability to superimpose an aggregated EEG and ECG signal on top of it to see how the brain reacts to any moment within a piece of communication, such as a presentation, video, website, or book. The black dot on the circumplex represents an experimental group's aggregate EEG and ECG signal.

The black dot represents an aggregate of the EEG and ECG signals of an experimental group in a neuroscience study. When participants process a stimulus—let's say a sales presentation—we can tell at any moment whether the buyer's brain is engaged by analyzing their level of attention, valence, arousal, cognitive workload, fatigue, and motivation. The lower-left quadrant is where boredom resides, and your goal is to keep people away from that quadrant.

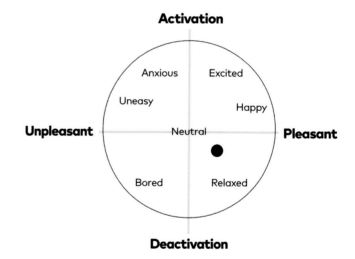

In this example, the EEG and ECG signals represented by the black dot indicate that at this specific point people are relaxed. Let's image people are two minutes in while viewing a Zoom presentation—we can tell that the arousal is not high, and they are fairly calm while watching the presentation. We can also detect from the bars at the bottom, based on their EEG signals, that their fatigue is above threshold (vertical line is a zero point), and so is working memory (a form of cognitive workload). Attention is low, however, and while motivation is high, this is a signal we observe for the seconds unfolding after this screenshot because if the valence shifts to negative, it means that people are motivated but not to keep going: they are motivated for this presentation to be over.

The following example shows how we can pair the EEG, ECG, and eye tracker signals to detect engagement. For the "Quality leadership" slide, attention and working memory are low, and the eyes are scanning mainly the

We pair EEG and ECG signals with eye tracking to further determine whether people are engaged or bored.

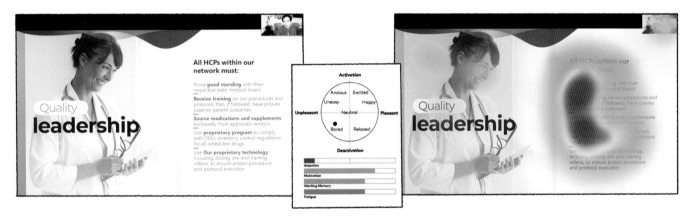

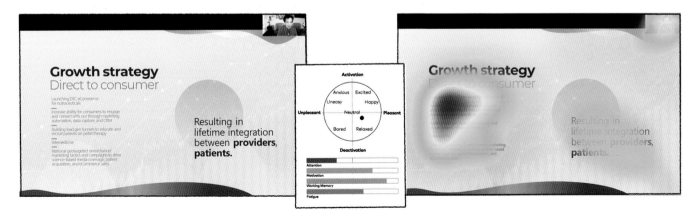

beginning of the sentences, which have the bolder words. For the "Growth strategy" slide, we can see that attention and working memory are higher (as the EEG signal indicates), and visual attention is more distributed over the slide and more focused on the presenter (as the eye-tracking map shows). So we can conclude that the Growth strategy slide is more engaging.

Knowing whether one person's brain is engaged with business content is interesting. Knowing whether multiple people's brains are engaged—and in the same way—is even more interesting because it has material consequences. Brain synchronization is essential to monitor because decisions are typically group-based, not individual-based, especially in large organizations. For all neuroscience research we complete where participants are watching the same thing at the same time, we use a method called intersubject correlation (ISC), which helps us calculate the correlation across participants' EEG signals. This method tells us whether participants' brains within one group engage with the content in the same way, which is likely because they pay attention the same way and have a shared understanding of what they are viewing. The point here is that there are a lot of methods to detect engagement, bypassing self-reports and focusing not just on the individual but on the group as well.

Now, let's consider a definition of *boredom*. Some people describe boredom as feeling unchallenged, restless, or trapped, perceiving activities as meaningless, or seeing no purpose. Artists and writers have described boredom as the dryness of the soul, paralysis of the will, or inexplicable sorrow. Russian poet Joseph Brodsky called boredom a "psychological Sahara." Danish philosopher Søren Kierkegaard considered boredom the root of all evil.

One definition that scientists agree on is that boredom represents a state marked by negative emotions and a low stimulation level. In the past, people used to measure these dimensions using various scales, such as the Boredom Proneness Scale, Job Boredom Scale, Academic Boredom Scale, Sensation Seeking Scale, and Sexual Boredom Scale. These scales include statements (which respondents agree or disagree with) such as, "It takes a lot of change and variety to keep me really happy," "I have no patience with dull or boring persons," "I feel empty," or "I get bored seeing the same old faces."

With improved technologies, we don't have to ask people if they are bored. From a neuroscience point of view, we return to the same circumplex as before, in addition to variables related to motivation and attention. This time, instead of high arousal, let's observe the opposite: low arousal and negative valence. This is how boredom sets in.

In the sequence exemplified next, the presenter shares with potential investors details about the market in the healthcare space; the product was related to improving vitality, especially for people over 40. Sharing a market overview is typical in an investor pitch because founders wish to demonstrate the potential of their solution. In the first set of examples, viewers start in a neutral state (the black dot is in the middle), but as the presenter introduces similar providers in the market, viewers get bored (the black dot is in the lower-left quadrant).

Then, as the patient population is presented, the state transitions toward the upper-left quadrant, and even though the engagement is slightly better through higher arousal, the presentation is still flirting with boredom. The point is that valence and arousal will fluctuate throughout a sequence. Some components in a communication will be more engaging than others. It's important to ensure that we're not keeping people in the lower-left quadrant for too long.

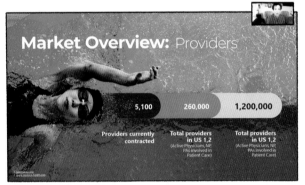

The EEG and ECG signals represented by the black dot indicate how quickly the brain shifts toward a state of boredom. Cognitive shifts are inevitable, so it's important to consider techniques to combat boredom throughout a communication sequence. Read on.

Break the Boredom Barrier

So how do we prevent boredom and create engagement instead? Scientists conclude that boredom can be *dispositional* or *situational*. *Dispositional* boredom is subjective, related to some individuals' propensity to feel disinterest and find no meaning or promise in life. *Situational* boredom means that something or someone in our surroundings is causing us to be bored, including the setting where communication occurs, the shared materials, or other people who are part of the context. Think of unchallenging meetings, long-winded sermons, or family members who tell the same story for the forty-ninth time. This chapter addresses situational boredom because when you create messages for others, you can control the *situation* in which the message is consumed more than you can their disposition.

The pro-engagement and anti-boredom guidelines included in this section are based on empirical studies and share common themes that have emerged from research on how to alleviate boredom to positively impact attention and, as a result, memory and behavior.

Variety

Joseph Epstein, acclaimed essayist and writer, recalls being six years old and telling his mother he was bored. She replied, "May I suggest you knock your head against the wall? It'll take your mind off your boredom." He never told his mom he was bored again, but she did have a point. You can provoke engagement and alleviate boredom by directing attention away from a boring stimulus. But it's not just about directing attention away from something; you must then direct it toward something else and keep it there for a while.

From an evolutionary standpoint, people tend to direct their attention to stimuli that shift in their surroundings: A loud sound, bright color, sudden movement, or unusual picture captures attention more than a smooth patch of grass. Neuroimaging studies show dopamine release when people engage in constant attention shifts, such as playing video games. However, when the novel stimuli stop providing rewards, people are off to the next new thing. One way to keep people's attention for a while and reward them for doing so is to vary the stimulation you show them.

Here is an example. The following slides are from the investor deck you saw previously, where the founder introduces the growth potential for a company in healthcare. To convince her audience that they must appreciate this growth potential, the presenter first discusses the growth they had in the past. Initially, investors watching the deck are in a neutral state, and the more historical facts are mentioned, the more bored people get (it's interesting that the moment we say the words, "here is the history of . . . ," people instantly get bored, image 2). When the presenter introduces the notion of "today," people are more relaxed (image 3). And they stay relaxed until the presenter mentions plans for the product (image 4). There is also a lot of animation in these slides. But then (just 30 seconds after!), people get bored again (image 5), and it takes more information related to growth strategy to get them out of that state (image 6).

1

2

3

 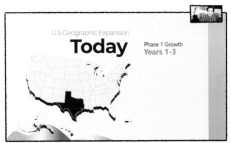

4

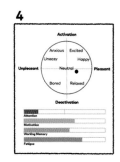 

5

6

We can extract two points from this example:

1. People get bored very quickly.

2. It takes a lot of stimulus variety to get them to shift from boredom to engagement.

If the stimulus does not change, people experience habituation, which means that as they get used to a stimulus, they pay less and less attention to it.

What leads to habituation? Tasks are simple, are repetitive, and can be carried out with minimum attention. Take a look at any message you create. Does it meet at least two out of these three criteria? For example, I remember a presentation where someone took 25 minutes to explain to an audience how to fill out a spreadsheet with several project deliverables. People quickly became bored because the task was simple and required minimal attention. A better approach would have been to send everyone a handout and reserve face-to-face time to answer questions about that task or present something about a more complex task.

Influential communicators vary the stimulus often, so the brain does not have a chance to habituate. But how often is often? The previous chapter on movement provides concrete guidelines on how often to change a stimulus. Here, let's focus on another concept. Be cautious about how much variety you orchestrate. Research suggests that boredom can also be caused by *too much* stimulation. I frequently see presentations, for instance, where each slide is at its most intense stimulus. You, too,

are probably used to seeing presentations with slide after slide offering abundant information, but often, it's just variations on the same theme (e.g., lots of charts). Data is important, but it can be more attention-grabbing when paired with a variety of stimulation, some more intense and some less intense, built with different message types and tones. For example, you can switch from visuals to text, from formal to informal, from monologue to dialogue, from facts to stories, from simplicity to complexity, and back again. Here is what I mean.

I once tested a sales presentation in a hyperscanning setting, meaning scanning the brain of more than one person at a time as they were viewing the presentation. The research aimed to see which method of presenting an introductory sales presentation was better: face-to-face, virtual, over the phone, or hybrid. The hybrid method meant one person viewed the sales presentation while in the same room with the seller, while another person joined via Zoom. We found no statistically significant differences among the modalities when it came to cognitive variables, such as attention, cognitive workload, fatigue, and motivation. But when measuring affective variables, such as valence and arousal, the hybrid condition performed the worst, while the virtual condition performed best (yes, it was surprising that face-to-face did not perform well, which could be a function of the variability that the medium introduces—the virtual modality may restrict the area of focus and provide a more similar experience). Based on these results, the practical conclusion

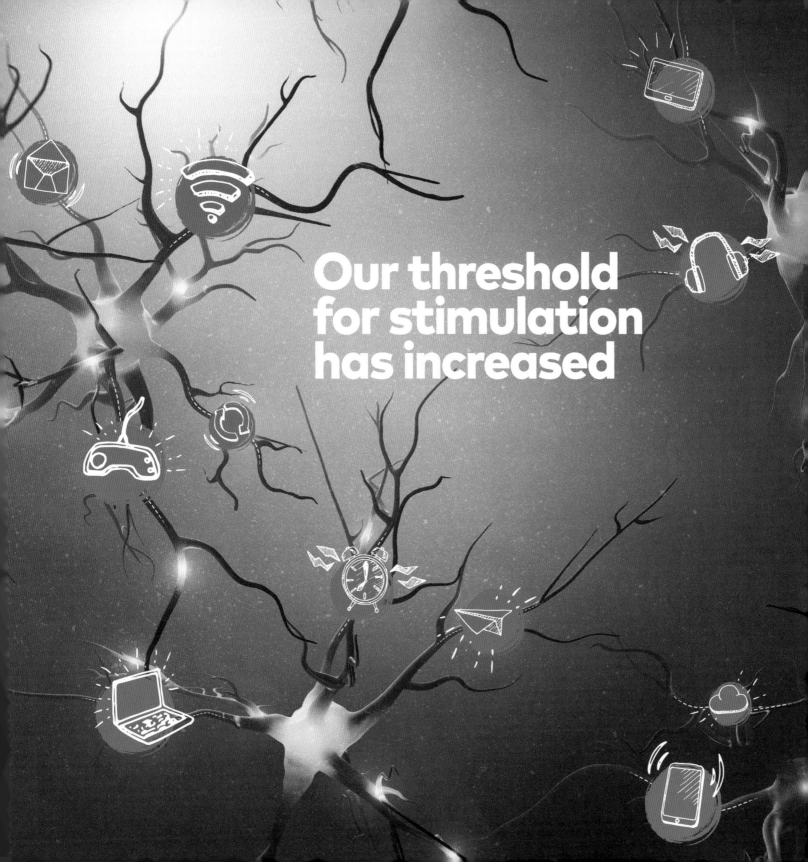

Our threshold
for stimulation
has increased

was to suggest a virtual setting for a first-time, high-level introductory presentation for a product. However, there are times when we cannot control the medium for presenting. In that case, we looked specifically at what the deck contained that made it cognitively successful even over the phone, when people did not see slides.

The script included many varied elements. The presenter was instructed to start with a *story*, a very concrete,

Varying the stimulus protects against boredom. In this presentation, we switched from concrete to abstract, from intense images to bullet points, and from stats to stories.

simple, and informal scenario that people could relate to. Then, he shared formal and complex *stats* about trends in the industry related to their software. Next he switched to simple *customer examples* and connected *their* stories with the merit of the platform he was advocating. Then he switched again to the predictable but more complex *logo* slide to show who their current customers were and how they were using several products. And then he switched again to a final punchy message about why organizations need the platform. This variety included different message types (story, stats, customer examples) that attracted and sustained attention.

Notice that in the presentation, while there was a great deal of variety, one thing stayed consistent throughout: The main message he wanted people to remember (see yellow boxes in the example). This is an important point because it can be easy to hop from one message type to another, get mesmerized by your own variety, and lose track of what ties it all together.

Regarding the frequency of change, where business content is concerned, there is no conclusive research on how little is too little stimulation and how much is too much. The frequency with which you switch depends on your audience's baseline and ability to detect a pattern. The brain needs awareness of the opposite state to detect the change. For example, adding another picture or video may go unnoticed if everything is visually intense or if the audience is used to a lot of intensity. But if you provide text for a while, a sudden image or video will be noted. In the previous healthcare example, I suspect the audiences' brains were ready for a bullet point slide after the third visual metaphor.

Challenge

In 2011, Oskar van Deventer, a Dutch designer, created the world's largest Rubik's Cube, measuring $17 \times 17 \times 17$ inches, which he called "Over the Top." The original Rubik's Cube is $3 \times 3 \times 3$. There are 66.9 quinquagintatrecentillion possible positions to solve Deventer's cube. In math terms: $6.69 * 10^{1054}$. This is a number with more than a thousand zeros of possibilities. So how long does it take to solve this monster puzzle? It took Kenneth Brandon almost eight hours of focused work. Look him up on YouTube to watch a brief time-lapse of the full eight hours for an example of a challenging task that keeps someone laser focused.

While a $17 \times 17 \times 17$ Rubik's Cube may be an extreme example, it shows that the human brain can have significant periods of focus if given a good challenge. Ponder your messages right now. How often do you take your audiences over the top and give them a good challenge?

We often baby audiences too much, so it is no wonder they get bored. Science confirms the association between challenge and boredom. For example, in Germany, researchers studied 9,452 high school kids, starting with the premise that test performance may depend not only on ability but also on motivation and emotions involved

Our brains are overloaded but understimulated.

in test taking. The subjects completed a math test, a test-taking effort questionnaire to gauge motivation, and a boredom/daydreaming survey to gauge emotion. The results showed a correlation between individual ability and boredom/daydreaming. In addition, when test items are too easy or too hard, the test-taker will likely experience increased boredom. This is why you may be noticing an increase in the popularity of computerized adaptive testing.

How do we include challenging segments in business content? In my workshops, I ask business executives to give me examples of information they use in their content to "stretch their own audiences intellectually"—in other words, to provide a challenge. Many give examples of sobering statistics tied to their messages. For example, an executive from a data security company cited these statistics: "80 percent of business data is files, 50 percent of users bring their own devices to work, there were 79 zettabytes of data generated worldwide in 2021, and over two-thirds of all new integration flows will extend outside the enterprise firewall." These numbers were meant to challenge the audience to think about intelligently managing their files to avoid the loss of critical or sensitive data, limited reporting, process breakdowns, and administrative burdens. He had the entire room's attention because most of us handle hundreds of files monthly. His presentation was nicely titled "Where Is My File?" and had the right mix of challenging and easy-to-understand concepts.

For some, challenge implies an *accelerated pace* of performing an activity. For example, imagine that you typically run eight-minute miles. Now, try running six-minute miles. In business, any time we give an audience the task of doing something more quickly than they are used to, they will perceive it as challenging. For instance, following the prior example on file management, imagine asking viewers how long it takes them to locate an important file on their computer. Now give them the task of creating a technique to find it twice as fast. Venture capitalists often tell entrepreneurs that they have 30 minutes to speak, and once they start, they tell them to do it in 10 minutes to see how they handle the pressure. As long as the tasks are realistic, audiences challenged by speed find it difficult to get bored.

Some people consider *deep, complex,* or *creative* content to be challenging. Notice the difference between these two questions when you meet someone: "Where are you from?" versus "What is the strangest thing about where you grew up?" Or "How was your weekend?" versus "What was the best part of your weekend?" I remember a marketing executive who wanted to persuade people to join him on a project in San Francisco to rescue one of the town's most challenging districts: the Tenderloin. He opened his presentation before a committee with a profound statement: "The Tenderloin isn't the home for San Francisco's problems. It's a haven for them."

I've seen numerous presenters deliver complex slides well because they challenged cognition and

Are you creating messages that are

too hard,

too easy,

or

just right?

invited deeper thinking. If well-organized and logically explained, complexity can be a path toward challenging an audience. You will learn more about complexity in Quadrant 4 of the book.

Challenge can also mean the *absence of information in a way that gives people the joy of getting it.* I remember a Nikon ad that showed no pictures but displayed this text: "A three-year-old boy saluting at his father's funeral. A lone student standing in front of four tanks. An American president lifting his pet beagle by the ears. A woman crying over the body of a student shot by the National Guard. . . . If you can picture it in your head, it was probably taken with a Nikon." I enjoyed the ad because it was not obvious; it challenged viewers to engage and complete a message.

Complexity invites deeper thinking and conversations. These two examples contain a lot of information that is varied and connected. In the first example, the eyes have to "jump" between items. The improved version leads the eye around the screen, making complexity easier to manage.

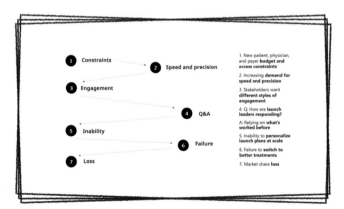

Choice

I grew up in Communist Romania, and the only way you could watch Hollywood movies was to get them on the black market. A group of "professionals" smuggled tapes into the country and used a kludge setup to dub them: One VCR played the movie, a woman with a microphone translated the audio track, and the two were recorded onto a new VHS tape. The only drawback: It was the *same* woman dubbing *all* the smuggled movies. Her name is Irina Nistor, and she has one of the most recognizable voices in Romania. If you ever want to impress an older person from Romania, go beyond mentioning Dracula or Nadia Comăneci. Ask about Irina Nistor.

During Communism, Irina Nistor was in demand, dubbing six to seven movies daily. She was Bruce Lee, Chuck Norris, Jean-Claude Van Damme, Bruce Willis, and Sylvester Stallone. By the time I left Romania, I heard she was Jesus. Given that the Romanian population did not have ready access to popular Western movies, the

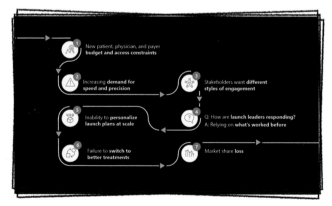

Being trapped in an unwanted situation is the hallmark of boredom

demand for speed completely obscured the need for voice inflections. Despite her high-pitched voice, we paid attention for hours because there was no other way to get the "content." We had no choice.

A forced-choice approach is one way to get people to focus, but there is a difference between staying focused because you have to and staying focused because you want to.

In academic studies, lack of perceived choice is predictive of boredom. For example, when teachers tell students what to do or offer suboptimal options such as, "If you've finished the assignment, do more work or help other students," that is conducive to boredom. In contrast, when students have choices, they show greater engagement, learn more, perform better, and have higher levels of aspiration. Studies show that many gifted students leave school, and many gifted employees leave jobs because they feel they don't have the opportunity for self-determination, the power to change a situation, or the authority to implement choices.

Choice is intricately connected with control. Choice means you have sufficient power to act on it. With regard to both, the research is clear and consistent: Control or choice leads to motivation and sustained effort to pay attention and learn. When you speak to your audiences, are you encouraging autonomy and providing interesting options?

How many choices are too many? Don't think about numbers; think of the *time* when you offer those choices. If you want to influence people at the outset of attaining a goal (e.g., to sign up for a long-term fitness program), giving them four or five choices is motivating because they can see many ways to get there. As they get closer to the finish line and have progress under their belt, people enjoy fewer choices because choosing implies thinking, which disrupts the momentum to get to a desired endpoint. When they are already following you and have a specific goal to reach, offering a more rigid approach works because it simplifies the task. For example, suppose you were running a fitness club. In that case, promoting one fitness program to already fit people is more beneficial because they are already on the right track, while offering several choices to people who just joined after New Year's Day works better because they are just at the beginning of their fitness program. For people in the middle stage, providing choices driven by social information may boost motivation. Use this fitness example as a metaphor for your field: offer more choices to neophytes and fewer to those close to attaining a goal.

I remember working with a sales executive who wanted to show customers how to use a software tool to create targeted marketing campaigns. The goal was for a prospect to buy the entire platform, but we agreed it was too ambitious because more features came at a higher cost. So we divided the features into three categories: smart email, smart online, and smart marketing. He presented all three options to prospects along with two subsets for each to build the larger context, advising that they buy the first choice to "start small and succeed big." In subsequent conversations, he did not need to reiterate all these choices after prospects became customers with more knowledge about the system. Instead, he could zoom in and focus on a selected choice, ensure it was completed successfully, and then move on by offering the next set of choices.

Consider giving your listeners choices in the following areas (at least one must be flexible to decrease boredom):

1. **Content:** Are the topics you speak about relevant to your audience? Can they express a preference prior to interacting with you and your content, which will determine what you choose to share?

2. **Process:** Do your listeners have a choice on how and when they listen to you?

3. **Environment:** When you address others, are the time of day, place, or group size flexible?

Boredom and a Meaningful Life

Ample research confirms a causal relationship (not just correlational) between life meaning and boredom. Scientists agree that boredom often represents a failure to develop meaningful life goals. People who claim to live a meaningful life behave according to their definition of meaning or a sense of purpose. For some, it is making a difference in the world; for others, it is making money, achieving status, or simply enjoying oneself. Whatever the meaning, when it exists, it erases boredom.

Joseph Brodsky, the winner of the 1987 Nobel Prize for Literature, delivered a commencement address at Dartmouth College in 1984. He warned students that the amount of boredom they had experienced because of teachers would be minimal compared to the amount of boredom they would experience as adults. He cautioned that escaping boredom would be a constant effort, involving a frequent change of jobs, locations, wives, lovers, and interests. In a philosophically sad way, Brodsky concluded that boredom would teach a valuable lesson, the "lesson of your utter insignificance." However, he reminded graduates that this knowledge of insignificance leads to a sense of mortality, which leads to a sense of passion and purpose.

With each message you deliver, you're not just adding to a repository of information; you can touch people's lives and inspire them. For example, boredom is alleviated when people can answer these questions:

1. Do I have a clear purpose?

2. Do I have autonomy?

3. Do I have mature relationships?

In helping people find these answers, you can magnify the meaning of their existence.

Don't
make it
just about
content.

Magnify
to people's
purpose.

CHAPTER 5

Give Them Something to Think About

Previous chapters have shown how to share content that makes people look outward and keeps them looking. You can also capture attention by inviting people to look inward and think deeply about something. However, not all thinking is equal: Some thinking can be superficial, and some can be deep, meaning critical. So your challenge is to guide people to look *and* think critically. Why is this important? Consider this example.

In season one of the show *Breaking Bad*, there is an episode where drug dealer Jesse Pinkman uses hydrofluoric acid to dissolve a dead body in his upstairs bathtub. Jesse is stunned to see how the toxic substance turns the body into a bloody, lumpy mess that eats through the tub and the ceiling and splatters onto the ground floor of the house. Intrigued by this scene, Adam Savage and Jamie Hyneman from *MythBusters* investigated whether this was realistic. To replicate the context, they built an elevated bathroom in the desert, equipped with a cast-iron tub set on solid flooring. They used a pig carcass for the body, and three times as much hydrofluoric acid, fortified with a "secret sauce," which they did not divulge to viewers. Despite the increased quantity and potency, the toxic mix did not even make a dent in the floor.

Critical thinking helps us analyze, assess, and verify information. And while it's fine not to invoke it in entertainment, in business, triggering critical thinking in your audiences will help them dig deeper, pay attention, and understand better, which translates to better memories and decisions.

We'll assume you're already a critical thinker and want to share with an audience something you know is true. How do you guide people to think as deeply as you do and arrive at the same truth you hold? To answer this, let us first define truth, and then look at five types of claims you are likely to make in your messages and the kinds of evidence your listener's brain is likely to accept and find reflection-worthy.

This chapter is important because people often create messages in a rush; accurate content is usually at a disadvantage because it is time-consuming. To paraphrase a journalism adage: Opinions go around the world while accurate content is still putting its pants on. The guidelines presented here will help you find a pragmatic and fair way of inviting people to focus inward on something accurate and rewarding.

Going back to the prior example, using critical thinking and scientific principles, Adam and Jamie formed a hypothesis ("this toxic mix will eat through the floor"), designed an experiment, gathered results, and interpreted them ("the TV scene was not accurate"). These are typical steps in the scientific method, and I recommend using them when you share content and make people think. When you invite your audience to ponder your content, you will help them by not just telling them *what* to think but showing them *how* you've arrived at your conclusions so that they can see them too, even in the absence of any visuals from the external world.

Beyond Black and White: The Complex Nature of Truth

Let's look at techniques for sharing information with your audience that enables them to see what is true. But what is truth? I propose the definition: a statement that is most probable in proportion with the evidence available at the time. This definition is helpful for three reasons.

Truth Can Change in Time and Context

In many contexts, truth is not transcendent; it can take new forms based on new evidence. There are many such examples of scientific U-turns because, in the quest for new knowledge, scientists observe that old knowledge needs correcting. For instance, there used to be evidence that drinking one glass of wine daily was healthy; new evidence shows that this is not true.

Alan Alda, the actor and host of the PBS program *Brains on Trial*, labels truth as "workable units, useful in a given frame or context." Reflecting on your own messages, consider using phrases such as, "This is what I consider true *now*, in this *context* . . ."

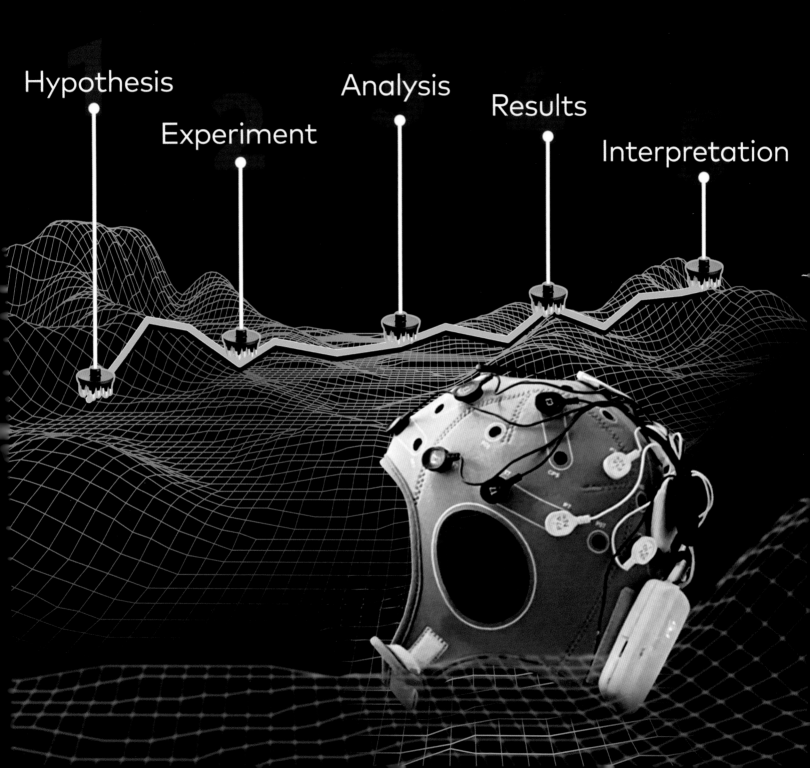

In these slide examples, I am presenting myths related to communication, such as "human beings have short attention spans," "pictures are more memorable than text," and "less is more."

Here are some slides I've used in my own presentations, challenging past truths that have changed in light of new information or experiments.

Probabilities Matter

The definition of truth mentioned earlier included the phrase: "a statement that is most probable." Probability means the likelihood that an event will occur: "There is a 90 percent chance of sunshine." Unfortunately, probabilities are not easily understood. If there is a 90 percent chance of sunshine and it rains, it does not mean the information was false; it just means that the lower probability event occurred. If you ride on a train 500 times a year to and from work, and the train is 99 percent on time, it means that about 5 times, you will either be late to work or late getting home.

The problem is that we don't have a strong intuition for odds, or when we do, it is inaccurate. For example, consider this question: Which place has a higher probability of rainfall, London or Naples? Even though intuitively, we may think it rains more in London, Naples has 50 percent more precipitation yearly. The trouble with the truth, when considering probabilities, is that quite often, we look at things not from the angle of what is probable but from what is congruent—what we *expect* to happen. And expectations do not always equal the truth.

Understanding probabilities and their link to the truth is critical if you want people to reflect and pay attention to something accurate. A helpful tip: when you advocate something as highly likely for your audience, give them strategies if low-probability events occur.

These are slides from a presentation in which I was debunking the myth "simplify complexity." You will learn more about this in Quadrant IV. The visuals are intended to show what happens when you remove complex elements (keyboard items) and assume an audience is not equipped to handle complexity.

Seek Evidence

The definition of truth mentioned earlier emphasizes the proportion between probabilities and evidence. This is not easily done because often we don't have enough evidence. Too many people create and deliver messages based on *convenience* instead of *validation*. Content based on convenience is self-serving; it selects only those facts that confirm an audience's beliefs, gain others' loyalty, and convert it into financial gain. Content that is based on validation places high importance on accuracy and authentication. An ethical hybrid approach is necessary.

When you create your own content, be mindful of the balance between the number of claims you make and the amount of evidence you have. The more claims, the longer the message. This is why it is better to make fewer claims with substantial evidence than more claims with superficial evidence.

The rest of this section focuses on the balance between claims and evidence. When you provide them in proportion, you make people reflect on what is true.

Your Claims

Almost every business claim you ever make falls into one of these five types: definition, fact, cause, value, and policy. Knowing details about each and combining them in your messages will help you and your audience examine your content deeply, think critically, and pursue the truth.

| Claim of Definition | Claim of Fact | Claim of Cause | Claim of Value | Claim of Policy |

Claim of Definition

With this type of claim, you investigate what something is or how something should be defined. For example: "Human trafficking is the illegal movement of people, typically for forced labor or commercial sexual exploitation." To be perceived as truthful, people must agree with you on a definition. How would you define the word "yellow" to someone? Would that definition be the same if your listener was color-blind?

I once wanted to convince a CEO of the importance of brain science in corporate presentations. I had a full speech prepared, which I quickly abandoned because we took the entire hour debating the definition of a presentation. Analyze your claims and ask: Do your listeners define your terms the way you do? And are your definitions still valid and current?

Take big data, for example. The subject of big data is so ubiquitous that if you talk to any business professional long enough, regardless of the field—technology, finance, healthcare, telecom—it will come up at some point, along with the definition that includes the three Vs: volume, velocity, and variety. Yet no one mentions where the three Vs came from. It turns out that an analyst's report on the challenges of data management first identified the three Vs in 2001. So if people are talking about how current big data is, do *old* definitions still apply?

Reflecting on your own content, ask: Are you using current definitions of what you're claiming?

To get to the truth, focus on defining simple words deeply instead of defining complex terms superficially. In the book *Physics of the Future*, scientist Michio Kaku discusses artificial intelligence (AI) and comments on the trouble with AI, which is the lack of consensus on the definition of consciousness. He then takes a stab at a

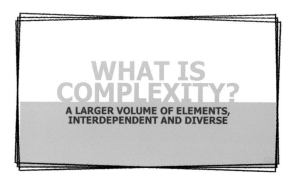

Here are some slides from my presentations, which I often start by defining the concepts I share. Note how not all slides have to be absolutely stunning because this is not about getting the brain to look outward for long. Instead, these are intended to use a visual stimulus to direct attention inward toward deeper processing of the information.

definition. According to his research, consciousness includes three components: (1) sensing and recognizing the environment, (2) self-awareness, and (3) planning for the future by setting goals. Even if some may question his definition, you can see how offering *a* definition makes it easier to have a conversation and quantify technological progress in a field as complex as AI.

Take a look at a project you're working on right now. Pick a small part of it and define it completely first. This has several advantages:

- It exposes your knowledge gaps, if any.

- It helps you get to the essence of truth.

- It enables you to create attention-grabbing and more memorable messages because when you give your listeners *only one* deeply detailed topic to pay attention to, you avoid overload.

Claim of Definition	Claim of Fact	Claim of Cause	Claim of Value	Claim of Policy

Claim of Fact

When you make factual claims, you observe whether something happened or something exists: "Facebook bought WhatsApp for $19 billion." You most likely include factual information in your content because facts bring credibility. And when they sound impressive or disruptive, they also give you social currency.

Provide your listeners with shareable facts, but constantly check their validity. A fact is objective, discovered, and verifiable. It is presented with unbiased words: "Brussels sprouts are a source of vitamin C and vitamin K." An opinion is subjective, interprets reality, cannot be verified easily, and is presented with biased words: "Brussels sprouts taste awful."

Using the definitions of facts as compared with opinions, you will now find it easy to spot them in other people's content, such as this Realtor's statement: "Two-bedroom, one-bath house with scenic valley view, on a quiet street. Centrally located. The town report says home is in need of major repairs. Sellers say all it needs is love."

Opinions do not need to lose the battle with facts. Our conversations would be sterile and dull if we did not

Opinions

Evidence

add opinions to facts. However, acknowledge anything speculative. So much speaking these days is unscripted and unprepared. Who has time to vet and verify? We live in a culture of immediacy. But ask yourself: Am I passing along opinions? If so, how did I form them? Am I selecting only specific facts that serve a point for persuasion? Are there competing facts that I have considered?

Claim of Cause

Definitions and facts alone may grab attention, but will they sustain it? The brain seeks meaning to keep going, and sometimes we are quick to provide it by looking for cause and effect. When you make claims of cause, you note the effects of a phenomenon. "People who drink tea are healthier" is an example of a claim of cause. The conclusion could be that tea prevents health problems. Whenever you see such inferential leaps, immediately ask: Is this cause justified? Maybe tea drinkers generally lead healthier lifestyles, so they have fewer health problems. Maybe it's the antioxidants in tea that reduce the risk of disease.

Identifying causes makes a message reflection-worthy because it appears relevant and useful, attracting additional attention. Humans love to jump to conclusions. This is because conclusions help decide actions. From an evolutionary standpoint, if we identify cause and effect, we can predict the effects of our decisions and improve our survival rate. When we compose cause-and-effect frameworks—which is why storytelling is so appealing—we think we know how the world works, which feels good.

cause

A .A

effect

Many elements in our environment feed our illusions of mastering cause and effect, such as factories and computers, where we can see which specific input leads to which specific output. This one-way relationship is visible and controllable. However, we must be cautious because some systems, such as the economy, social media, or human behavior, are too complex to fit neatly into predictable cause and effect. Inferential leaps can get us in trouble because they may obscure the truth.

To understand the danger of drawing conclusions when the effect is not linked to a specific cause (the famous "correlation is not causation" adage), analysts create spoofs to show how seemingly correlated data could lead to bizarre conclusions. For example, using actual data and correlated numbers, there is evidence to conclude the following: Super Bowl outcomes could predict the stock market. Living in a poor country increases penis size. The more babies named "Ava" there are, the more housing prices increase. Chocolate consumption per capita leads to Nobel Prize winners. Lonely people are more likely to take long, warm showers, and black cats give you allergies.

If correlation does not imply causation, how are you supposed to invite your audience to look and make sense of anything? While you must be cautious about jumping to conclusions, you have to be able to make predictions so you can help your audience think about what to do next. There is a middle ground between being statistically cautious and evolutionarily pragmatic.

We are learning much from fields that seek substantiating causation: Biomedicine and the social sciences are two examples. Scientists from these domains claim you can show causation if there are randomized samples from a large population and randomization of assignments during a scientific test. Here are some additional guidelines you can use as you reflect on claims of cause in your content:

Temporal relationship: Always note whether the cause happens first and then the effect appears. Do you remember the popular anti-inflammatory drug Vioxx? The pills became controversial when they were associated with cardiovascular risk. However, there was a debate in individual cases that some *other* conditions could have caused cardiovascular risks, such as age, gender, hypertension, obesity, or smoking. Those conditions appeared *before* people took the drug.

Dose-response relationship: Using another pharmaceutical example, imagine that 10 percent of those exposed to a drug develop a disease compared to only 5 percent of those who are not exposed. The disease occurs twice as frequently among the exposed group. The relative risk is 2 (10 percent divided by 5 percent). A relative risk of 1 does not show an association between exposure and risk. Despite criticism, many US and UK judges accept the *doubling of risk* as a minimum

When you become skeptical about knowledge, you develop a

scientific and critical thinking mentality.

And you help your audiences do the same.

threshold for determining causation. For example, consider a context of using a certain software application to incentivize sellers by showing them their compensation on mobile devices. When sales leaders use this software, they report a 65 percent improvement in the way they design comp plans compared to when they are not using the software.

Reversible association: This means that the concentration in one component affects the concentration in another. For example, if you remove a stuffy nose, sore throat, hoarseness, and cough, the concept of a cold would not be applicable. In a business presentation, someone claimed that cloud, mobility, social collaboration, and big data are causing corporations in healthcare to rethink their tactics. If these four factors were removed, would healthcare corporations still need to change their business models?

Consistency and coherence: This means that multiple studies in other locations show similar effects on what you claim, and the information is coherent with other known facts. Following the business example above, if we notice that the four factors also impact technology, environment, and transportation businesses, we have a stronger claim.

To practice critical thinking and help your audiences do the same, constantly poke holes into causal relationships you may be sharing. Does breastfeeding really lead to increased IQ, or is there another variable that makes them both increase at the same time? If something is simple enough and you can make sense of it quickly, do it. For complex issues, look for alternative or rival hypotheses or alternative explanations to interpret the data.

Claim of Value

It is impossible to view the world entirely through the lens of definitions, facts, or causes without adding a sense of value. One could know many facts without knowing which facts are *important*. It is also impossible for your audiences to pay attention and make decisions solely based on facts, so you must clarify value if you want to impact attention and deep thinking. When you make claims of value, you're essentially telling others if something is good or bad, for example, "Technology has a positive impact on education" or "Cell phones have changed human interactions in negative ways."

For the most part, value is opinion-based, meaning it is biased. Bias is not always bad. You have developed your opinions based on something, even if it was just curiosity at first. But be sure to combine curiosity with discipline. You must have curiosity *and* a hypothesis to explain why

Claim of value

something has value. If you are not disciplined, messages become arbitrary, and you will find it difficult to predict their impact on your listeners.

To demonstrate value methodically, provide parameters by which value is decided. For example, if you say, "Restaurant X is better than Restaurant Y," what are the criteria by which you make this value claim? Zagat, for instance, uses three parameters to assign value: food, decor, and service. Having some generally agreed-upon criteria helps you to balance ethical knowledge with empirical knowledge and make reasonable value judgments. Gartner offers four dimensions of value related to introducing new technologies and implementing them: Leaders, Visionaries, Niche Players, and Challengers. What criteria do *you* use for claiming value, and how many entities agree on those criteria?

Claim of Policy

Claims of policy tell people what to do. For example: "Use public transportation more frequently to protect the environment." Claims of policy are the toughest for listeners to accept, particularly when they have a different view than yours or are quite happy with the status quo. Psychologically, persuading people away from a position they already hold is more complicated. Moving away from prior beliefs and attitudes feels unpleasant.

You will also see resistance when your claim of policy is tied to people's existing habits. For example, what is the impact of telling others that they should eat healthier, be on time, swear less, not interrupt others when they speak, use less screen time, and not gossip? They may agree with you theoretically but not do any of it. This is why claims of policy work best when you design them with your audiences' habits in mind. Modern research has identified three components of habits:

1. Environmental cues
2. Routines
3. Rewards

For example, each time I sit in a specific chair, I eat chocolate because I think it energizes me for the morning. The cues are the area where I am sitting and the time of day. The routine is eating chocolate. The reward is that I feel energized.

Neuroscience studies confirm that when people repeat the same action, the decision-making areas of the brain become less active; a stable environment triggers those actions automatically. In this regard, *disrupting* the environmental cues that trigger habits renders those habits open to change. This is why one of the best opportunities for change is to deliver your claims at a time when your listeners are already undergoing natural shifts in routines, ranging from major (getting a new job, relocating, earning more or less, starting a family, getting a divorce, becoming a leader, going global) to minor (changing computers or using a different software program).

Reflecting on your own messages, if you're in the business of telling others what to do (claims of policy), ask yourself: What are the larger contexts in which people's behaviors are embedded? Which cues in the environment trigger the current habits that you recommend changing? How can they avoid exposure to those cues? How can you change their context so that your claims of policy are perceived as true and, therefore, worthy of turning into action?

We have discussed five claims you typically make when speaking with others: claims of definition, fact, cause, value, and policy. Combine them in your messages and treat them according to the guidelines included here to protect the truth and invite critical thinking in you and your audiences.

Your Evidence

The definition of the truth mentioned earlier—"a statement that is most probable in proportion with the evidence available at the time"—emphasized the need for evidence. If you use the five claims and follow the guidelines, you already have a solid foundation for evidence.

However, given today's audiences, who are more discriminating and often cynical, you may need *extra* evidence. In the past, you may have spent a week or two researching the proof of your claims. Today, your listeners may be equally informed on the same topic, which means that your level of evidence must be even higher.

There are several types of evidence: *statistics* (the use of numbers to make a case), *testimonials* (the use of endorsements from experts), and *anecdotal* (the use of observations, experiences, ideas, examples, or analogies). Use them in combination to create a solid foundation for your messages. On the next page is an example of a sequence that uses all three components in one of my presentations. In the first slide, I am sharing stats from a neuroscience study I was running on evaluating the impact on the brain of four delivery modalities for a sales pitch: face-to-face, virtual, hybrid, or over the phone. The second slide includes testimonials from a memory test that customers received 48 hours after viewing the sales pitch. And the third slide shares an anecdote about how the sales pitch was created. In that slide, I was sharing the slide sorter view of the actual pitch deck and details about how each slide had been created to support the main message. The overall sequence of my presentation is intended to make the audience look and think about the implications of the evidence in their work.

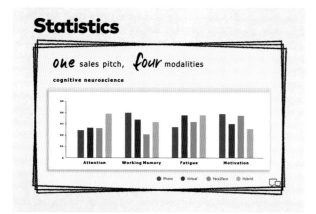

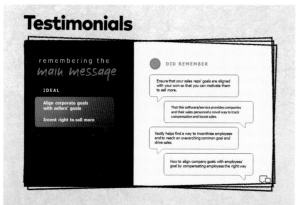

Combining statistics, testimonials, and anecdotes helps you fortify the level of evidence for your arguments.

Seeking evidence from multiple sources and choosing a path you believe is right will make your message more reflection-worthy. Avoiding a constant cheerleading style for presenting the evidence makes the message more influential yet. For example, suppose you hear a presentation on big data from those who sell big data solutions; the content typically focuses on more accurate data sets, risk management, better decision-making, and fraud avoidance. It would be so refreshing to hear a salesperson include other angles on big data at least occasionally. For example, even if we have the best algorithms for a lot of data, sometimes we still may not know what the data means. Sometimes we can get wrong correlations. Datasets are not always objective; humans still create them. Sometimes "how many" is not as important as "why" and "how." This approach is not meant to cast doubt on what someone is proposing. It is intended to enhance credibility by looking at evidence from various angles and then focusing on solutions that have been shown to work.

Regarding the *amount* of evidence you include, your listeners may be satisfied with *less* evidence if the information is simple and uncontroversial. However, for information that is challenging and disruptive, provide *more* proof.

In addition to the amount of evidence, consider the meaning you attach to that evidence. We can have the greatest amount of evidence, but when we don't attach a meaning to it, it does not make people look and

Elevate your level of proof

think. Imagine you had a lot of evidence about wine, including the ability to test how many acids, varieties of alcohol, esters, aldehydes, types of sugars, and hundreds of aromas you could detect in a wine sample. But if we don't attach any of this evidence to the meaning of the social use and the pleasure of wine, why go through the trouble of gathering all that evidence?

Deriving meaning is critical because, as cognitive scientists note, meaning fuels our success in internal processes such as efficiency in learning, problem solving, planning for the future, and deciding between options. In short, strong meaning bridges external looking and internal thinking.

It takes skill to organize facts and evidence, analyze them, and organize them in a way that provides meaning. Have you listened to a speaker make sense of complex information in a way that you understood and was meaningful? I was listening to someone speak about the importance of recruiting talent. He shared many stats about new job skills that did not exist five years ago, how there isn't enough talent to feed the economy, and how customers expect more from recruiting platforms that work like a marketing funnel. This recruiting funnel was built throughout the presentation. It all became meaningful when the funnel turned into a martini glass to symbolize that behind all this data, the most important factor was the great experience employers and candidates would have using the system. His facts were impressive, but the meaning of the facts helped me remember his presentation. And while the funnel model often comes under scrutiny, the classic martini attaches a timeless feel to his message.

One final thought: If you're sharing information that is still unfolding, tell your listeners what you know and what you don't know. They will appreciate your transparency and humility. Keep in mind that the more time passes after something has occurred and the more meaning you add to your message, the more evidence you must provide.

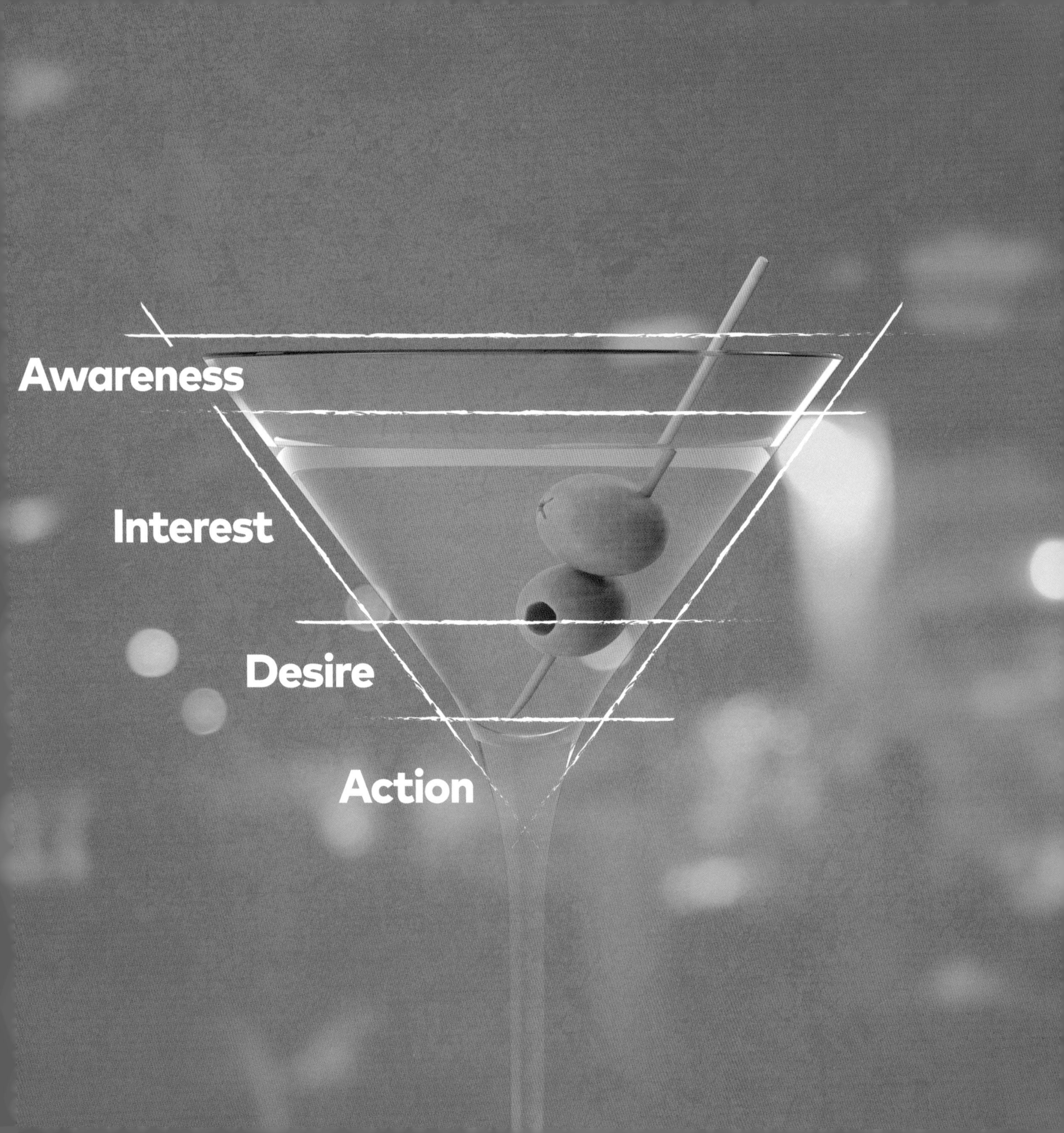
Awareness
Interest
Desire
Action

Mastering Metaphors

"Hotel California," the Eagles' best-known song, is ranked among the Top 100 Classic Rock Songs, but if you ask people what it means, you receive at least that many explanations. The band has described it as a metaphor for the high life in Los Angeles, as seen from their humble Midwest upbringing. Glenn Frey, one of the Eagles' founding members, compared the song to an episode of *The Twilight Zone* that jumps from one scene to the next and doesn't necessarily make sense. Some bolder interpretations imply that the hotel was a psychiatric hospital, an old church taken over by devil worshippers, or an inn run by cannibals. It's even been suggested that Hotel California is the Playboy Mansion. Such a bountiful metaphor paired with striking guitar skills earned the Eagles a Grammy Award.

You may not be an expert guitar player, but you can create metaphors to make people look and think. It's a perfect way to craft an *external* stimulus that guides attention *internally*.

A metaphor is a figure of speech that denotes one thing through the lens of something else. Metaphors are often used in songs, poetry, and fiction, but they work in business content, too. What are the most prevalent business metaphors? At some point, you may have used mountains, ladders, steps, or buildings to symbolize success or progress in your field. You may have used sports to

target

source

denote peak performance (or lack thereof) and chess to showcase optimal strategy. You may have helped someone understand the features of your solutions through puzzles, gears, time devices, or tools to imply precision, efficiency, speed, or convenience. You may have used ships to show how you navigate hazardous environments or planes to indicate liftoff, defying all odds. Animals, fish, insects, and plants are no strangers to business content to indicate results, leadership, and evolution. Agriculture offers metaphors to symbolize business growth through farming or gardening. Food items convey something desirable or a step-based process, such as following a recipe. And nature has appeared on many slides to symbolize a business path or journey.

Metaphors include a *target*, which typically belongs to abstract, complex, unfamiliar, and often poorly defined domains, and a *source*, which is usually concrete, simple, familiar, physical (often connected with our bodies), and well defined. Think of "life is a journey" as an example.

While there is much research on the use of metaphors in education, advertising, and politics, there is not that much scientific research on the use of metaphors in business content, especially B2B. Yet business professionals frequently use metaphors. Step into the Metaphor Gallery to see. In fact, you would be hard-pressed to find a business context that does not employ metaphors. It's just that we don't have much scientific evidence of how the business brain reacts to metaphors. This chapter intends to fill that gap and offer practical guidelines on using (and not abusing) metaphors to make people think and influence behavior.

How does the business brain react to metaphors? I had the opportunity to conduct three neuroscience studies to observe the impact of metaphors in B2B sales presentations, and I am excited to share the results. But first, let's look a bit more closely at the merits and potential drawbacks of using metaphors in business. When we understand these aspects, the results of the studies will be easier to apply to your content.

NOT A PURPOSE
MBA / PhD

To lead the Authentic
Leadership Institute

PURPOSE
Help others live more
meaningful lives

To wake you up and have
you find that you are home

WHAT IS YOUR
PURPOSE?

fortune
favours the
prepared mind

TIME TO
ACCELERATE

CONTROL THE
MEANING

FOCUS THEIR ATTENTION

Metaphor
Gallery

INFORM

INTERACT

INSPIRE

WE MAKE **WORK**

WORK BETTER

BUYER PERSONA
research

ENABLING
CROSS-FUNCTIONAL
COLLABORATIONFOR
SHARED SUCCESS

UNAVOIDABLE CHANGE

CURIOSITY
IS OUR MOST VALUABLE CURRENCY

What is **our**
approach to
Partnering with
IPSM?

OUR JOURNEY

Persistence + Learning from Failures + Taking Smart Risks

Why Do Metaphors Work?

The chapter on movement in Quadrant I includes evidence that cognition is not confined to our brains. Our attention, memory, planning, and decisions are influenced by moving our bodies in space. The scientific literature demonstrates that you will judge the temperature in your room to be five degrees warmer if you're made to feel good about something. If you're asked to think about the future, you might lean slightly forward, and about the past, slightly backward. Holding a heavy clipboard makes you judge a currency as more valuable. From this perspective, think about the metaphors you use to express thoughts and emotions in reference to the body: "He is in over his head," "This is under my control," and "I am warming up to her." Metaphors often rely on physiology and are created at the intersection of perceptions, thoughts, and emotions.

Using this embodied cognition view, here are several tangible merits of metaphors, demonstrating how sensory inputs and motor outputs are integral to the cognitive processes.

Metaphors Facilitate Universal Understanding of a Subjective Experience

Nobody can have full access to anybody else's experiences and the emotions they feel during those experiences. Let's consider migraine sufferers. Can you truly feel the pain of someone with a migraine? A metaphor can bring you closer to understanding. Check out Ian McEwan's description of the heroine's migraine in his book *Atonement*:

> She felt in the top right corner of her brain a heaviness, the inert body weight of some curled and sleeping animal; but when she touched her head and pressed, the presence disappeared from the coordinates of actual space. Now it was in the top right corner of her mind, and in her imagination, she could stand on tiptoe and raise her right hand to it. It was important, however, not to provoke it; once this lazy creature moved from the peripheries to the center, then the knifing pains would obliterate all thought, and there would be no chance of dining with Leon and the family tonight. It bore her no malice, this animal, it was indifferent to her misery. It would move as a caged panther might: because it was awake, out of boredom, for the sake of movement itself, or for no reason at all, and with no awareness.

Comparing a migraine to a panther moving around a cage is a visually striking way of helping readers understand a subjective state in a universal way. Reflecting on your content, consider whether there are some experiences that *only you*, an expert, might have and understand fully. Then link this experience through a metaphor to an abstract concept you want to help others see and feel in the same way you see and feel it.

For sustained attention, when you speak about your subjective experiences, turn a metaphor into a story (or allegory). The caged panther example has a narrative structure, mapped to different stages of experiencing a migraine: At the onset of pain, you're aware of a sleeping animal's weight; the sensation of increasing pain corresponds to the perception of the animal moving around; later in the story, there is the realization that the attack is over, which corresponds to the perception that the animal has left. You know your metaphor is like a story if there is action across time, with a beginning, middle, and end.

Metaphors Offer a Unique Interpretation of Everyday Experience

I remember a software engineer who wanted to instill the idea of an e-commerce solution as "giving you the best of both worlds" in terms of cost and capabilities (implying that competitors' solutions offered many capabilities but

> Metaphors as stories frequently appear in business content when they involve movement along a path. "Business success as a journey" or the steps of a business process are common choices to show action across time.

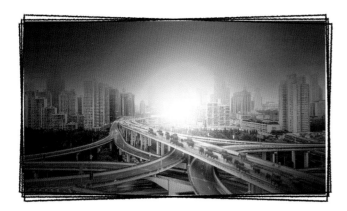

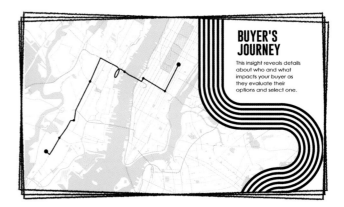

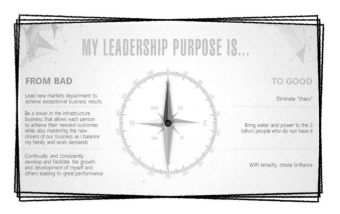

at a high cost, or were low cost but had only a few capabilities). To visualize the best of both worlds, he invoked some pleasurable experiences, such as skiing and swimming, and remembered a time when he could do both on the same day. We created a slide that showed the beach on one side and a snow-covered slope on the other, so he could tell his audiences that using his solution "was as satisfying as swimming in the morning and skiing in the afternoon." Audiences paid attention because they had not considered associating the benefits of a software solution with swimming and skiing on the same day.

Metaphors, we used to believe, were based on existing similarities between items ("a lion is fierce in the face of competition, and so are we"). A bolder approach is to consider that similarities don't have to match real life; they can be *perceived* similarities, such as in the example "life is a gamble." To avoid the cliché, however, think of personal experiences that on the surface may not be connected to business but may offer an unforced connection to a business concept anyway.

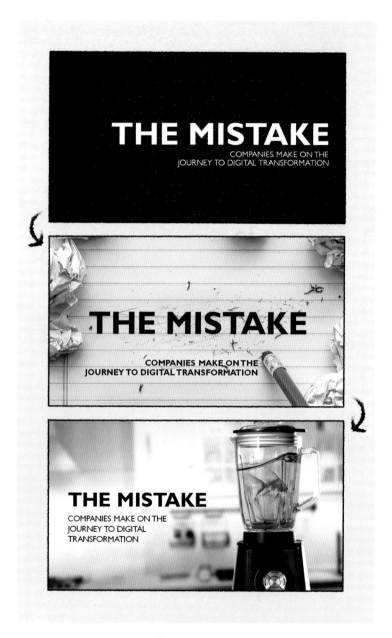

Showcasing similarities between the dissimilar makes the viewer look and impacts their memory too.

Here is a business example of two concepts that are not linked on the surface, but their connection offers a unique viewpoint for a business solution: you could compare a solution that pairs two benefits to culinary artistry that fuses the bold flavors of Mexican cuisine with the delicate precision of Japanese sushi.

The following slide collection exemplifies the way to *showcase similarities between the dissimilar.* You can see our take on visualizing a "mistake in digital transformation." The left vertical row shows how we progressed from no metaphor to a conventional metaphor showing a crumpled piece of paper, to associating a mistake in digital transformation with putting a goldfish in a blender.

You can also see the progression in visualizing the mantra "customer experience first, technology second." A giraffe in a bathtub (as opposed to predictable medals or no metaphor at all) startled some participants, but we did manage to positively impact their attention, memory, and motivation.

Metaphors Emphasize Specific Concepts

Using unique or vivid metaphors, business professionals can emphasize some aspect of a phenomenon and question or downplay others, impacting audience attention. For example, looking at the design of the slide in the upper-left corner of the following collection, you cannot help but notice first the pencil shavings, which are a metaphor for resilience. The slide that symbolizes augmented human capabilities through the hand-drawn wings on a person's back invites attention to that part of the slide, while downplaying the trees in the background. In the series of coffee cups, the design emphasizes one and dims the others, suggesting that it's important to create memorable—not forgettable—messages.

These examples were not about automobiles, pencils, ice, or coffee. These were just metaphors using contrast to substantiate a business point about old versus new, grit, techniques to approach customers, or enhanced human capabilities.

Use metaphors to add oomph to abstract concepts, adorning them with concrete elements.

Metaphors Deepen Understanding by Making the Abstract Concrete

Attracting attention with metaphors is one thing, but you must ensure that people *understand* the concepts you are sharing. Metaphors help describe or provide a simpler vocabulary for complex business or scientific phenomena that cannot be observed.

The visual examples on this page show how a metaphor enables better understanding of a concept by linking the abstract to the concrete. For example, in the top sequence, we were helping a client visualize the concept of data not being used (abstract concept); so in one slide, we showed a computer, and in the next image, the computer and its surroundings were covered by moss (a concrete concept). The bottom sequence is from a presentation in which I was talking about controlling what audiences remember, and the slide sequence clarified the abstraction through a vivid and concrete treatment.

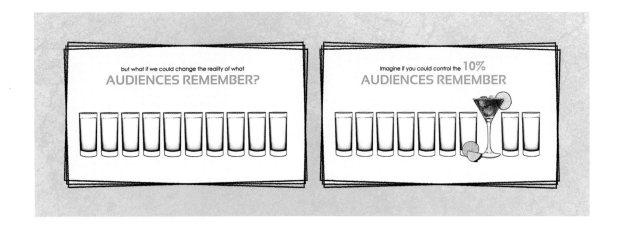

When building metaphors, effective communicators also use elaboration by adding details in an unusual way. Take a look at a literary example from the novel *Thinks* by David Lodge, in which he adds details to make us feel the depth of depression:

> For six months I languished at the bottom of a deep hole, like the shaft of a waterless well, while kindly, puzzled people . . . peered down at me over the rim of the parapet and tried to cheer me up, or lowered drugs and advice in a bucket.

It's possible to elaborate on metaphor in business content too. In the example to the right, I elaborate on the watermelon metaphor in sharing results from studies related to the neuroscience of attention. In the first slide, I simply showed a piece of paper to remind viewers that text is a viable attention-grabbing element. In the next slide in the sequence, I was speaking about the importance of adding extra details to keep customers focused and pleased, and help them remember, so I added some extra elements paired with the watermelon metaphor. And in the third slide, I mentioned the importance of uncertainty and an element of surprise and sophistication, so I elaborated on the watermelon metaphor further by combining it with an orange texture.

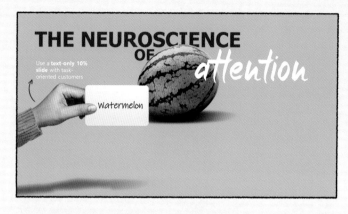

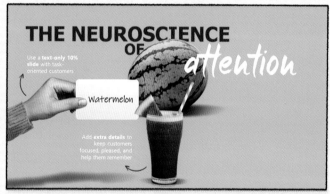

Attract attention using elaborated metaphors.

Metaphors Frame Complexity in Manageable Terms

With metaphors, you can help your audience understand complex content even if they aren't experts. Here is an example in which the presenter uses a plumbing metaphor. In the beginning, he talks about a very complex web architecture. Then he reminds the audience that all that complexity is in service of an optimal user experience (like a functional and beautiful faucet) before showing how those complex processes support the software platform he is proposing. The metaphor eases cognition momentarily before it transitions to an increasingly complex screen.

Metaphors Are Great, But . . .

While metaphors can make the complex easier to understand and highlight some aspects of the target domain, they do downplay others. For example, think of the "code" metaphor scientists use to describe DNA. Physicist Erwin Schrödinger first used the term *code-script* in 1944 to describe the role of chromosomes in individual development, but this term turned out to be too narrow. Even

In this sequence, the metaphor is "sandwiched" between two technical slides, guarding the brain from cognitive overload or boredom.

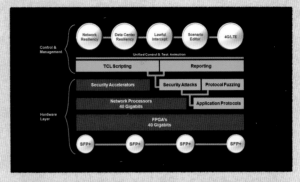

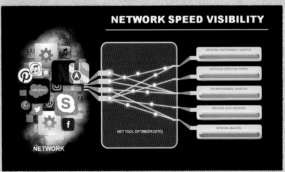

Schrödinger says, "The chromosome structures are at the same time instrumental in bringing about the development they foreshadow. They are law code and executive power—or, to use another simile, they are architect's plan and builder's craft—in one." Notice how even Schrödinger switches from DNA as code to DNA as architecture. You will see later in the chapter how this switch was helpful in a study I conducted on mixing metaphors when one metaphor is insufficient for explaining complex phenomena. When something is complex, you might need multiple metaphors.

In the example of DNA, scientists have started to be careful about the metaphors they use because they are aware that metaphors are not just relevant to making research understandable, they can even impact public and political opinion, including policymaking. What if people whose genes did not have "the right code" or script were not allowed to have children? So scrutinize your metaphors as they might carry intended implications and lead to confusion.

What Neuroscience Teaches Us About Using Metaphors in Business Content

Many of the merits and drawbacks of metaphors mentioned so far come from surveys or other self-assessment research. In this section, let's look at the results from three neuroscience studies I conducted related to the type and number of metaphors you can use in business content. (As I have mentioned, neuroscience research helps us bypass self-reports, which may be inaccurate.) The specific research questions I was asking about metaphors were related to selecting original versus clichéd metaphors, varying metaphors across a presentation, and using one metaphor throughout an entire presentation.

Fresh Versus Clichéd Metaphors

"What does the giraffe have to do with anything?" This was a question I heard a few times during the study, which was set up as follows. I divided participants into five groups, and asked them to watch a sales presentation on a software application related to digital transformation. Group 1 viewed no metaphors. Group 2 viewed clichéd metaphors on 5 slides (out of 11). Group 3 viewed clichéd metaphors on nine slides. Group 4 viewed original

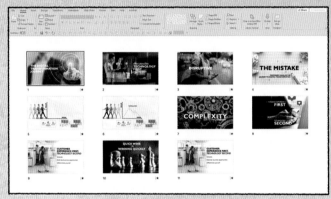

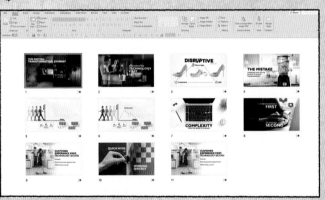
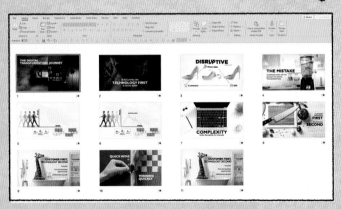

This was the setup of the study, indicating a progression from no metaphor to five clichéd metaphors, to nine clichéd metaphors, to five fresh metaphors, and lastly, to nine fresh metaphors (out of 11 slides).

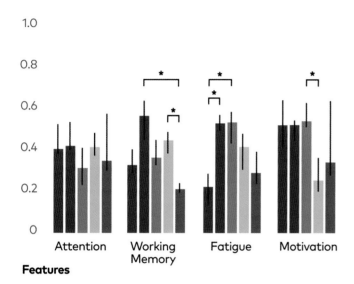

metaphors on five slides, and Group 5 viewed original metaphors on nine slides. Before the neuroscience study, I conducted a pilot test to ensure that other people agreed with what I considered clichéd metaphors and fresh metaphors.

With regard to *affective* variables, we noted statistically significant differences in arousal, with Group 5 (the group that witnessed the most original metaphors) being in the most excited or engaged state. In terms of *cognitive* variables, Group 2, which saw five clichéd metaphors, showed the highest level of working memory, a form of cognitive workload.

So, if your content lends itself to metaphors, *use multiple original ones*, as people remembered the content better (a 12 percent increase compared to the clichéd condition) without experiencing a heavy cognitive workload (meaning a higher mental effort). Participants who saw the highest number of original metaphors were also more alert and excited, paid more attention to the presentation, and experienced a stronger Eureka effect, which we measure by analyzing the gamma frequency.

Affective and cognitive variables for the five groups who viewed the presentation on digital transformation. Four out of the five groups viewed the content paired with metaphors.

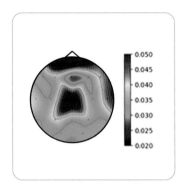

Group 5

Gamma power for Group 5, which saw the highest number of original metaphors, indicating a Eureka effect.

Based on the results, I also recommend avoiding cliché metaphors because they increase buyers' fatigue (as demonstrated by EEG data) and decrease recall (as demonstrated by long-term memory test scores).

Mixing Metaphors

In the previous study, the fresh metaphors we used were abundant but also *varied*, linking different targets to different sources. An easy way to picture a variety of metaphors is to look at a pop culture example. Notice how singer Michael Bublé, in his hit song "Everything," combines analogies of a falling star, a getaway car, a line in the sand, and a swimming pool to describe the perfect partner.

The mixed metaphors I used in the neuroscience study included comparisons between landing a B2B buyer and finding a needle in a haystack, using a solution and making progress on a board game, and adding precision to a business strategy and a robot looking into a crystal ball. When the business brain is asked to jump from one semantic domain to another, does it appreciate and engage with the variety, or does it become confused and fatigued?

A combination of metaphors might be helpful because it produces a more complex and elaborated set of connections between concepts, which increases the likelihood of more memory traces. In other words, the *combination* becomes more impactful than each individual metaphor. When you need to explain complex concepts, you may also need multiple metaphors because one metaphor may not be able to cover all the layers of depth.

But how does combining metaphors impact the business brain? In the neuroscience study I conducted to discover the answer to this question, I divided participants into four groups and asked them to watch a sales presentation on the merits of a complex software solution. Group 1 viewed a presentation that contained 12 slides with no metaphors. Group 2 viewed the same presentation but with two different metaphors on two slides. Group 3 viewed four metaphors on four slides, and Group 4 viewed eight metaphors on eight slides.

Groups 3 and 4, the groups with the most mixed metaphors, had high motivation, especially toward the end of the presentation, low fatigue, 13 to 15 percent better

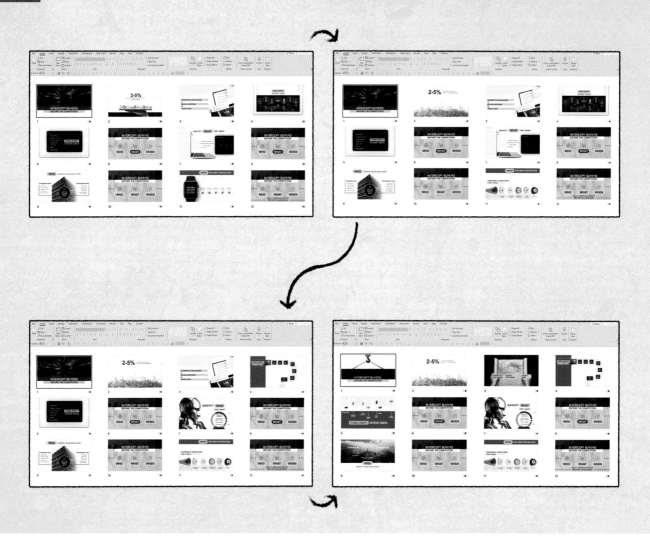

This was the setup of the study, indicating a progression from no metaphor to two varied metaphors, to four and then to eight (out of 12 slides). My hypothesis was that the more varied metaphors we offered, the worse the participants' brains would react. I was wrong.

memory than the group with fewer mixed metaphors, and also higher brain synchronization, meaning that people engaged with the content in a similar way. Group 3 even experienced a Eureka effect and approach-related behavior, meaning participants leaned in and wanted to learn more (versus withdraw). And Group 4 experienced significantly higher motivation and the lowest fatigue level throughout the presentation.

After these two studies, the firm conclusion is that if you use metaphors, use many different ones (anywhere

Values

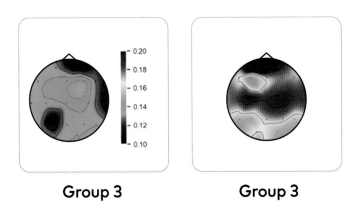

Group 3   Group 3

Advantages of Groups 3 and 4, the groups that saw the most mixed metaphors. The top charts show the cognitive variables, and the plots below show the approach behavior (left) and the Eureka effect (right).

from 30 to 80 percent of a presentation sequence), as they decrease fatigue and increase motivation. In some cases, they even provoke approach-related feelings and a Eureka effect.

Invoking the Same Metaphor Multiple Times: Useful or Dreadful?

The inspiration for this study was born almost a decade ago when I saw a template that an event organizer had created for all speakers. The theme was "crushing the competition." So they built a visual that showed a fist coming down and "hitting" the bottom of each slide. That fist was mighty the first time you saw it. Maybe the second and potentially the third because the theme became apparent. But by the fiftieth time, it was too much. The designers' intent was good: Establish consistency, coherence, and impact recall. But how much is too much, especially given metaphorical thinking? It bothered me. But would I have become bothered if that fist metaphor had been replaced with an actual image of their product as superior to the competition?

That question about consistency versus metaphor abuse stayed with me for some time. Finally, I had the opportunity to conduct a neuroscience study on the topic. I divided participants into four groups and invited them to watch a sales presentation about a software platform that promised four steps to customer success for complex organizations. Group 1 saw a presentation

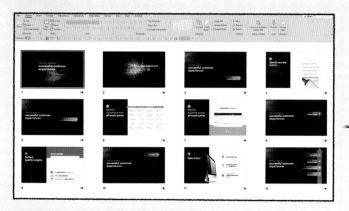

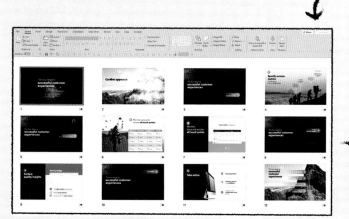

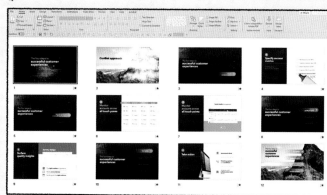

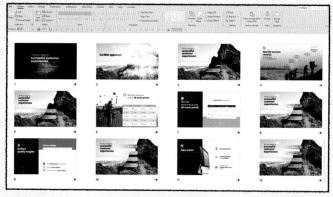

This collection shows the progression of the mountaineering metaphor across the four groups, from no metaphor to two mountain metaphors, to four and then to eight (out of 12 slides). My hypothesis was that the more cliché metaphors we offered, the worse the participants' brains would react. I was right on this one.

with no metaphors, while the other three groups were exposed to an increasing number of metaphors on the same theme: mountaineering. I chose this metaphor because in a pilot test, I had asked a group of 232 B2B participants to select the most prevalent business metaphors, and climbing mountains was deemed the most popular.

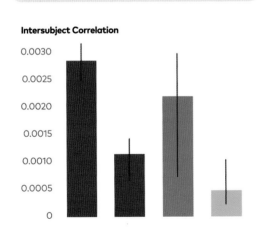

Cognitive variables and ISC (intersubject correlation) score for the four groups in the study.

So, Group 2 saw a mountaineering metaphor on 2 slides (out of 12), Group 3 saw the metaphor on four slides, and Group 4 saw it on eight slides.

Group 4, who saw the presentation with the mountaineering metaphor in the most slides, performed the worst. They had:

- Lower motivation and working memory (as evidenced by the EEG signal)

- Increased fatigue in some participants (as evidenced by the EEG signal)

- Lower excitement (as evidenced by the GSR data)

This group also showed the lowest synchronization score, meaning that despite the metaphor providing visual consistency, participants did not experience the presentation the same way.

In contrast, Group 1, who saw no metaphors, experienced the highest synchronization score and Eureka effect, and had the highest memory scores. So, in the other groups, the metaphors may have acted as distractors. Keep in mind that the overused metaphor was clichéd. This study confirmed that you're better off with no metaphor than an extended metaphor if you use a clichéd one.

Of course, generating fresh or original metaphors takes work. In fact, in one study, participants were administered a metaphor generation task that assessed the cognitive processes in both novel and conventional metaphor generation, along with a battery of cognitive measures such as vocabulary, divergent thinking, working memory, and selective attention. Results indicated that although both novel and conventional metaphor generation are linked to attentional resources and inhibitory control, the greater creativity inherent in creating fresh metaphors involves more complex cognitive processes.

One goal that all modern communicators must have, then, should you need to create original metaphors, is to develop cognitive flexibility, which means the ability to shift your thoughts and actions based on the demands of a situation. This happens because several networks become active in your brain when you engage in various mental tasks. For example, when you focus on your external environment, you engage your frontoparietal network. When you focus on relevant items, the salience network is activated. When you focus internally, the default network is active. When these networks become active, two types of connections support how you process the environment. The first type of connection represents your crystalized knowledge, which is your encoded prior knowledge and experiences. These connections are less flexible because it took you years to form them (that's why it's often hard to go beyond the conventional metaphor). But other pathways in your brain are flexible and can form the second type of connection, which is related to fluid knowledge, which is the ability for abstract thinking and problem solving in new situations, regardless of prior knowledge.

Here is how you can develop cognitive flexibility and, in the process, original metaphors:

Transition your thoughts. Cognitive flexibility depends on how quickly you can switch between different thoughts. For example, imagine you're in a group conversation, and someone is talking about nutrition. Suddenly someone changes the subject to baseball. Your ability to switch from one train of thought to another and contribute to the new discussion is considered flexibility of cognition. To transition easily, you must be focused on the moment.

Update your beliefs. Are you typically "set in your ways"? Or are you willing to change your mind when presented with new or better information? Keeping an open mind helps you improve your cognitive flexibility. We kept an open mind when we added a twist to known metaphors, such as those that follow.

Observe multiple dimensions. Do you notice just one aspect or multiple dimensions when you look at an object? For instance, when you look at a table in a room, do you note its color, shape, texture, quality, and sturdiness? Or imagine that in a meeting, someone says you could earn a few thousand dollars each month by starting your own business. Do you become immediately excited and agree? Or do you first ask if this is the right thing to do for you and your family? Cognitive flexibility implies your ability to connect elements around

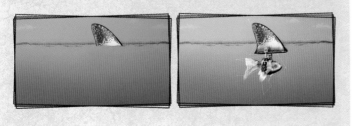

you. This also requires that you not be easily distracted.

Build domain knowledge. Ensure that you have a great deal of knowledge in the subject you are creating communication about. Creative metaphors require divergent thinking, meaning that you must consider many viewpoints on a topic. This can only happen if you have enough knowledge to explore.

Overall, we've demonstrated the many merits of metaphors. Some people you interact with, who might not be aware of this evidence, may consider metaphors cosmetic, just mere decoration. We experience this often when clients feel that a presentation needs to get straight to a solution, without a preamble, which typically includes metaphors. So, in addition to the guidelines included so far, make sure you overcome this objection by creating metaphors that are relevant to your business messages and not just providing seductive detail.

This collection shows how we added a twist to the proverbial iceberg metaphor, which indicates that there is more to the story. For example, in the two slides in the top row we show the famous Easter Island statues, and then in the next slide, we show there are aliens under the ground. In the middle row, we first show the top of a mountain, but in the next image, it turns out it's the top of an ice cream cone. In the last row, we first show the shark fin, and then the smaller fish wearing a fake shark fin.

Metaphors:
are you using
them for meaning or
mere decoration?

Practical Guidelines from Quadrant II: Guided Action

1. Offer a variety of stimulation types (such as stories, stats, customer examples, abstract conclusions) to avoid habituation and challenge people's cognitive abilities by accelerating the pace of your message or providing deeper, more complex, or creative messages.

2. Offer more content choices to new customers and fewer choices to existing customers. Invite your audience to select the type of content they prefer to receive from you, the process of working with you, and/or the environment in which they meet with you.

3. Present your solutions in terms of probabilities, and offer your audience specific approaches on how to handle low-probability events.

4. Gather enough evidence to substantiate your claims. It's better to present fewer claims with more evidence than more claims with superficial evidence.

5. Define your key terms to discover if you have any knowledge gaps in what you present and get to the essence of the truth.

6. To the extent you can, offer your audience information based on experimental studies that follow the scientific method to show how one variable causes another.

7. Base the claim of value you make on generally agreed-upon criteria in your field.

8. If you're making claims of policy (telling your audience to do something differently), prepare to offer information or guidelines at a time when people's routines are already disrupted (such as during a leadership change or transition to other software, going global, or taking on a new role).

9. Consider whether there are some experiences that only you, an expert, might have and understand fully. Then link this experience through a metaphor to an abstract concept you want to help others see and feel in the same way you see and feel it.

10. Use metaphors to link the abstract to the concrete and to protect the brain from cognitive workload.

11. Pair a common concept with a unique metaphor.

12. If your content lends itself to metaphors, use *multiple* and *original* ones, as people remember the content better without experiencing a heavy cognitive workload.

13. Avoid clichéd metaphors because they increase fatigue and decrease recall.

External Focus

**Initiated by
the Individual**

**Initiated by
the Environment**

Introspection

They orient their own
attention internally
toward something they
consider rewarding

Internal Focus

Introspection

In this quadrant, you will learn:

| What mind wandering is and isn't (the definition will surprise you)

| The good and the bad of mind wandering

| How to bring the buyer's brain back to focus on essential messages

The
interesting
in-between

CHAPTER 7

Mind Wandering

Help Them See When They Are Not Looking

Until a few years ago, I did not know the word "phubbing," which means snubbing one's companions in favor of a phone—or in other words, trying to maintain eye contact while texting. It is a humbling word that describes a harsh reality: Even when people are talking to you and you think you are in focus, their attention may be elsewhere. If sometimes people are not focused when you're "live" with them, how would you get their attention when you're not even around to guide them or when they focus inward? The purpose of this quadrant is to offer practical guidelines for getting attention in the situation when your audiences are not looking externally and are left to their own devices, often doing something else.

This phenomenon of off-task thinking can be voluntary or involuntary and is called mind wandering. It is important to address mind wandering because business professionals often look externally, but internally, the brain is steering elsewhere. If you ever reach for that last potato chip in a bag while thinking of a bad conversation, you have experienced this interesting in-between—looking outward but focusing inward.

Is it possible to help audiences still see you, the business communicator, and your message, even when they are looking inward? Is out of sight really out of mind? Or can you prompt business audiences to reflect on your content, even without a physical stimulus and despite the wealth of choices of thoughts, feelings, biases, and desires they have at their disposal?

These questions must be answered because mind wandering is so ubiquitous. We all stray from the here and now in favor of thoughts unrelated to the current task. According to some accounts, the brain is not fully focused about 50 percent of the time during waking hours, which varies according to some factors. For instance, older adults mind wander less than younger people, and most of us tend to mind wander more during an easy task versus a difficult one.

The chapters in Quadrant II offered guidelines to combat mind wandering in a way that guides the brain to focus. If you address those topics well, when the business mind wanders, you and your content will be there to greet it. What distinguishes this quadrant from the previous one is that *you* were present for an audience, as an external force, to guide attention. What happens when you're not around, and someone's brain decouples from the external world and focuses inward for a while? Can you still give your audiences an invisible wink—reminding them of something important, even when they are not externally engaged? Let's look at practical techniques that any content creator can use to be part of someone's inner dialogue.

First, let's define mind wandering in greater detail and understand how it impacts the brain. Once we have a definition and know its inner workings, establishing and applying practical guidelines will be easier.

What Is Mind Wandering, and How Does It Work?

To define mind wandering, let's first ask: Where does the mind go when it wanders? Attention can sometime transform into rumination, fantasizing, analyzing, or planning. Because of this, the phrase *mind wandering* is often used as an umbrella term for concepts such as daydreaming, task-unrelated thoughts, stimulus-independent thoughts, zoning out, or conscious fantasy, meaning spontaneous thoughts. It is fair to equate mind wandering with some of these concepts. For instance, *daydreaming* is often used colloquially in place of mind wandering, as it implies a series of thoughts that distract one's attention from the present (picture a person doodling during a business meeting something he had seen before but unrelated to the task at hand). If you are in a meeting and hope to get people's attention, their daydreaming would be a negative because it means they are not focusing on your content. However, daydreaming can be a positive during a leisure task, such as taking a walk.

Absorption and rumination are often associated with mind wandering; we can define these processes more granularly. *Absorption* is engrossment in an intellectual idea, and *rumination* is fixation on one's distress. Sometimes rumination can be goal-directed; for example, I obsessively consider how to improve my forehand after a subpar tennis match. Absorption is similar to the idea of "flow," which occurs when one's attention is completely focused.

Mind wandering also shares some characteristics with meditation. Consider *concentration meditation*, which implies focusing entirely on one thing, like your breath or the sound of an electric fan. This is typically not task-related, so if we think of mind wandering as task-independent thinking, then concentration meditation is close. Another type of meditation is *mindfulness meditation*, during which you are aware of what's going on and allow your mind to wander from thought to thought in a stream of consciousness. From this perspective, mindfulness meditation equals mind wandering plus meta-attention. You're aware and choose not to get attached to any thought.

For our conversation, let's define mind wandering as task-unrelated thoughts—meaning that if you're giving your audiences a task, they think of something other than the task at some point. When someone's brain decouples from the external world, you have two choices, and these choices have material consequences in business:

1. Bring the brain back to focus on the task.

2. Meet it in Wanderland, so that even though the brain is focused internally, it reflects on something you said.

Wouldn't it be nice if they were daydreaming while "listening" to your competition, all the while thinking of you? We'll address these scenarios in a moment, but first, a few more clarifications about the process of mind wandering.

It is important to clarify that mind wandering involves a form of attention because when someone's mind wanders, the lights don't go off. Instead, people have a vivid stream of thoughts in which they consciously and selectively focus on various bits of information, such as memories, internal speech, or fantasies. And many scientists define attention in terms of the selective focusing of consciousness. It's just that during mind wandering, attention is often unguided.

Bringing the brain back

What happens during this conscious, selective, and inner focus of attention? Cognitive scientists attest that mind wandering involves two specific alterations in cognitive processing. First, attention is directed away from the external environment, and this attentional lapse reduces the cognitive processing of perceptual information. This process of perceptual decoupling can lead to failures in the performance of external tasks. Second, mind wandering often involves stimulus-independent thought, where attention is directed toward internal information derived from memory.

Using these stages of mind wandering, we can consider that the phenomenon is not a dichotomous process, meaning that your mind is either focused on a task or it isn't. When we decouple from the external world, it's not in an all-or-none fashion. Perceiving the external world starts failing with different degrees, cascading downward through the cognitive system and causing decoupling at weak and deep levels. This is why it is possible to perform some automatic tasks (such as copying and pasting information from one document to another with minimal attention) while thinking of something else.

In addition, you may consider that all mind wandering is unintentional, but this is not so. Mind wandering can be intentional, too. In one study, participants were given easy or difficult computer tasks. Even though participants reported about the same amount of mind wandering in both easy and difficult tasks, it was more intentional during the easy condition. The difficult task led to more unintentional mind wandering.

How Do You Know When People Are Mind Wandering?

An easy way to measure mind wandering is to ask people when you give them a task, "Were you focused on it?" This is called a thought sampling method, but it is not highly reliable because when participants report their inner experiences of mind wandering, they might not answer truthfully. Social desirability might prompt some participants to reply, "On task" if mind wandering is perceived as negative. You could also bias an audience based on how you ask the question. If someone asked you, "How focused were you?" versus "Were you mind wandering?" your answers might differ.

Given that mind wandering is a subjective, often spontaneous experience, the better way to measure it is indirectly, with eye tracking, facial features, and body movements. With the recent advent of fMRI and EEG studies, scientists are linking mind wandering with a special network in the brain, the default network, in which the focus is internal and related to imagining past and future events or thoughts about goal setting.

Once we know how to measure mind wandering more reliably, then we can ask: Is mind wandering always

Not all
mind
wandering
is the same

detrimental in business? Scientists observe a significant cost to performance when mind wandering sets in. This has been tested in reading, sustained attention, and applying skills. This is important for business practitioners to understand because all business audiences engage in tasks that include reading or involve sustained attention and applying skills. When someone's mind wanders, it's harder for them to understand a message, build mental models, retain what is essential, or withhold automatic responses (meaning that if people have automatic habits, like checking their phones, they are more likely to do these instead of refraining). But this does not mean that people have zero cognitive control or that they always experience cognitive failures.

Let's consider the good and the bad of mind wandering. This is important because in your communication practices, there will be some mind wandering aspects you will want to keep for your audiences and some you will want to fix.

The Upside of Mind Wandering

While some aspects of mind wandering are disruptive, others are beneficial. Mind wandering is positively associated with *creative thinking*. There are lots of anecdotes about people stumbling on great ideas while mind wandering. Many are scientifically documented, but some are not. Was Archimedes really in a bathtub when he exclaimed, "Eureka!"?

Setting some exceptions aside, abundant scientific literature indicates that individuals' propensity to mind wander positively correlates with creative solutions to problems via incubation. The Unusual Uses Test (UUT) is one way to measure this. Imagine conducting this study: Some participants receive a difficult task; some an easier task. Some have a break to rest, and some do not. When people engaged in an undemanding task could rest and have incubation time, they came up with more creative solutions to the problem they had to solve. This group also reported the most mind wandering.

In recent years, more scientists are connecting mind wandering with innovation and building a stronger sense of self. Some researchers recommend scheduling periods when you allow your mind to roam in search of creative ideas, relaxation, and . . . you.

Mind wandering is also a technique to relieve boredom. For example, if you give people a repetitive and tedious task, they will report feeling unhappy about it, but less so if they are mind wandering during that task. Mind wandering also impacts the perception of time. People typically overestimate the length of a tedious task but underestimate it when they mind wander. So, mind wandering acts as a way to speed things up.

Mind wandering is also associated with future thinking, planning, and processing of self-relevant goals. Throughout the day, you likely have multiple goals, so it's beneficial to allow your attention to cycle and pay attention to different information—what you're looking

at, what you remember from the past, how much you've accomplished, and what you plan to do next.

Overall, scientists agree that mind wandering is a function of the healthy brain, which needs neural oscillations in cognitive engagement and executive control. While there are times when letting your mind wander feels good because it might fuel your creativity and offer a cognitive refuge, there are times when it feels bad because you recognize that your brain has gone astray without your permission. The negative aspects of mind wandering may also come from the fact that some people attempt to rectify personal problems during mind wandering. If attempts at problem solving are ineffective, mind wandering heightens the salience of current life concerns, and if you're in a negative mood, this can be a problem. Let's explore the darker side of mind wandering for a moment.

The Dark Side of Mind Wandering

Have you read the same paragraph twice in an email, article, or book because your mind was elsewhere? When we mind wander, there's a risk of reducing both perceptual and cognitive processing and, as a result, comprehension. In one study, when people's minds wandered and the text switched to gibberish, they found it harder to detect the switch quickly and accurately because they did not understand the entire sentence. Mind wandering also negatively impacts working memory (meaning the ability to keep track of information until completion of a task) and more global comprehension. For example, while reading a Sherlock Holmes story, mind wandering participants found it harder to identify the villain.

When you mind wander, there could also be a disruption in monitoring how you perform a task. This is because mind wandering can reduce controlling or adjusting behavior. When we perform motor tasks and the mind wanders, we make more mistakes.

There can be a serious price to pay for mind wandering. Missing critical parts of a conversation, traffic accidents, medical malpractice, or military mishaps are just some examples.

Mind wandering has been considered a form of repetitive thought, which is why it may be associated with rumination and a negative state of mind. Rumination is characterized by repetitive thinking or dwelling on unwanted negative experiences that can cause distress. Can introspection become a burden? When we focus too much on responsibilities, appearances, and the passage of time, overanalyzing what we do, second-guessing ourselves, and replaying conversations we had, too much self-awareness can leave us paralyzed. As a result, mind wandering has been linked to a lack of productivity, anxiety, and depression. A clarification is needed here because scientific studies demonstrate that unhappiness is not necessarily a *consequence* of mind wandering. Science suggests that negative thoughts during mind wandering, rather than mind wandering per se, bring the mood down. In other words, *what* you think during mind wandering impacts your mood.

It's also interesting to note that sadness may bias mind wandering toward events from the past, whereas anxious thinking is considered future-orientated. We will see how these observations can inform practical guidelines in a moment.

How Do You Bring the Brain Back to the Present?

Although evolutionarily, there are benefits to mind wandering, in business, it's essential to bring the brain back at some point because a focused mind has more chances to build memories, which can influence decisions. How do you refocus the wandering mind? Some techniques would not be readily applicable in business settings. Practices such as meditation, breathing exercises, and physical activities will refocus the mind, but it is unrealistic to ask a client during a presentation to breathe in slowly while you count to four. Walking, cleaning your workspace, or taking a shower are equally unfeasible in a corporate setting.

There are also some personality traits that contribute to mind wandering, and factors such as neuroticism,

conscientiousness, and openness to experience are predictors of task-unrelated thoughts. Neuroticism and conscientiousness correlate negatively with mind wandering. Findings on openness are conflicting, and it may be because high-openness people engage in frequent everyday mind wandering when circumstances allow but

can concentrate when necessary, such as during artificial laboratory tasks.

Despite these factors, there *are* some things you can do to refocus the wandering mind. Here are several intervention techniques that apply in corporate contexts and build off the positive benefits of mind wandering.

Tax Their Perceptual and Cognitive Load

Scientific literature shows a connection between mind wandering and perceptual load, meaning how much your audiences' senses are impacted. When the perceptual load is low, there may be more opportunities for mind wandering. This can be explained through perceptual load theory, which suggests that the degree to which people are distracted critically depends on how much attentional capacity is available to them at any given moment.

You can prevent distractions when sharing a relevant task with your audience by including a high perceptual load and engaging all their attentional capacity. A high perceptual load can also overcome individual differences in distractibility and even the effects of highly salient distractors, such as a phone ringing or someone moving around. In the example on the next page, you can see the materials we created for a neuroscience study on mind wandering, in which we aimed for a high perceptual load. Interestingly, we noted that people's minds wandered more during a Zoom call versus reading the same content in an e-book. This may be because on Zoom, a live presenter might be taking the cognitive load to extremes, either easing it or exceeding it too much.

It is important to consider the difference between perceptual load and cognitive load. Let's look at perceptual load first. One study that used eye tracking to measure mind wandering found *shorter* fixation durations and *more* fixations when participants played an episode with high perceptual load and *longer* fixation durations and *fewer* fixations when they played an episode with low perceptual load. As an aside, such effects demonstrated that fixation-related parameters could be used to index mental workload at different (perceptual and cognitive) stages of mental processing. Even if you're not using eye-tracking devices, consider increasing the perceptual load to guard against mind wandering. And remember that a high perceptual load does not always have to come from abundant images. Text is a graphical element too and can impact your audience's perceptual load.

While a higher perceptual load decreases mind wandering, a higher cognitive load tends to increase it by reducing the ability to suppress irrelevant information. This is not to say ease the cognitive load entirely, but rather tax it to reasonable limits. This is best understood through the concept of working memory, which is the process of temporarily holding small amounts of information in your mind until you complete a cognitive task. It is a form of cognitive workload because it impacts how many items you can hold in your mind at any given time. This type of memory is necessary because working memory is essential to most cognitive tasks. Anything that requires you to think, understand, solve a problem, plan, and make decisions involves working memory—in short, everything you are asking your customers to do. What is the maximum capacity of working memory? Typically, people can keep in mind three to four items for about 30 seconds to a minute. So consider creating messages that tax this capacity. When you do, you are more likely to keep distracting thoughts away simply because you're *stopping the production of thought.*

In my neuroscience study on mind wandering, I selected an e-book on artificial intelligence (AI) and machine learning (ML). I asked people who were not data scientists to read it and remember the points about the positive impact these technologies can have. During the project, I wanted to detect when mind wandering sets in and how we can bring the brain back (the technique is described later in the chapter). The point I am making here is that we did not select an easy topic. We chose something that taxes people's attention and understanding, but we eased comprehension by applying techniques you have already encountered in this book:

- Gradual display of complex information

- Clear charts that also build complexity gradually

- Maintaining the same mental model throughout the materials

- Repeating an important message four times

This is the slide sorter view of the presentation we used in the mind wandering study, where we aimed to tax cognitive load to reasonable limits. The deck also had a high perceptual load.

In this presentation, I was talking about principles related to creating video files that attract attention and impact memory. I intensified the perceptual load and also taxed cognition so that participants did not have time to produce additional thoughts.

These techniques were intended to avoid overtaxing working memory while maintaining interest by offering a challenging topic. The scientific literature shows that people tend to disengage when the cognitive workload is too low or too high.

The examples on the right from my presentations and client files demonstrate a higher perceptive load using intense images, icons, lines, and shapes while reasonably taxing cognitive load by presenting three or four items at a time.

Link Content to Your Audience's Goals

On the surface, mind wandering might seem purposeless as it contrasts with goal-directed cognition. However, empirical evidence suggests that our minds

This is a collection of slides from a company's sales kickoff, which were created with the intent to energize and motivate an audience of sellers.

frequently wander toward our goals. We also know that the mind tends to wander during low-importance or low-cognitive tasks or tasks that exceed cognitive capacity. So, engaging in goal or autobiographical planning is one of the ways that mind wandering justifies its function.

Knowing that when people have enough mental resources to indulge, they engage in prospective mind wandering, a practical guideline is to create content that connects them better to the future. The next chapter in this quadrant has additional guidelines on meeting the brain in the future.

Manage Their Mood

One aspect of mind wandering is the tendency for the mind to go to unwanted places: fears, anxieties, and ruminations. While both positive and negative moods can lead to equal levels of arousal, in a negative mood, arousal is related to the processing of self-relevant information, leading to inattention, which is why people have fewer attentional resources to devote to the task at hand.

Current perspectives on psychological science accept that cognition and emotion are inseparable. In daily life, one area in which emotion and cognition can overlap is through their joint contribution to the experience of thoughts unrelated to the here and now. So, while experiencing a negative mood, people fail to pay attention to a task more frequently, have even more task-irrelevant thoughts, and become less inclined to reengage their attention after a lapse. A positive mood, in contrast, is typically associated with a better ability to reengage after a lapse, and even when more mind wandering occurs, it's the positive kind that can influence creativity and problem solving, both beneficial to business outcomes (you want your customers to be creative and find solutions with you). So, how do you get your audiences in a better mood?

1. **Prime with positive words and images.** Even if people may mind wander, they at least do so in a positive state of mind. This also helps them transition from dark rumination to light introspection and makes them more likely to return to your materials. For additional ideas on priming, refer to Chapter 1.

2. **Offer a framework** to help them sort their thoughts. One of the reasons for negative feelings may be a lack of order: chaotic thoughts that often occur with shifts in the economy, company restructuring, or political environment. Frameworks address this because they can help you filter content and share only the essentials. One of the examples in the collection on the next page demonstrates how a company we were coaching used a framework based on classic leadership principles to showcase three pillars to their employees: "believe the best in our people, want the best for our people, and expect the

This is a compilation of slides we have used as positive primers because of their optimistic outlook and design.

These are examples of frameworks that bring order and stability and help the brain create a "template" through which to process new information.

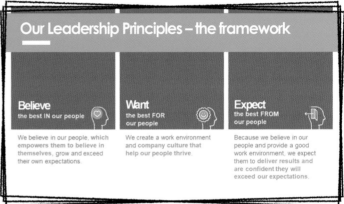

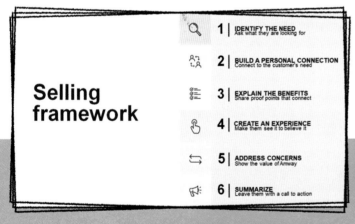

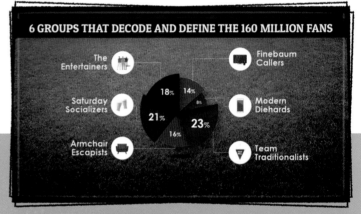

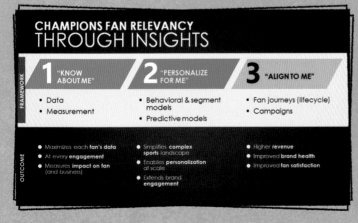

best from our people." The rest of the presentation included only information that mapped to these three pillars.

Once you establish a framework, maintain it consistently throughout your content so the brain can sustain a schema. Mind wandering correlates with the inability to form and maintain a model through which information can be processed.

3. **Bring their focus to the present.** In other words, load the perception. Research suggests that the relationship between negative mood and mind wandering might be explained by the extent to which individuals are attentive to present-moment experiences. Use the guidelines in Quadrants I and II to bring the brain into the present. If it's critical that people don't steer away from the task, don't let them. For example, in video games, researchers noted that fixation (indicative of mind wandering) often occurred in games that allowed players to pause what they were doing without consequence or provided a window of time when players cannot or do not need to act.

Feeling sad leads the brain toward retrospective focus during mind wandering, while anxiety biases mind wandering toward the future. Knowing that business decisions are made in the future, it's possible to induce brief moments of anxiety so that people can be directed toward future states. You can do this by presenting industry trends, challenges customers must overcome, or unexpected teaching moments. These examples showcase brief moments intended to create tension within a communication sequence.

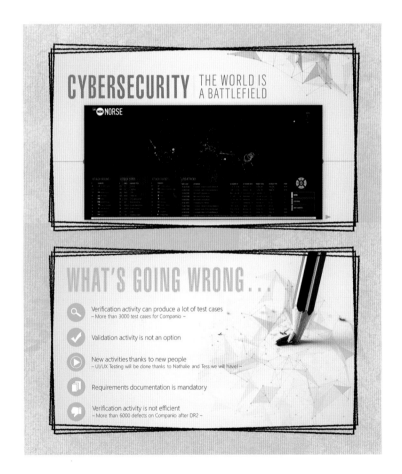

These are excerpts from several engineers' presentations, in which they were sharing with their teams problems or challenges from their work.

Make Allowances for Some Mind Wandering

We've already seen that there can be benefits when our minds stray from a task. It's possible to leverage these potential cognitive benefits and ease off pressuring people into action. Sometimes business practitioners are too eager to get things done. Allow for some distance, and for periods of silence.

Mind wandering can lead to successful problem solving, which is crucial in closing business deals. Problem solving depends on two related processes:

1. A capacity to imagine conditions, allowing an audience to move forward on the problem

2. A capacity to selectively implement the most effective strategy

These steps depend on imagining events unrelated to the present moment. So, create spaces where your audience's imagination can roam.

Let's talk about imagining the future next.

Imagination

is not just for

escaping

reality, it's for

creating it.

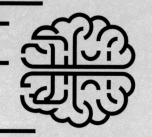

the future
is the brain's
preferred
state

CHAPTER 8

What Happens Next?

The Neuroscience of Predicting the Future

In early 2018, Mahathir Mohamad was reelected Malaysia's prime minister . . . at the age of 92! He first served as prime minister in 1981 and was applauded for his ability to modernize the country. If you remember seeing Sean Connery in the movie *Entrapment* dangling off the lights hung from the bottom of the bridge linking the super modern Petronas Twin Towers, you have Mr. Mohamad to thank.

Even though he lost his third bid (at the age of 97), in an interview after his last win, Mr. Mohamad said something we could all learn from. He admitted that he "should not be here," but he felt a duty, despite his readiness to retire, read more books, and take an Alaska cruise. Given that at some point he would not be running for office any longer, he mentioned that the challenge for the next prime minister would be "to live with the consequences." This statement struck me as applicable to creating business messages, too. When you're trying to capture an audience's attention, your content can have consequences. Is your audience ready to live with them? Are you?

Asking these questions means having a future perspective on how you create content. This isn't hard to do because the future is the brain's preferred state. Research suggests that people think about the future approximately once every 15 minutes when asked to record their thoughts throughout the day. Future-oriented thinking happens two to three times more often than past-oriented thinking. This is because the brain is a prediction machine, constantly anticipating what will happen so it knows how to guide your next move. From a content design and delivery perspective, the most important question must be: What happens next? What happens *after* your audiences see or hear your messages? Can they still see you in the future *when they are not even looking*?

The idea of thinking about the future is a relatively modern notion. Before the seventeenth century, most people believed that the world would last only 6,000 years, and they were already nearing the end. Even though some had long-term goals like planting for harvest, going on trips by boat, or building cathedrals, not much was expected to change. It was only after the 1900s that the word "futurism" took off, and with the advent of technology, the term *new* started having value in itself.

The notion that we should discard the past to make room for the new has been a popular strategy in business for the last few decades. However, given that the modern world is obsessed with the future, it is helpful to maintain a future-tense mentality when creating content and ask: What will people see in their mind's eye in the future when they are not exposed to me or my materials?"

What does it take for someone to steer their thoughts toward you in the future, even when they are mind wandering? It takes:

1. Simulation
2. Prediction
3. Intention
4. Planning

Let's discuss how you can appeal to these four stages in your communication.

 ## Help Them Simulate the Future

To help an audience think of you in the future, you must help them simulate it in the present. Helping your audience imagine the future in an explicit and detailed way is important because they may be too tired or lack the cognitive energy to do so on their own.

In the following examples, you can see how we help an audience explicitly visualize the future. In the first example, the presenter discussed the "middle office," explaining that there are currently many solutions for the front office, which is customer-facing. These solutions include sales methodologies, call centers, forecasting, and marketing opportunities. There are also many solutions for the back office, which keep all business on track, such as compliance, balance sheets, manufacturing, and talent management. But at the time, there were no solutions for the middle office, which would include better tools for configuring quotes, creating contracts and renewals, managing orders, offering promotions and rebates, and facilitating approvals. The slide simulates a desirable future state, showing the tools that can be automated for the middle office.

Not all future-oriented designs have to involve complex architecture. Some might be metaphorical, like the example on the next page, presented in a sales context, which indicates an intersection between the seller's and the prospect's mindsets.

The composition of the slide offers a framework for a future state: one in which the audience could picture opportunities for a gap in the market (the middle office).

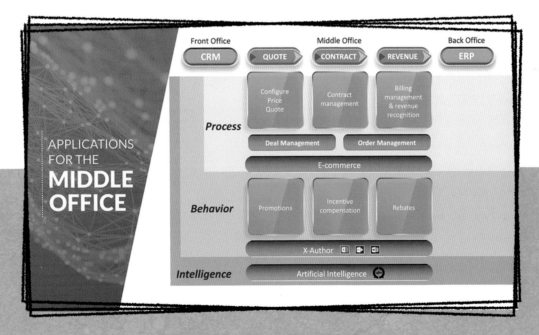

We used the highway metaphor to ignite in the audience's mind a future state in which sellers need to do prospecting for a particular context.

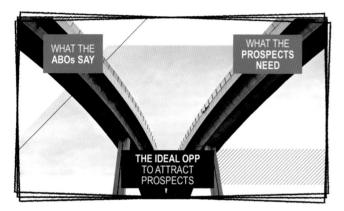

In the next examples from a different context, the presenter acknowledges that people always have choices in the future. However, when it comes to those choices, she clarifies which one will have advantages. The purpose of the presentation was to introduce a new probiotic, which is compared to other popular probiotic choices, such as kombucha, kimchi, and yogurt. Each slide builds contrast between the proposed new product and the current choices, building a picture of what an audience should select in the future.

In the slides on the next page from another presentation, we enabled people to picture the future and placed the solution in a physical context. The company presenting the slides was promoting products and services for improving pelvic health for women over 40. To design it and appeal to a future state, we were looking for where ideas and products "live" as they do their job. In this case, if the

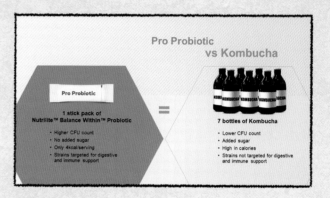

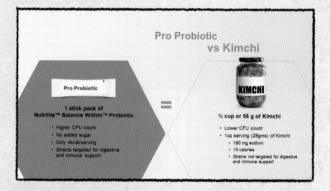

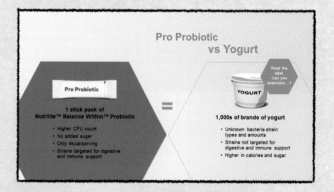

target audience had better pelvic health, they would enjoy a few hours at the beach without having to run to the bathroom. Thinking of natural habitats for the consequences that result from using a product or service makes it easier and much more fun to visualize a concept, too. Of these, the client chose the middle slide.

If you are using slides in your presentation, you don't need to create every single one as a visualization of the future, but take any opportunity you can to speak to the future. Always consider the difference between aesthetically pleasing but disposable design versus visualizations that simulate future desires.

Help Them Predict the Future

Your audiences' brains are constantly engaged in prediction. In fact, many scientists currently believe that our brains are essentially prediction machines that frequently compare expected and actual outcomes. By exercising this ability, people have learned to anticipate events in their environment and work toward correcting prediction errors.

Take a look at the images on the next page. Initially, you might see just some black lines and shapes, but if someone offers more details, you might see them differently. Imagine someone saying the one on the left is not a fishhook but an umbrella handle and the one on the right is not a sunset by the sea, but rather a fried egg, sunny side up, seen from the side. When you read these details,

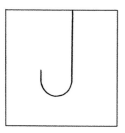 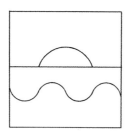

your brain accesses memories, going beyond the present perceptual elements and making meaning. In the process, your brain changes the firing of its neurons. Even though you might not have seen these objects without the prompts, a new meaning shapes up for you. The lines and shapes haven't changed—your perception has.

Predictions enable you to read the black lines on this page and understand them as words and ideas. Predictions are also why it feels frustrating when someone does not finish their . . .

While making predictions, your brain is, in a sense, having a conversation with itself. Based on past and present conditions, a series of neurons guess what will happen in the immediate future. If your brain has performed well, its prediction matches your perception, and it has efficiently prepared you to act. Your predicting brain creates your reality. However, when it's wrong, it learns from its errors and updates its predictions for better performance next time.

We know the brain steers toward the future during mind wandering and wants to predict that future. How do you help an audience improve their predictive power? Consider these two techniques:

1. Teach them new things.

2. Involve them in new experiences.

Everything people learn today prepares their brain to predict tomorrow differently. Novelty may seem hard to generate because it takes work to create new things, but sharing something new does not necessarily mean it is new for the entire world. It just needs to be new for most of your audience members.

I remember reading a story about American musician Frank Zappa, who once performed in Stockholm in 1971. He had just finished two shows at the Konserthuset, the main hall for orchestral music, when two kids approached him and said they had been to both shows that night, but their brother Hannes had seen only the first show and went home to sleep because he had school the next day. They asked the musician whether he would go to their house with them, which was about 20 minutes outside of the city, sneak into Hannes's room, and say, "Hannes! Hannes! Wake up! It's me, Frank Zappa." The musician went along with it! The parents were just as surprised as Hannes, and once the humor wore off, they all sat in the kitchen until 5:30 a.m., talking politics.

Zappa's attitude teaches us something we can all benefit from: Have an experience you would not usually have. Live a little! As a result, you could share new perspectives with an audience. What could be a new and unusual experience for you that you can link with your main messages?

Be aware of the fine line between helping an audience *predict* what happens next in their fields and *becoming predictable* in the way you deliver a message. Some research studies indicate that when the brain is in predictive mode, it has difficulty encoding new memories. In one study, when participants saw a series of images, and some images always followed others (e.g., a mountain consistently appeared after a beach picture), recall was worse for the predictable images than for new images. The results suggest that predictive images trigger the hippocampus to shift gears toward prediction—and away from encoding a new memory.

Another way to help the brain predict better is to offer *specific* content rather than speaking generally. Sharing details and elaborating on a concept helps your audience see what you see.

 ## Help Them Set Intentions

What enables or determines humans to act in the future? This has been a question in scientific research since the inception of psychology. One way to tackle it is to convert it into two questions: What intentions guide our behavior? How do we act on these intentions?

Let's imagine a person who might have the intention to lose weight or achieve success in a small business. One way to improve this person's likelihood of acting on his future intention is to be clear and specific about this statement: "When x occurs, I will perform y." This makes the memory more accessible and automatic. Relating to the weight loss context, an example would be: "When I am craving dessert, I will have some raspberries drizzled with honey instead of ice cream." Relating to a small business, an example would be: "When customers request a proposal, I will use an automated tool instead of creating one for each customer from scratch."

In your communications, help your audiences formulate a clear intention for the future. For example, a formula you can consider is: "When you need x, choose y because you'll be able to do a, b, and c, which will mean d and e to you." More recently, I've seen companies reverse the formula in business content and start with: "What would d and e mean to you? You could have them if you did a, b, and c. To do those, you would have to choose y when you're in situation x."

The following examples show how we formulate most messages as actions that customers can carry out in the future. The "calls to action" slides are typical in most persuasive presentations, but the difference is in setting up the condition or the environment, not just presenting a disembodied action. In the first example, the presenter shares an action for the future as their organization faces layoffs. The broad future action was "Make the best of the resources you have," but then it switches to *specific* conditions and settings for those resources, which were related to a certification program. Then the message became broader again, encouraging the team to keep moving

forward. One of the drawbacks of inspirational keynotes is that they thrive on generic aspirational messages, but they often don't provide specific conditions and actions associated with those conditions to be carried out. Even in this example, there is an area for which the team did not have something specific (fourth column in the second slide), but they left it there, knowing that it needed to be addressed at some point.

It is important to note that there is a difference between setting goals and acting on intentions in the future. Setting goals means clarifying what to do (e.g., eating healthy), while intending to act means clarifying specific *conditions and means* needed to realize the goals (e.g., "When I have breakfast tomorrow, I will add a piece of fruit" or "When I meet with a customer, I will share two industry trends that must prompt a shift in their business strategy").

The following example is from a biotech company, showing the specific steps a few critical teams needed to take to interact better. The purpose of the presentation was to ignite efficient, cross-functional teams. The "Deliverables" slide includes specific actions that can be carried out in the future. The slides are also accompanied by information related to constraints, resources to complete those actions, and measures of success.

This sequence of slides was intended to set a context for a business shift and also to provide specific steps on how to handle upcoming business changes.

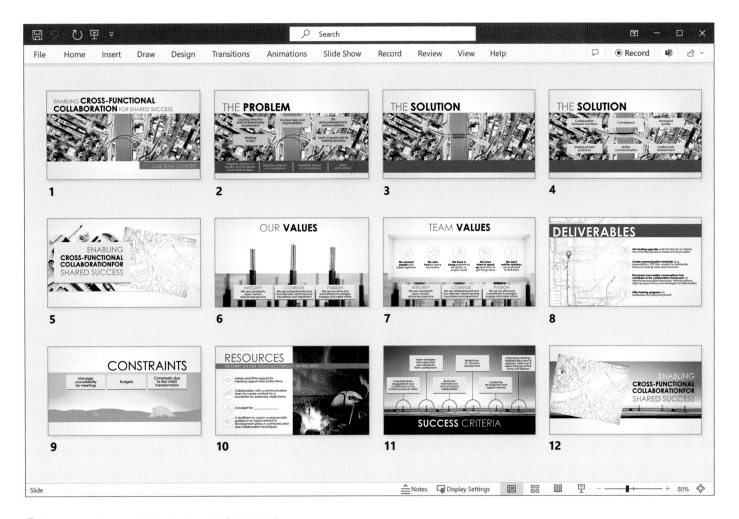

This presentation included balanced information in terms of context and specific steps that a team must take to handle business challenges. This renders realism to future actions. It's not just setting the actions but also the specific conditions around those actions.

Help Them Plan

Planning for action is essential because most future intentions are more complex than if-then statements. For instance, changing an IT system requires serious planning. To ease the complexity, consider these techniques.

Offer Organized, Consistent Steps

Offer your audience a set of organized steps or checklists to achieve a goal. I often see wishy-washy endings, where there is no clear indication of what should happen next, or the steps are nebulous, such as "Let's continue the conversation." This hardly ever leads to action. Offering frameworks is a critical initial phase. When you add steps to clarify how to achieve goals, make sure you keep the framework consistent. Another mistake I often see is the inclusion of too many frameworks throughout a communication sequence, making it more complicated to stay organized around only one set of steps.

The first example is from one of my presentations on neuroscience findings from a study on using videos in sales emails. The second is from a client presentation related to prospecting. Both examples include steps to achieve specific goals.

Use Your Experiences

Draw on your own experiences when you create a plan for others. This will make it easier for you to help them simulate and predict the future. You could invoke other people's experiences, but it would be harder for you to build a vision because experience enables you to offer vivid explanations backed by confidence. Take, for example, Amancio Ortega, who started Zara, one of the biggest international fashion chains, in 1974. When outlining the plans and vision for the company, he relied on his extensive knowledge of the fashion industry and his expertise in textile manufacturing. He also had deep knowledge of supply chain management, which was useful in responding to emerging fashion trends. With experience and skills you can paint a plan and a future for others to follow; in his case, Ortega was able to establish a new business model (fast fashion) and turn Zara into one of the world's most recognizable fashion retailers.

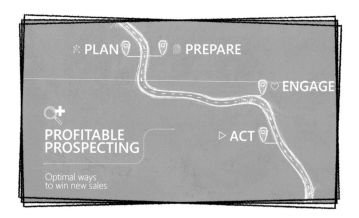

Get Them Talking

Invite your audiences to generate their own narratives. For example, ask: How do you see the future? What do you intend to do next? What do you predict as an outcome of our partnership?

Build Anticipation for the Future

If you watch any home improvement show, a formula quickly becomes clear: A couple picks a house, one or more home improvement specialists help them redesign it, work begins, something goes wrong, the wrong gets fixed, and everyone is happy in the end. One aspect of these shows that all business presenters will benefit from learning is how the show's creators and hosts build anticipation to keep us watching. A soothing voice tells us what we are in for at the beginning of each show and at each transition points to a commercial. The showrunners know that we can click away at any second, so they keep us watching by telling us:

> Tony and Veronica are in the market for a renovated property that can be updated to suit their style. Realtor Jonathan Scott saw great potential in the last property they toured. But the couple is not convinced. So the hunt continues in other areas around the city.

The anticipation of seeing something new invites viewers to sit through the ads to see what happens next.

After the commercials, we are rewarded by novelty: We are shown new house options in different parts of the town, and the couple narrows it down to a few choices. Then right before the next commercial break, we hear, "Coming up: Seeing is believing as Jonathan reveals the design plans to rejuvenate the fixer-uppers." In the next segment, the couple decides between two options, which are typically given fun names. Then before the next series of ads, the narrator offers another hook: "Coming up: Is the Peacock Pad the ideal home for Tony and Veronica, or is the Arch Nemesis's transformation too good to pass up? Plus, the Property Brothers remodel the couple's new home."

This balance between flashbacks and flash-forwards enables content creators to impact the audience's brain in two ways:

1. By repeating important points, they indicate what counts and create deliberate memories.

2. By saying what happens next, with a combination of specificity and surprise, they keep the brain hooked until the uncertainty is made certain.

Consider for a moment that the constant goal of your brain is to minimize prediction error. In fact, some scientists believe that error prediction is the only goal of your brain. So, as you build anticipation for your audiences, you're allowing them to find out whether there is a match between their prediction and what happens in reality.

In the *Property Brothers* excerpts presented, the narration builds anticipation, as do the show hosts, who are masters of the tease. "Today, I am meeting Tony and Veronica to discuss an offer," says Jonathan Scott. "However, I have some news they will not like." No doubt, many will stay to hear what that is.

Analyze the way you're currently delivering your content. Whether or not you're presenting with slides, are you giving a punch line away too soon, killing anticipation? If you are revealing too much early on in the sequence, consider holding back some information to guard against mind wandering. Build anticipation for these important points with phrases such as "Finally," "I've been looking forward to," "Just wait until you see the next part," or "There are four important tools that will serve you well. Today we covered three. Let's look at the fourth one when we meet next."

When you create anticipation, reward your audiences for their emotional investment by fulfilling your commitments. For instance, if you promised something surprising, make sure it is. If you promise three ways to fix an issue, make sure there really are three ways.

It is humbling to acknowledge that when people listen to your messages, they will be holding in their memory multiple intentions they need to carry through. Acting on *your* suggestions is hardly ever the single most important thing they must do. Keep this final guideline in mind: Many participants in your sessions will be well intended to act. Thoughts about one's intentions correlate with a break in an activity. Longer periods between activities provide people with opportunities to evaluate their goals. Don't push your customers and audiences too much by sending constant reminders of what to do. When they have a break from you, your absence makes their brain grow fonder.

We'll see you back here after a quick break. And then, we'll learn about an underutilized but potent technique in messaging and getting effortless attention.

CHAPTER 9

Transitions

Help Them See Your Message When You Aren't There

Your success in life is partly due to your brain's ability to form associations between unrelated objects or entities. You meet a new boss or prospect and immediately associate her face with her name. You hear a song and connect it with the place you're in or the person you're with. You link the name of a restaurant with a dish that made you sick once. Such associations, which can be summed up as associative memory, help you pay attention to what serves you well and avoid what doesn't.

Your audiences are no different from you. They will attend to your content, and at some point, as described in Chapter 7, their minds will wander from one thought to another. This wandering is often powered by associations, meaning that one thought will lead to another, and to another. One way to be on your audience's mind wandering path is to be part of the associations they will make. In this chapter, let's discuss techniques that enable you to influence the notorious "this reminds me" train of thought that most people have as their minds wander.

First, let's consider that moving from one thought to another implies transitions. So if you influence transitions when you're *with* your audience, then transitions can help you be part of what they think of next, even when you're no longer there. Good transitions connect one idea with another.

The Benefits of Proper Transitions

Surprisingly little research has been dedicated to studying transitions or connectors in business content. However, a few academic studies point out the merits of transition words for better fluency in speech and writing.

Transitions can have a positive influence on the person creating the content *and* the person consuming the content. Good transitions allow the content creator to organize the content well, showing the logical relationships and sequences between ideas, which results in a better message.

The benefit of transitions for audiences may be more pronounced in verbal than written content because written content is not so time-bound. When people read, they have more time to think about how the ideas connect. In an oral presentation, ideas move quickly, and there is less time between speech production and reception. With good transitions, you're also likely to make content more engaging because you may be giving your audiences the joy of getting it, of understanding how concepts connect and conclusions form.

Whether written or verbal, what I observe frequently is that too many content creators have no transitions, jumping from one point to another with no apparent logic; while others transition too quickly or in the same way, making content dull. The use and misuse of transitions can become obtrusive. What are some practical ways to include optimal transitions in your content and impact your audience's attention and associative memory?

Types of Transitions

Any business content you create will be composed of small segments, such as slides in a presentation, paragraphs in an article, scenes in a corporate video, or segments on a website. These small segments are combined to form a larger entity, such as a presentation, article, video, or website. With this composition in mind, consider two types of transitions: One helps you tie thoughts *within* sections of your content, and the other helps connect those sections. Whether you're thinking of your transitions in the micro or macro sense, they can be divided into these four subtypes.

 **Temporal Transitions**

When you speak, you typically share ideas in a sequence, with elements preceding or following others. To help your listeners detect and follow a sequence in time, use transition words such as:

first	then
second	next
the first point	previously
the second point	before
the final point	after
before	meanwhile
after	later
during	in the end
at the same time	

You may use these temporal transitions to describe a process or to order arguments in your discourse, which is how persuasion is born. These phrases are effective because they help your audience follow and understand how things unfold.

Some standard techniques for temporal transitions include:

- **Previous/next:** Tell them what you said and then what you will say: "You've seen a broad picture of what this product can do. Now let's look at some individual features."

- **Pose a rhetorical question:** "Do you think we're done after entering the information in Salesforce? Not quite. Let's take a look at what happens next."

- **Let your audience know that you are about to switch ideas** with words and phrases such as: *next, first, last, on the other hand, finally, now let's consider.* For example, "Now that we understand what is important to you, let's look at some customer service options."

- **Guided tour:** Present a structure, process, or theme and reference each part. For example, "Here's the six-step process for effective prospecting. Now let's take a closer look at each step. In step one . . ."

In this example, the presenter talks about a valuable product that helps surgeons by illuminating close to the surgical site, compared to lights in the operating room that are farther from the patient. As early as slide 2, the presenter asks, "Which surgeon ever complains of too much light?," announcing how the product is valuable. Then, as the presentation unfolds, on slide 7, the presenter reveals the unique features of this illuminating system, using "previous/next" (he outlines problems with illumination in the operating room and announces a solution) and "guided tour" (there are three features the audience will benefit from knowing, and these three features will be detailed in the rest of the presentation).

In this example, the presentation is created around a "guided tour" reflected in the slide with the solid green background. This slide includes the sections detailed in the rest of the presentation and acts as a transition between the different segments.

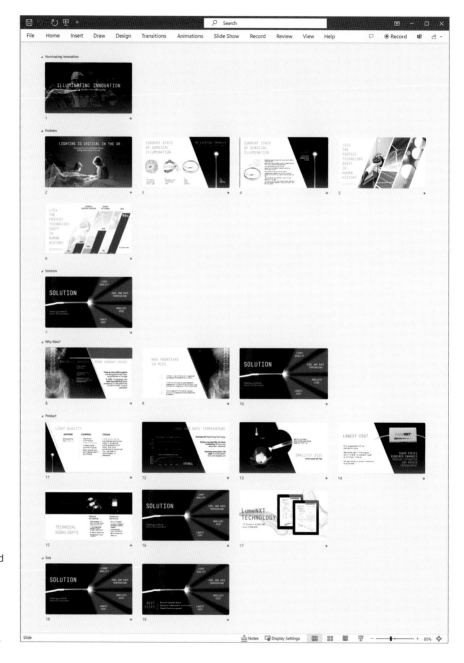

Additive Transitions

Additive transitions are used to link ideas to those you've already stated. These include:

again	and
besides	in addition
also	for example
another	

In the presentation mentioned previously, the presenter talks about the advancement of LED technology in various fields. Then, using additive transitions, he gives specific statistics that reflect the fast growth of LEDs in multiple areas, such as electric vehicles and solar panels.

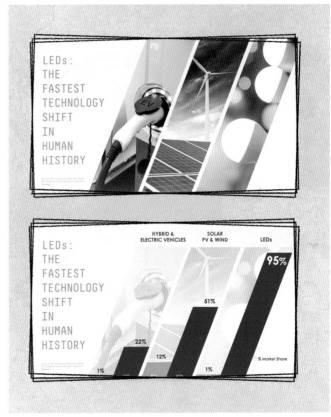

These examples are accompanied by additive transitions, which enable the presenter to move from slide to slide and maintain interest by elaborating on concepts related to the main theme.

Additive transitions can be powerful in capturing attention and sustaining engagement. Here is a progression from one of my presentations, in which I talked about psychological aspects that hinder growth. Each entry is a mouse click, and when done quickly, it generates a heavy feeling, which was the intent.

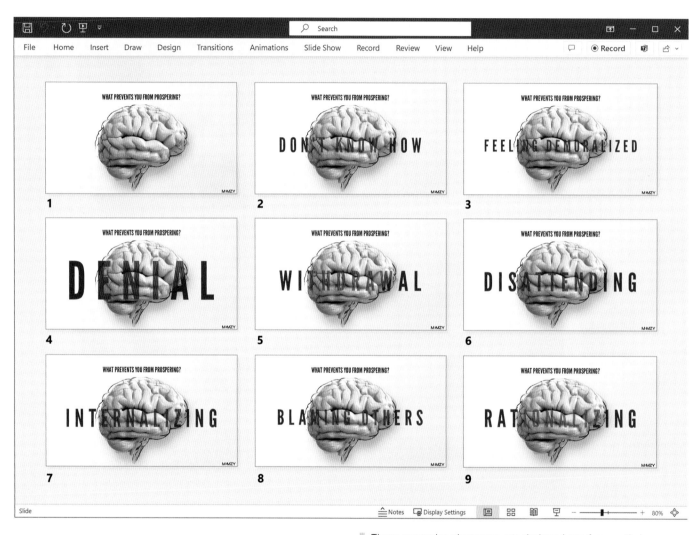

These examples showcase a technique I use frequently in my presentations where I keep one element constant and immovable, and I transition from phrase to phrase in rapid fire to give the impression of urgency and conceptual heavy weight.

In this example, I was using additive transitions to build a point from the movie *Her*. The film reveals a future in which it is possible to develop deep relationships with our computers and even fall in love with our operating systems. In the progression to the right, I detail the premise (Boy meets operating system. Boy falls in love.), and then I ask, "Which is the real Her?" as I show a meeting between the main character and his soon-to-be ex-wife. And then, I make some cautionary remarks about living a super digital life that excludes humans. The transitions build on each other to reveal a sobering point related to what futurist Ray Kurzweil has called "singularity": the moment at which the cognitive abilities of computers exceed those of humans, with unpredictable consequences for human history. Each click is an additive transition, building these points conceptually and visually.

◯△ Adversative Transitions

Some transitions help you contrast ideas and offer arguments contrary to expectations. Common adversative transitions include:

but	although
yet	despite
however	on the one hand
nevertheless	on the other hand

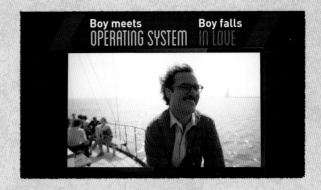

In this example, the additive transitions form through elaborating on a concept around digital versus real relationships, and the engagement is created through visual changes and an unusual perspective on the movie.

An idea can become clear and create the ground for persuasion when it imposes tension. For example, "On the one hand, people know they must eat healthy foods; on the other hand, they don't eat the recommended servings of fruits and veggies. Therefore . . ." Contrast also solidifies the meaning of what you say, and meaningful content is attention-grabbing.

In this presentation example, I discussed the importance of a growth mindset. Within such a conversation, self-awareness is mandatory, as you cannot distinguish whether you have a growth mindset unless you reflect on your present state. So, the first slide presents the importance of self-awareness. Then, I include a quote—I typically avoid quotes in presentations because audiences prefer a fresh voice, but this time, it gave me an excellent adversarial transition. The philosopher, mathematician, and physicist Blaise Pascal reflected on humans' inability to sit in a room alone. The third line acts as a punchline to this adversarial transition, asking the audience if they really are self-aware.

This is a sequence that exemplifies setting up a thesis, then setting up an anti-thesis, and resolving the tension with a question or a statement.

In the example below on the importance of automation, I use the adversarial transition to caution against an overdependence on machines and algorithms. For instance, after relying heavily on computers, some pilots report they are not as adept at flying in crises, doctors are starting to lose their ability to diagnose, and architects can no longer draw as well as they used to. The machines are making us more distant from our work. These adversarial transitions are intended to point to a bleak irony that automation frees us from what makes us feel free, such as the ability to work and to find our unique artistry in it.

> In this sequence, I first built up the argument around human versus machine with the classic trolley problem, and then used adversarial transitions to add gravity to the potential issue of humans' overreliance on algorithms.

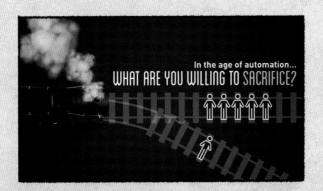

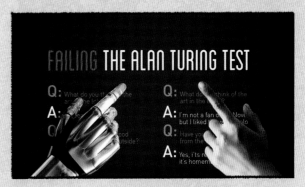

Causative Transitions

In a causative relation, you're showing how a concept is the cause or result of another. Common causative transitions include:

so	as a result
therefore	consequently
because	for this reason

These phrases are helpful because the brain is constantly looking for meaning, and such transitions help your audiences draw meaning from what you're sharing. In addition, sharing meaning with your audience removes the possibility of misinterpretation.

Using causative transitions while sharing a story adds teeth to your arguments. For instance, in a presentation I was delivering on the advent of artificial intelligence, I was sharing the story of David Cope, a math professor at Santa Clara University, who had taken on the project of composing an opera but then decided to create a computer algorithm to do the job for him (this was long before ChatGPT). When he played the final composition in front of an audience, people were moved by the music. But when he confessed that a computer had created the piece, someone in the front row got up and punched the composer in the face because he felt tricked. The slide titled "The composer without a heart" presents implied causation.

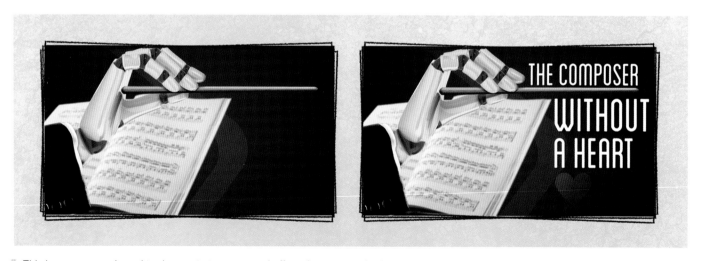

This is a sequence I used to demonstrate cause and effect. A composer had used algorithms to create music that touched an audience who did not know the music had been created by the machine. The on-click animation added a punch line intended to make the point that it's not so much that algorithms may become human but rather that humans may become robotic.

In the same presentation, I implied a "because" with this transition when I asked whether we could stay human in a robotic age. The answer was an implied yes because robots do not create demand; humans create demand.

Overall, you may use any of these transitions between thoughts in a section or between sections within a presentation or other type of communication. Remember, transitions help your audiences build associations, so later on, when you're not in front of them, and they may be jumping from thought to thought as their minds wander, they might experience a "this reminds me" moment. To do that, make sure that you present an unfamiliar perspective on a familiar topic at some point in your message. For instance, in a presentation on digital transformation, we talked about Uber *not* being innovative because the application was based on existing technology such as GPS, mobile apps, and shared services. This was seen as unusual because many business practitioners associate Uber with innovation. So next time they call an Uber, a "this reminds me" moment brings you to mind, even when they're not looking at your materials.

Create a Solid Storyboard

Storyboards are not often habitual for content communicators because they take time, and a lot of content creation is rushed and usually done by copying and pasting elements from existing pieces of content. This is unfortunate, because in the absence of an approved storyboard, people start moving content around, and transitions are either lost or are no longer smooth and meaningful.

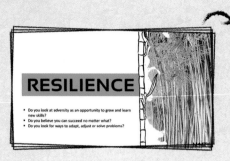

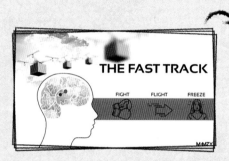

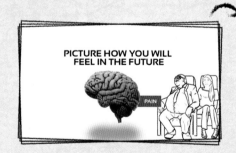

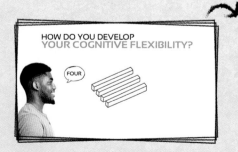

A solid storyboard prompts you to *plan* transitions and implement them well. The example on the left shows transitions in the finished slides initially created in a storyboard. It indicates that some elements build on previous elements or take one element and "carry it" to the next slide. For example, the first row of slides is from a presentation on building resilience. The first slide asks the audience some questions about the concept. Next, the design transitions to a more filled-in composition, alluding to the Robison Crusoe story. It then reverts to the initial questions, accompanied by a Likert scale so viewers can gauge their resilience.

In the slides in the second row, I spoke about how, when faced with a changing environment, reactions in the brain travel on a fast track, and the classic ways humans respond are fight, flight, or freeze. Then, with on-click animations, certain parts of the brain are highlighted on the slide, and I explained the brain's reaction to change on the slow track. The other slides in the collage also show visual transitions from one concept to another. With these transitions, complex explanations are manageable because some of the elements from the previous slide appear consistently, and there is not much novelty to process with each slide.

Overall, if you're using slides, think of the transitions between slides in each section and between the presentation segments.

Integrate Text and Pictures

Let's stay for a moment at the micro-level of transitions and use neuroscience to focus on the two most mistreated aspects of text and graphics in business content.

The first flaw is that too much business content includes images and text presented as separate units with too little or no integration, which makes it harder to

The sequences exemplify visual design that is based on transitions, not just a talk track. Each slide builds on the previous, adding elements to showcase cause and effect.

build associations between them. The following example shows how the brain does not need to consume extra cognitive energy because, even though the slide is fairly complex, the design composition and color coordination are created such that it is easy to understand how different parts relate.

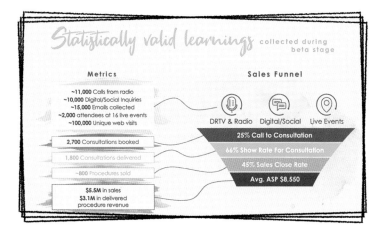

Whenever you use slideware for content creation, you must be extra cautious because some default layouts in PowerPoint invite you to add "text on the left, picture on the right," which does not lead to reliable memory. Those layouts are OK if you're after distributed attention and "gist" memory. However, if you want focused attention and verbatim memory, make the connections between text and image clear in a way that does not strain the brain.

An Apple ad from 1980 is a great example of how text and pictures complete each other's narrative. The commercial opened with a text-based story of a person who had an Apple computer, which he took home for the holidays. While he was out, his cat knocked over a lamp, which caused a fire, which made his TV melt on top of the computer. The conflict was settled by referencing all the Apple dealers available to fix problems. The verbal and visual stories went hand in hand.

There are also situations where pictures and text are used together but in intentional contradiction. An art director from Saatchi & Saatchi titled a print ad for the British Tinnitus Association, "Some of the things we removed from people's heads." The picture showed a medical tray with mostly metal objects such as a faucet, whistle, doorbell, knife, and a small airplane. Also on the tray were a piece of bacon and three flies. Tinnitus is a condition that means "ringing of the ears," which can also include roaring, clicking, hissing, or buzzing. The purpose of the ad was to invite patients to a special clinic with solutions for such debilitating symptoms. The incongruence between the text and the picture caught immediate attention.

The following examples are from business presentations we designed for clients or my speaking engagements over the years. They are intended to exemplify how text and pictures work better when integrated versus separated in typical designs showing the image on the left and bulleted text on the right.

"Fuse text and images"
gallery

In the following example, I used slides to speak to a business audience about embracing change. I used a concrete context, a gym locker, because starting a new workout routine (and embracing change) is difficult. I then associated the section on the mindset with posture, the brain with the head, and resilience with the gym bag, using a design that integrated text within the physical context of the image.

In this sequence, the composition integrates text with the image by placing it in a physical context, which is not typical for B2B content.

If some images have borders, place other elements to connect them to what is outside the border. In this example, we first see the image in the middle, and the message is related to the company splitting the market in beauty-related processes. On the left are the med spas, and on click, this image appears related to the picture in the middle. On the right, plastic surgery appears, and the image is also connected to the picture in the middle. Everything is interconnected, even though the slide is divided into three parts.

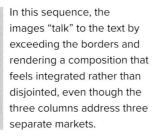

In this sequence, the images "talk" to the text by exceeding the borders and rendering a composition that feels integrated rather than disjointed, even though the three columns address three separate markets.

Use Transitions for Cognitive Closure

You can glue together different parts of your message by using transitions to summarize what you have said, how each important point fits the overall structure, and what's to come. If you deliver a formal presentation, an agenda slide typically provides this guide. We call this "the 10 percent slide" because audiences tend to forget 90 percent of content after 48 hours, and the little they remember tends to be random. To be deliberate in influencing what people take away, you can design a 10 percent message distinctively and display it repeatedly throughout a sequence. Most people intuitively include this 10 percent message in an agenda slide, but a common mistake is showing it only once, in the beginning, and displaying a summary at the end (and typically, these do not match). For better memory and audience experience, consider repeating the agenda slide in a consistent way multiple times throughout a sequence.

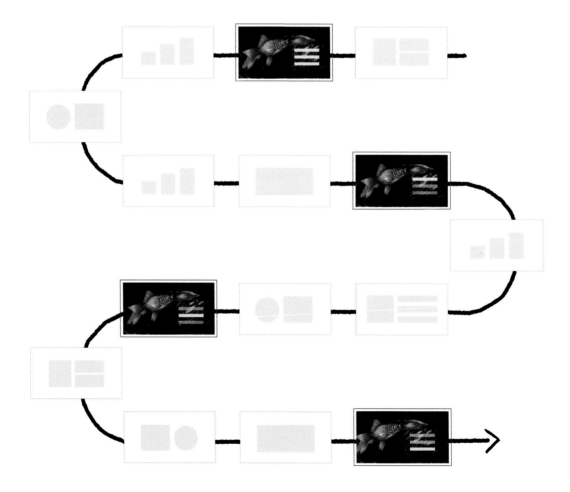

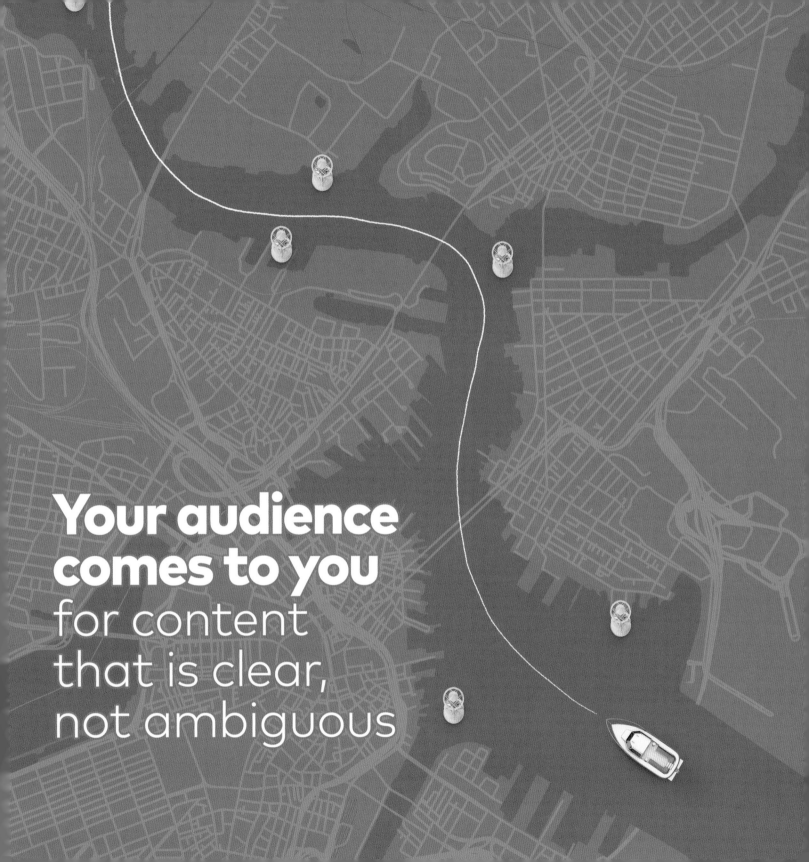

Your audience comes to you for content that is clear, not ambiguous

This type of repetition and transition between sections offers your audiences cognitive closure. Why is this useful? The human brain is constantly constructing knowledge for optimal everyday functioning. Knowledge construction is indispensable, whether you are making mundane decisions (what meal to order) or sophisticated decisions (what B2B solution to buy). In a business context, knowledge is valuable when it's clear, not uncertain or ambiguous. From this perspective, the business brain seeks closure, meaning it looks for definite knowledge regarding a concept.

The need for closure is assumed to derive from two general human tendencies: urgency and permanence. This means that when constructing knowledge, individuals typically wish to obtain it quickly and hold on to it for a while. Such seize-and-freeze motivations are helpful because when they are achieved, the brain can conserve energy—it can stop looking, form hypotheses, and take action. Cognitive closure offers a myriad of benefits because it:

- Frees people from continued information processing (which can become tiring, dull, or both)

- Makes action-taking more likely and faster

- Promises order and stability

Even people who may not desire closure because they appreciate the flexibility to suspend judgment or keep their options open are shown to appreciate closure because it helps them with the need for accuracy. So, overall, if you're operating in environments that value confidence, order, and clarity, your customer's brain will appreciate cognitive closure.

In one neuroscience study I conducted on the concept of cognitive closure, and also to detect whether the famous T3 adage (tell them what you're going to tell them, then tell them, then tell them what you told them) works, I asked participants to watch a presentation about a B2B solution intended to attract more customers by using intent data, which includes prospects' web searches and the content they consume, indicating their level of interest in a particular topic. Participants were randomly assigned to one of the following four experimental groups as they watched presentations that were identical except for closure frequency. Specifically:

- Group 1 watched a fluid presentation with no concepts fully "closed," meaning no decisive knowledge offered on critical concepts around intent data.

- Group 2 watched the same presentation as Group 1, except this group viewed an agenda at the beginning of the presentation, which clarified three critical points to remember regarding intent data. These main points were mentioned together only once, then explained gradually throughout the presentation.

- Group 3 watched the same presentation as Group 2, except, in addition to an agenda, this group also saw a summary of the three main concepts at the end. This was the group exposed to the T3 approach.

- Group 4 watched the same presentation as the other groups, including an agenda and a summary, but in this condition, the three essential concepts were repeated or "closed" two more times in the middle of the presentation.

In terms of affective variables, we noted that both Groups 1 and 2 had high valence and low arousal, with Group 2 being slightly more alert, which may suggest that inserting an agenda and providing some closure (decisive knowledge) stimulates the brain. Is an agenda sufficient for cognitive closure? Analyzing the affective variables for Groups 2 and 3 (the T3 condition), we noted that surprisingly, the audience does *not* enjoy the agenda-plus-summary condition. This difference between the groups is statistically significant for both valence and arousal. A possible interpretation is that when people are presented with the key components of a message and the summary, they are also reminded how much critical information they have forgotten. This is confirmed by the Eureka effect we found that was only exhibited by Group 3 in the experiment.

Analyzing Groups 3 and 4 (T3 approach versus frequent cognitive closure), we noted that Group 4 was also

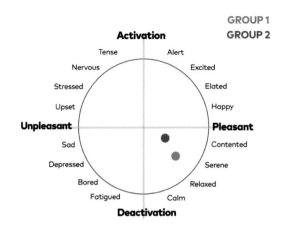

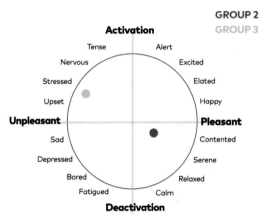

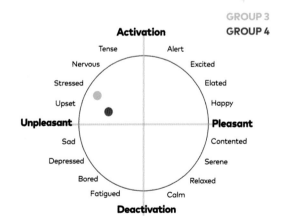

in a negative but less stressful state. This less stressful state was marked by a statistically significant reduction in valence. When participants were administered a long-term memory test after 48 hours, the only group that showed superior and precise memory for the essential concepts was Group 4, which showed 58 percent more precise memory for the main message compared to Group 3. Group 4 also showed better memory for understanding the problem presented in the sales pitch (42 percent), better memory of the details related to the proposed software solution (34 percent), and better overall comprehension of the content (29 percent). Participants' memory answers also demonstrated that only Group 4 could identify the three components that supported the main message with precision. Twenty percent of the participants in Group 4 could *state verbatim* the three components important to the client. *No participants in the other experimental groups were able to achieve this precision.* So, while the repeated cognitive closure may have seemed slightly unpleasant (most likely derived from the learning process and the short presentation length), Group 4 showed superior memory for the critical concepts.

Only Group 3, the T3-principle group, experienced a Eureka effect, which may have been because they were told the main message in the beginning of the presentation, and when the presenter repeated it at the end, it acted like an aha moment. They were reminded of the essence, but by then the presentation was over.

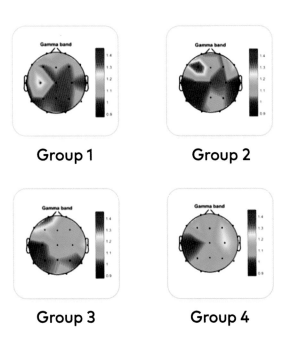

Group 1

Group 2

Group 3

Group 4

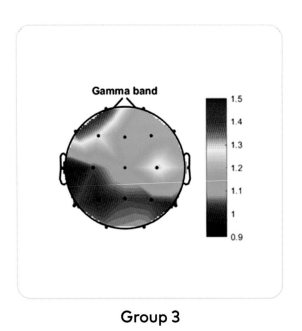

Group 3

Regarding cognitive variables for the entire presentation, we noted that Group 1, which saw the fluid version, experienced the highest fatigue. In contrast, Group 4, the condition with repeated cognitive closure, experienced the lowest fatigue. This confirms existing research, according to which one of the benefits of cognitive closure is the ability to discontinue information processing, stop looking, and avoid fatigue. In addition, the repeated cognitive closure group was the least tired despite feeling slightly uneasy. Group 4 did not have the highest working memory/cognitive workload, which supports the notion that with increased repetition, the brain does not have to exert extra cognitive energy as familiarity sets in, which, in turn, allows for more fluid processing and better comprehension of the message.

Practice Transitions

If you're in the business of delivering your content live, transitions will polish your speech. Using any of the transition words and phrases in this chapter will make you sound more polished because you will eliminate filler words such as "um," "uh," and "like."

When you practice delivering your content, you will likely notice awkward transitions. Please correct them, and then practice the proper transitions as much as you practice the actual content. Doing so will clarify your own thinking. You may even prompt yourself to add examples (using "in addition" or "for example") or propose contrasting points of view ("in contrast") or substantiate a logical sequence ("as a result"). Typically, transitions inspire writers and speakers to rework and revise content to best convey their intended meaning.

Remember that disjointed thoughts lead to forgettable content, while tightly linked ideas help the brain to remember more easily because one thing reminds people of another and another. The more associations your audience makes, the better they understand and remember your content, and their thoughts can "stumble" onto your ideas even when you're not around or when their minds wander.

Transitions

although then also for this reason the final point during then although also

although then also for this reason the final point during then although

Practical Guidelines from Quadrant III: Introspection

1. Tax the perceptive and cognitive workload within reasonable limits to engage all attentional capacities and prevent distractions.

2. Link content to your audience's future goals because the brain tends to mind wander to a future state and unfulfilled ambitions.

3. Make allowances for *some* mind wandering, which is often associated with problem solving and imagining creative solutions.

4. Help the brain plan for action by offering a set of organized steps, showing how your experiences map to the steps you're advising, and building anticipation for the future.

5. Use temporal transitions to describe a process or to order arguments in your discourse, which is how persuasion is born.

6. Include additive transitions to link ideas together and adversative transitions to contrast ideas and offer arguments contrary to expectations.

7. Use causative transitions to help the brain draw meaning and remove the possibility of misinterpretation.

8. Develop a storyboard to plan transitions, and implement them well.

9. Integrate text and images to help the brain build better associations between them.

10. Use transitions for cognitive closure, giving the buyer's brain clear, unambiguous knowledge.

External Focus

Visual Search

They orient their
attention externally
toward something they
consider rewarding

**Initiated by
the Individual**
**Initiated by
the Environment**

Internal Focus

Visual Search

After reading the guidelines in this quadrant, you will learn how to:

| Convince a buyer's brain to look at your content

| Help the brain pay attention even when content is complex

| Influence not just individual but collective attention

CHAPTER 10

The Decision to Look

Mixing Business with Pleasure

To ensure the survival of our species, evolution offered us a bold trick: pleasure. Food and sex are the *basic* pleasures that keep us going. But once those basic pleasures are satisfied, we have *higher-order* pleasures, such as social, artistic, monetary, and transcendent pleasures. These employ the same or similar brain mechanisms as the basic pleasures, and we know this because neuroscience tools provide evidence for the overlap.

Since pleasure is essential to humans, it is intuitive that people direct their attention to what is pleasurable. We will approach this quadrant by considering that when your audiences look externally and perform a visual search of their own accord, they decide to focus on one location instead of another. From this perspective, it is worthwhile to ask: How do you make business content pleasing and convince the brain to look at what you have to offer? Since you're not there to guide your audiences' attention, in this quadrant, we will specifically answer these questions:

- What ignites their decision to look? Is your content pleasurable enough to keep them from looking elsewhere?

- What happens when the external environment you're creating is complex? Will they still look and keep looking?

- What are the implications of collective attention? After all, in business settings, often marked by complex problems and solutions, the decision to look is hardly ever individual. How do you ensure that more than one person finds the same thing pleasing and worthy of attention? And, as a side note, who is influencing *your* attention?

In this chapter, we will first define pleasure and understand how pleasure happens in the brain. Then we will look at practical guidelines you can use in your communication that act as motivational magnets for your audience's attention.

What Generates Pleasure in the Brain?

Let's consider pleasure as the hedonic quality of stimuli—something you consider rewarding and you're willing to adjust your behavior to get. But what does the brain find pleasurable or *rewarding*? There are several components of rewards that are important to understand because if you know what it takes for your buyer's brain to perceive something as rewarding, then you can create messages that motivate them to pay attention and act on what you say. Conversely, without clear rewards, people may pay attention but not be motivated to act.

Three main components of a reward influence your audience's attention and actions. The division of these components is necessary because we may think of rewards as something the brain likes and wants, but liking and wanting operate in dissociable circuitry. Here is how—and what it means to the way you create content.

1. Wanting

This is the process related to motivating the brain to get the reward, to set the body in motion. It is supported by strong brain networks fueled by a well-known chemical: dopamine. Wanting is based on cravings, also called "incentive salience," which add a visceral oomph to mental desire. Wanting processes have a subconscious component; we can call this an objective component, which can be measured with neuroscience tools, bypassing self-reports. Wanting can also be expressed consciously through cognitive goals, but this can be subjective, and measuring it is not always reliable. For example, a team in an organization may express "wanting" to follow up with a vendor for a new marketing solution when, in fact, they prefer their status quo. Wanting depends on the physiological state when seeing a cue that triggers the process. For example, your nose catches the smell of someone barbecuing in their backyard, and even though you are not particularly hungry, you may get an instant craving for chicken. However, acting on that craving depends on whether you just had a heavy lunch. This means that someone's current physiological state can change the value of a perceived reward. The impact of this observation on how you develop content will become materially important in just a moment.

 2. Liking

This is the hedonic impact of a reward and includes subconscious reactions as well as conscious experiences of pleasure expressed through cognitive awareness. Liking is based on more feeble and fragile neural networks, and its chemical currency relies on opioids and cannabinoids. Since liking relies on a weaker network, and it may fluctuate, it's a good idea to keep sending your audience multiple media types and iterative messages. They will not like *all*, but you increase the chances that they will like some. In a behavioral study my colleagues conducted at Corporate Visions, they noted that 14 touches were necessary for a customer response and many content creators give up after 3.

 3. Learning

This process includes associations, representations, and predictions about future rewards based on past experiences. Learned predictions can be both explicit and implicit. For instance, think about people who sort of "know" the perfect time to deliver a pitch during a customer meeting (implicit or tacit knowledge) or those who can predict that a meeting with a client will go well based on previous experiences (explicit knowledge). Learning also includes associative conditioning, such as instrumental associations. For example, if you are rewarded in some way when you volunteer for a project, you're more likely to volunteer again.

The three processes—wanting, liking, and learning—can occur together at any time during the reward-behavior cycle. However, wanting processes dominate the initial phase when you're craving something, while liking processes dominate the subsequent phase when you're consuming that something and satisfying your craving. Learning happens throughout the cycle. In the following sections, let's look at how you can enable these three processes through the communication materials you create for a business audience.

Offer Intermittent Reward Schedules

As any pet owner knows, the brain can modify behavior based on rewards. Humans are no different. But there is more to rewards than simply receiving them. Differences in *when* and *how often* you reward others can also impact how they experience the reward and whether they will engage in that activity again.

In behavioral psychology, reinforcement theory states that people and animals respond to rewards and change behavior according to schedules. The simplest type of behavior reinforcement is continuous, in which you reward a behavior every time it occurs. This can happen in two ways. First, you can determine a specific number of actions that must occur before you dispense a reward. Coffee or juice shops do this, when you buy nine coffees and get the tenth one free. This is called a *fixed ratio schedule.* You may also use a *fixed interval schedule,* which implies that a specific time must pass before you offer a reward, like paying someone a salary every two weeks. *Continuous reinforcement* is often helpful in training a new behavior. Loyalty cards for department stores, airlines, and restaurants all increase the likelihood of our continued use of those services. Consider continuous reinforcement in your initial interactions with your audiences. For example, predictable rewards such as timely responses to customers and clear, relevant communication are likely to sustain engagement.

It's not just what rewards people get, it's **when** they get them

Intermittent reinforcement means delivering a reward at random intervals, based on a *variable ratio schedule*, meaning that you give rewards after a varying number of behaviors—sometimes after 4, sometimes 5, and other times 20. This method has been determined to yield the most significant effort from people because *the reward is unpredictable.* Slot machine gambling takes advantage of this principle; the machine doesn't guarantee a consistent rate of reward, so players continue, hoping that the next button press pays off. For your content development, can you consider offering rewards after varying, unpredictable intervals? For example, sometimes you might send a customer a white paper, sometimes a video testimonial, sometimes some case studies, and sometimes nothing at all.

When you offer rewards according to a variable ratio, you are likely to reinforce behaviors more effectively because when people don't know when they will be rewarded, they continue to act, just in case. Think of your own situation: If you have a boss who drops in randomly, this is more likely to reinforce your hard work. Psychologists describe this persistent behavior as *resistance to extinction.* Even after the reward is completely taken away, the behavior remains for a while because people aren't sure if it is just a longer interval before the reward than usual.

Using intermittent reward schedules when creating business content gives you a productivity advantage, too, because you don't have to create the most intense, amazingness-filled materials all the time. Sometimes you can give your audiences a smaller reward, sometimes no reward, and sometimes a bigger reward.

The following example is from one of my own presentations, where I addressed the importance of understanding how the brain handles change. Some slides are more visually intense (stronger reward) and some are simpler (weaker reward). The interplay between them keeps the audience paying attention.

In this presentation, I offered an intermittent visual reward by varying the amount and type of stimulation in each slide. Some slides are more visually and conceptually intense, and some are simpler.

The same technique is used in the following example of a tech solution presentation, in which some slides and messages are more stimulating than others, varying the degree of reward. The good news is that not every segment you offer has to be at the same level of intensity. When it is, the brain habituates (the process is also called hedonic adaptation), or gets bored, and may start looking elsewhere.

In this sequence, the presenter keeps one message more intense (the slide that is most important to remember) and tapers off the intensity on the other slides.

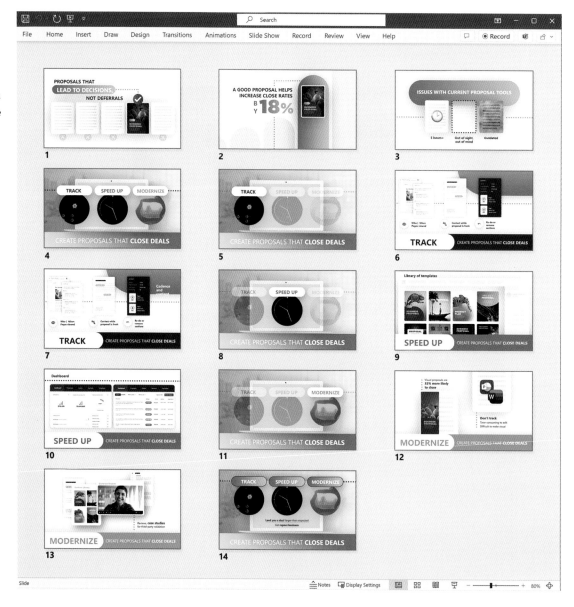

Create Incentive Salience

To understand rewards, we must understand how the brain builds enough wanting and motivation to get them. The brain manages the external world by dividing it into two regions: peripersonal and extrapersonal. The peripersonal includes things you can reach and control right now using your body. For example, if a pen is within your reach right now and you need it, you will not be that motivated to get up and pursue another pen. Extrapersonal refers to everything else you cannot touch, unless you move beyond your arm's reach, whether a small or large distance.

Things in the distance cannot be consumed yet. They can only be desired and consumed in the future. If you're craving chocolate and don't have it within reach, you can only enjoy it in the future when you go get it. The main chemical responsible for fulfilling future desires is dopamine, which has one job: to maximize the resources necessary to pursue things. One way for you to realize that some things are worth pursuing is for them to

have enough salience and incent you to come and get them, hence the phrase that psychologists use: *incentive salience.*

We know that incentive salience has two essential features. One is a cue that triggers a short peak of temptation. For example, if you smell someone cooking, you suddenly pay attention. The other feature is that the cue creates a motivational magnet, strengthening the attention pull further, making you treat the cue as if it was the reward itself. So, you are drawn to the smell of chicken as if it were the chicken itself.

How do you use this knowledge when creating content? Consider designing elements that contain cues that can trigger wanting. Food and sex, the basic rewards, can work when done tastefully (ha!). The collection of examples in this section includes business content concepts associated metaphorically with food items. For instance, the example with the excavator and exaggerated hamburger from the previous page symbolizes the idea of a software solution offering an abundance of features that modern customers in a particular industry crave. You don't have to use only food to trigger wanting, but it's a good and easy start as long as the metaphors feel fresh. In a recent neuroscience study on metaphors (mentioned in Quadrant II), I noted that business audiences do not consider business content associated with food to be clichéd.

These sequences build gradually to turn an abstract point into a concrete one. The first sequence offers a visual transformation of something undesirable (pile of rusty metals) into something desirable (ice cream truck). The second demonstrates the transition from ordinary to extraordinary. These examples were included in tech sales presentations to ignite wanting, much like ice cream or chocolate would.

Another cue that triggers wanting is sex, but in B2B content, if you choose to appeal to sex, it must be subtle, sophisticated, discrete, and fleeting. The collection below includes examples from various business presentations with a slight sexual undertone.

The appeal of a subtle sex-approach is broad, with one possible and unexpected exception: millennials.

Despite this generation being called "the hookup generation," they do not show as much inclination toward sex. Based on a sample of approximately 26,000 American adults, millennials born in the 1990s, aged 20 to 24, did not score high in terms of sexual partners compared to Gen Xers born in the 1960s. In fact, more than twice as many millennials had no sexual partners compared to

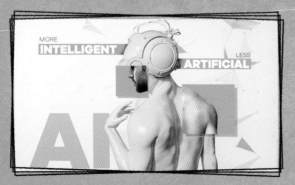

In this study, the eye-tracking signal clearly showed that sex organs attract attention.

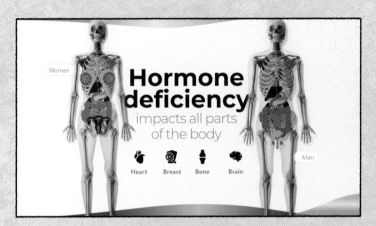
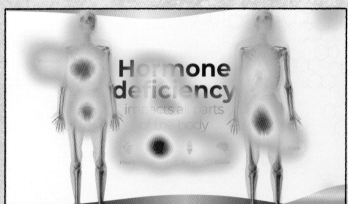

Gen Xers. There could be multiple explanations for this decrease in sexual activity. When digital communication abounds, face-to-face social skills may fade (so millennials might get a Tinder date but may not know how to flirt). Air-brushed photos that are abundant in social media may also lead to skewed ideas about body image and increased fear of being judged. The digital world presents less risk, while nonstop news reminds them of the seriousness of sexually transmitted diseases, so this might be a generation starting to withdraw.

But, this data is based on self-reports and theories, which may be inaccurate. The implicit attention toward sex-related items typically transcends demographics such as gender, age, and culture. I completed a neuroscience study a few years ago in an investor context. Participants included millennials who worked for reputable companies such as Goldman Sachs, Truist Bank, and Jefferies Group. I was observing how the investor's brain reacted to a presentation on hormone-related therapies. The main message in the slide in the example above is that hormone deficiencies impact both men and women. The skeleton images indicate the four critically affected areas: heart, breast, bones, and brain. The heat map shows the greatest attention on the sex organs, even though this slide was displayed briefly.

If you appeal to sex, you may have to trade the certainty of attention with the possibility of offense. What you create does not have to be a reputation killer if the

Hustle for greatness, be the good.

kindness
even when it's inconvenient

DISTANCED, BUT

NOT DISTANT

technique matches your brand personality, and you would not be embarrassed if your family saw the content. Keep in mind that attention and, subsequently, learning and memory are often associated with an unpleasant state of mind. I remember reading the case study of a dentist in the Boston area who increased the popularity of her cosmetic dentistry business by focusing on the link between a "healthy mouth and healthy sex." She was taken seriously because she took the topic of sex seriously, kept it clean, and stuck to accurate medical advice that people could use. It was also helpful that everything her team created (website, e-book, social media entries) was professionally designed rather than cheaply thrown together. It produced a positive image for readers and the media.

You may want to transcend the basic desires of food and sex and appeal to higher-order rewards, such as offering aesthetically appealing compositions, which rely on a combination of principles related to color, lines, shapes, balance, harmony, unity, and contrast. You can see these principles included in the compositions displayed in The Eye for Elegance Gallery on the next spread.

Higher-order rewards also include social rewards. Because this topic is broader, let's look at it in more detail in the next section.

Appeal to Social Rewards

An important aspect of rewards is that they help us filter many possible actions and motivate us to carry out those that offer a reward. For example, the prospect of a delicious meal might motivate you to travel to a distant restaurant. However, we hardly ever experience rewards in isolation. We live social lives, and the rewards we seek out and experience are intertwined with our social interactions and relationships.

How does this relate to attention? Social motives impact the importance of a task, so when people have a social reason, they may be more likely to continue to pay attention and see an action through.

I remember reading about the DJ Suna Duijf, who shared how one particular event changed her career. She was invited to play at a woman's seventy-fifth birthday party and was surprised to observe how older people really, really love to dance. Each time she played requested songs, many even got emotional. So Suna started her own company, Dance Palace, and her programs invite elderly people to dance and socialize. Her business is successful because the social motive is immediately persuasive.

Even though content creators might know that humans are a social species, they create content behind their desks at the last minute and don't take enough time to validate it in social settings and figure out how the message will impact their audiences' audiences as a group. To avoid this, always ask: How does my content attract not just the attention of the individual but the attention of the individual interacting with other individuals?

Much business content does not draw attention because it is developed in isolation, often resulting in something that is not useful in real life.

The Eye for Elegance Gallery

not **all minds** that wander are *lost*

past focus

future focus

THINK TANK

As a sidenote, you may think that older audiences have a harder time paying attention, remembering, and acting on memories. To a certain degree, this is true, because as we age, we have less cognitive capacity for *strategic monitoring*, or increasing attention when we expect something important to occur and decreasing attention when we don't. As we go about the day, some activities don't receive as much attention, and many things stop being important. However, age effects are diminished when you attach a social motive to a task. So if you're creating messages for older audiences, you will increase the chances that they will pay attention to and act on your content if you clarify the social motive.

In the following example, we were helping a presenter share characteristics of value propositions to entice potential buyers. His audience included salespeople who have their own audiences to impact, such as current customers or prospects. The information was shared in such a way as to offer salespeople techniques on how to please their own audiences. These slides prompted attention because the future social motive was clear.

Another benefit of social motives is that they tap into intrinsic motivation. They attract attention, and that attention does not come with a cognitive cost because they rely on automatic processes. When you analyze your content, are there opportunities for tying some of your slides or discussion points to a strong social motive your audience may have?

This deck was successful because it clarified and offered sellers a social motive: how to gain more customers.

Play with Time

Time is a fundamental part of our lives, whether we are rushing to catch a cab, relaxing on the couch, riveted by emotion, or mind wandering and staring into space. It plays a critical role in business content, too, because you will likely try to persuade your audiences to give you time and stay with you for a little while. To influence the amount of time you want others to spend with you, you must first understand how the brain keeps track of time.

The perception of time involves attention and memory processes; you probably agree that time passes more quickly when you are doing something interesting, important, amusing, or exciting. In contrast, a watched pot never boils. Minutes drag by when you are bored.

We now better understand the molecular mechanisms for the perception that "time flies when you're having fun." A great deal of research is converging to show that dopamine fuels time processing, namely that compounds

activating dopamine receptors tend to speed up our perception of time. For instance, cocaine enhances the effect of dopamine, creating the impression that time passes more quickly. In contrast, the neuroleptics used to treat schizophrenia inhibit the effect of dopamine, creating the impression that time is passing more slowly.

How can this information help you when creating business content? Your audience's *experience of time* can impact where they look on their own and for how long. When dopamine activity is high, the brain is more likely to judge a time interval as short. So a practical guideline is to offer enough rewards that lead to a high level of dopamine (e.g., speeding up movement or advancing slides, varying the embedded media, or transitioning frequently from formal to informal, simple to complex, or passive versus interactive). This technique can create the feeling that content unfolds quickly and works well when creating presentations; no one has ever complained of a business presentation being too short.

Is speeding up the perception of time in content processing *always* a good technique? Let's consider other scientific observations. One of dopamine's primary roles in the brain is to offer a reinforcement signal: We're likely to seek what serves us well and avoid what does not. Occasionally, we are surprised by an unexpected reward, and this happy forecast error leads to a dopamine burst. Time plays a vital role in this reward prediction error: a reward that comes *earlier* than expected triggers the dopamine signal.

Why would our sense of time and reinforcement learning converge on the dopamine system? It is possible that when we stumble upon a situation that's better than expected, *slowing down* our internal clock would lead us to spend more time in that environment. That's one way the brain is being helpfully rebellious; it's encouraging us to stay engaged in what is helpful and disengage sooner from what is not. The takeaway: when you offer your audiences a better-than-expected stimulus, they may want to linger longer.

One way to ensure you're offering something better than expected is to constantly test and retest various versions of your content to ensure you are hitting (and hopefully, exceeding) the mark. In the following example, we tested multiple versions of the introductory slide of a presentation on a marketing solution because we wanted to make a strong first impression and offer a better-than-expected stimulus. This was a presentation I had included in a hyperscanning neuroscience project, meaning I was scanning more than one person at a time using EEG equipment.

Hyperscanning is by nature a more involved research study, so the stimulus had to be of very high quality. You don't want to test a poorly created presentation because the EEG and ECG signals don't lie; they *will* reveal a boring presentation. Before most neuroscience studies, I conduct a pilot to determine business professionals' reactions to the content. It took quite a few tries to create the right introductory slide that presented the notion of marketing content that was not useful to salespeople, which was the essence of the presentation. Respondents did not relate to the spiderweb concept, but responded to the image of clothes on the treadmill. All this to say: strive to provide a better-than-expected stimulus, and the audience will stay longer.

In this sequence, I was testing out different versions of the title slide, keeping the same image across experimental conditions and varying the text. The treadmill-turned-closet slide outperformed the spiderweb. We used it in the neuroscience project, and it got the audience's attention, as later evidenced by the eye-tracking and EEG signals.

Our perception of time also depends on our emotional state. Neurophysiology research is beginning to show how emotions may speed up or slow down our perception of time. For instance, one study investigated how watching films that impacted subjects' emotional states also affected their sense of time. Subjects saw excerpts from films that induced fear (*The Blair Witch Project*, *Scream*, and *The Shining*) or sadness (*City of Angels*, *Philadelphia*, or *Dangerous Minds*). Other subjects viewed neutral footage, like weather forecasts and stock market updates. When asked to estimate the duration of a visual stimulus, researchers noted that fear, not sadness, distorted time. The fear-inducing stimulus was perceived as longer than it was.

The theory of embodied cognition helps explain how perceiving other people's emotions changes our sense of time. Embodied cognition contends that we have the ability to simulate other people's emotional states, and this enables us to understand their feelings. For example, in research where young people spend time with the elderly, who speak and walk more slowly, the young people's internal clocks slowed down. Research also suggests that slowing time enhances social interaction. So if you want audiences to slow down and linger with your content, *you* might have to slow down first.

Click to add title

Click to add subtitle

Simplifying
complexity
is a myth

CHAPTER 11

Harnessing Complexity

In today's increasingly globalized markets, communicating complexity is frequent and unavoidable because an organization's credibility often stems from offering a suite of comprehensive, complex solutions. It is often suggested that an optimal solution to handling complexity is to simplify it. In fact, if you type "simplify complexity" in a search engine, you get over 55 million results.

It's tempting to think that you could simplify your communication, but where attention and memory are concerned, *less is not always more*, and simplicity is not always the solution. It's true that *sometimes* simplicity helps attention and memory. When you feed your audiences' brains with simple content, they may focus on it better and show appreciation—which may help them retain your content. But even though simplicity is sometimes necessary, the degree of it is debatable. Where attention—and subsequently, memory—are concerned, there are four thoughts you must first consider about simplicity.

1. Question the adage "less is more."

Less is not always more; less can be a bore. You can only stare at a white painting in a museum for so long before you move on.

 2. Consider complexity versus randomness.

Often it's not complexity that annihilates attention and memory. Instead, it's randomness, which undermines the ability of your audiences' brains to detect patterns, which help with focus and recall.

 3. Avoid simplistic content.

Sometimes people simplify so much that they end up offering superficial content. Simplistic content is often ignored or, worse, not deemed credible.

 4. Offer a point of reference.

There will be moments when a simple message is appropriate, as you will see on the following pages. However, your audiences' brains cannot appreciate your simplicity unless they know the complexity from which it has come. This contrast will impact attention and credibility.

Overall, simplicity and complexity need each other. So, in this chapter, let's look at practical neuroscience-based guidelines that lead to a mindful balance of simplicity and complexity to preserve attention and build engagement and memories. Before we start, a quick definition of complexity. For our discussion, we're not analyzing the type of complexity associated with the stock market, political systems, or social groups, but rather the complexity that applies to sharing content with an audience.

A system increases in complexity depending on the number of items it contains, how varied those items are, and whether there is a set of rules that someone can use to retrieve the essence of that complexity (meaning a way to identify patterns and recreate the initial complex content). For example, if someone showed you the pattern 01010101010101010101, even if it has many items and the items are somewhat varied, there is a short set of rules (01×10) to retrieve it later. Contrast this with the random string 5 7 2 6 9 8 3 1 6 0; the only way to retrieve this would be to memorize the entire string. In other words, how complex something is can be calculated by the length of the shortest recipe or algorithm required to recreate it.

In business content, it's not complexity that kills us, it is randomness, meaning that your audience cannot identify a rule that governs a piece of content and cannot see any patterns. So, in the following sections, let's look at some practical guidelines you can use to help your buyer's brain manage complexity and detect what is essential in your content. But first, let's consider a question.

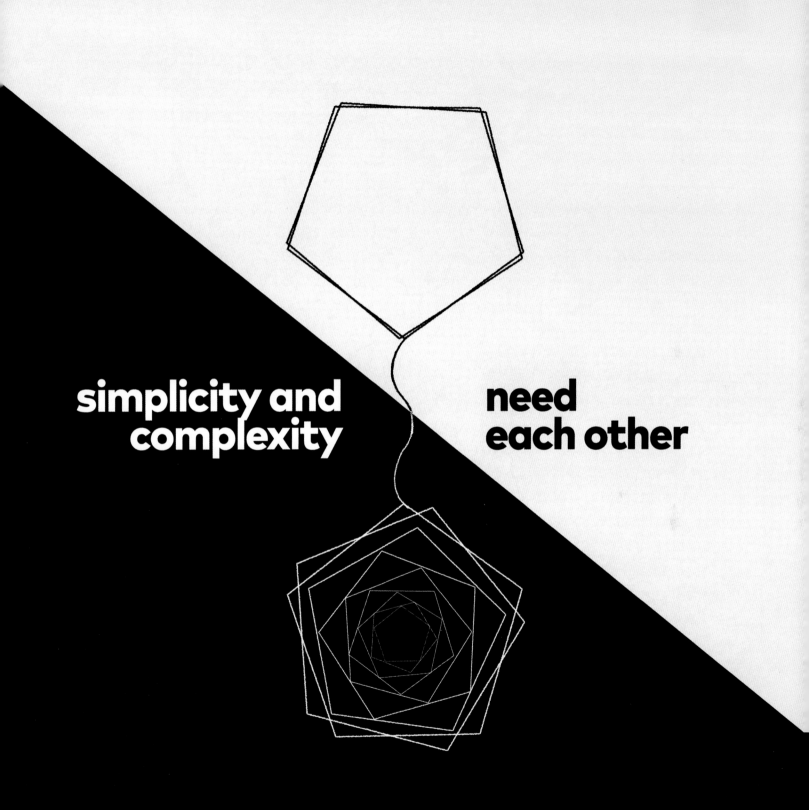

simplicity and complexity

need each other

Do People Crave Complexity?

If you were to listen to someone speak or receive some collateral from a vendor, would you prefer the materials to be simple, Zen style, with slides that had a picture and just a few keywords, representing stand-alone concepts? Or complex, with slides that included a lot of images and text, with various interconnected ideas? It has been suggested that different cultures appreciate different levels of detail during business meetings. For instance, some cultures strongly believe that going into detail is necessary to understand content deeply and avoid misunderstandings, while others prefer to communicate by "suggestion," or by generalizing the information and drawing personal conclusions rather than being given all the details.

Many of these observations on cultural preferences for detail have been based on survey studies or anecdotes. Consider this lighthearted narrative that epitomizes cultural differences in communication style and the preference for detail:

> Once upon a time, three journalists—a Frenchman, an American, and a German—were asked to write a fictional story about an elephant. The Frenchman wrote, "L'éléphant et l'amour." The American wrote, "36 Miracle Diets for the Modern Working Elephant." The German

wrote, "The Psychological Nature and Fundamental Dynamics of the Socialization of the Elephant: Volume 1, The Symbolic Importance of the Elephant, Chapter 1: From Julius Caesar to the Present."

Moving beyond anecdotes, I had the opportunity to conduct a cross-cultural neuroscience study that asked the question: What is the impact of culture on attention, cognitive workload, fatigue, valence, arousal, memory, and motivation when participants from B2B companies process complex content? And are there any other elements that play a substantial role when sharing complex content across cultures?

Participants from nine cultures (American, British, French, Italian, German, Irish, Australian, Indian, and Chinese) were exposed to presentations with different levels of complexity while we recorded EEG and ECG signals. We also used eye-tracking and GSR devices to monitor participants' visual attention and arousal levels. The presentations were recorded as simulated Zoom calls and introduced participants to a solution for managing cybersecurity threats for IT (information technology) and OT (operational technology). For this study, we considered one of the presentations to be more complex because it contained the three components typical to a complex system mentioned earlier: a large volume of varied and interdependent elements.

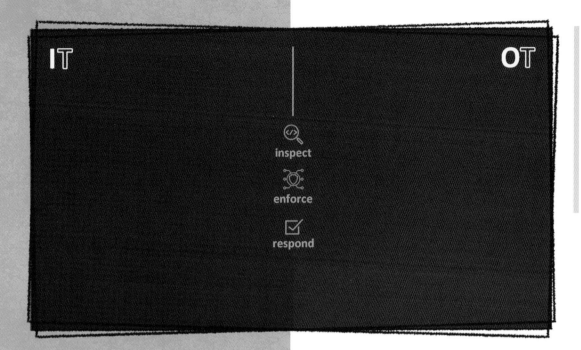

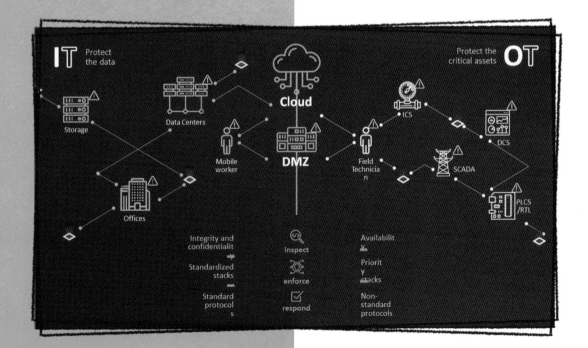

The two slides represent the contrast between the technical details included in the simple versus complex presentations that participants from various cultures saw during the neuroscience study.

We split participants into two groups: one was exposed to the presentation containing more details (Complex Group), while the other was exposed to the presentation addressing the same topic but with fewer details (Simple Group). The results:

1. The cultures in the Complex Group remembered the main message with more precision, understood the content better, remembered additional information, exhibited an approach behavior, and mind wandered less during the complex presentation.

2. An elevated level of complexity had a positive influence even on nontechnical participants. Even though they were more fatigued and showed greater stress, participants with lower levels of expertise also had better memory performance after watching the complex presentation. This is important because often in business, you must persuade someone nontechnical to buy your complex solution.

3. Non-native speakers also showed superior performance, demonstrating that complexity can transcend cultural and language barriers.

In the Complex Group, I also noted that participants' brains synchronized better in a way that was relevant to learning. This finding, along with the previous remarks, leads to the strong recommendation to share complex content in a cross-cultural virtual selling context.

How Do You Manage Complexity Well?

Sharing complex details has cross-cultural advantages related to increased attention, motivation, and long-term memory. But how do you manage complexity properly?

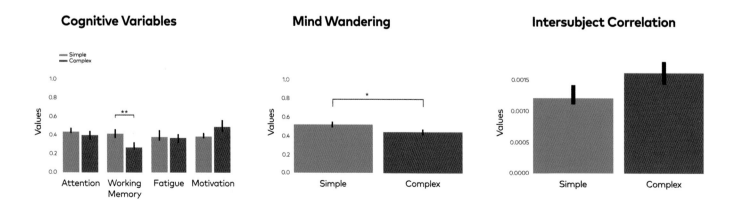

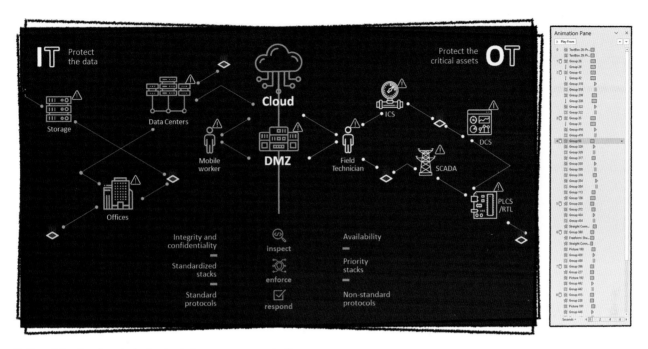

Tasteful animations help the brain to manage complexity.

In our study, the complex presentation included the following:

- Icons designed to reflect a meaningful concept.

- Variety in the icon design, intended to avoid confusion of the diverse concepts.

- Contrasting colors and positioning of elements (IT and OT presented on opposite sides).

- Abundant animations gradually displayed the varied and interdependent elements to avoid overwhelming the brain with too many details simultaneously. What are "abundant animations"? Even though the Complex presentation contained only two extra slides compared to the Simple presentation, the two slides included 104 animations (59 on one slide and 45 on the other). In Chapter 2, on motion, you learned the advantages of movement on attention, memory, and motivation.

How do we know that people paid attention to important elements the way we intended? We set AOIs (areas of interest) around critical factors, such as IT, OT, and the middle of the presentation, which contained the

US

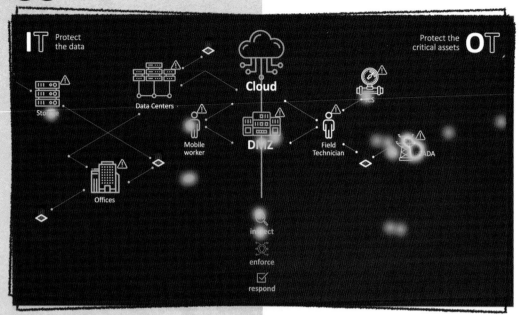

Germany

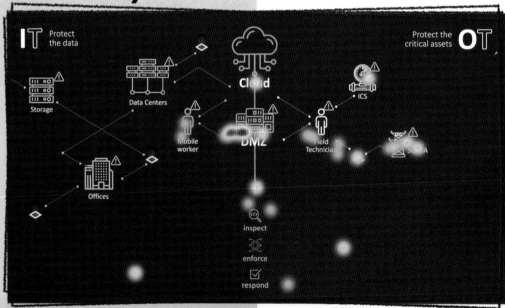

components of the vendor's proposed solution. Based on the eye-tracking data, we noted extra visual attention to the IT and OT elements, which we considered the main message that participants had to remember. In the Complex version, these items remained on the screen longer, but just because they were there, participants did not have to pay attention to them—they could have habituated. However, the voice-over emphasized the difference between these two items, which may explain the extra attention and the better memory for this information. Given this finding, when presenting complex content on slides, ensure that your narration constantly points out the essence of a message within a complex design. For a successful cross-cultural sales presentation that includes complex content, the design of the presentation and the management of the details are critical considerations.

I must also emphasize the uniqueness of the topic presented. The proposed solution included aspects that participants had never heard of before. For instance, after the study, many remarked that they had not heard about operational technology (OT) described the way it was in the presentation and contrasted with IT. So a pragmatic approach for a persuasive communicator is not to focus only on the importance of "detailed thinking" but also on "nonconventional thinking," which will make complexity more attention-grabbing and memorable.

The heat maps demonstrate that there is no significant difference between the US and German buyers in the way they process complexity.

Embracing Elaboration

According to our definition earlier, complexity implies volume, meaning *adding* elements to a concept, such as details, stories, or inferences. This type of addition—also called elaboration—positively impacts attention and memory, further solidifying the notion that less is not more. Why does elaboration work? Elaboration can help link new concepts to semantic networks that already exist in the brain, making it easier to process the content. Given extra details and examples or stories, elaboration can reveal multiple meanings and activate deeper encoding, further improving attention and memory.

I conducted a study a few years ago in which we created a presentation on digital transformation that included five slides delivered in five minutes. In one of the

These two contrasting presentations took the same amount of time to deliver. However, in the second sequence, I included more tangible examples to help the brain visualize abstract conclusions related to digital transformation.

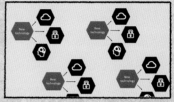

presentations, we made room for extra words and slides to elaborate on existing key points but stayed within the five-minute mark. We kept the length constant because we wanted to recreate a realistic situation; your customers give you and your competitors a similar amount of time. The materials you present within that time are up to you.

We elaborated on a core message with imagery and specificity. For example, we didn't stop at an abstract conclusion like, "Digital transformation helps you differentiate yourself." We showed how Target and Starbucks enable customers to place their orders online and pick them up in the store. We didn't just say, "Digital transformation enables you to be more innovative." We showed how Home Depot provides reserved parking and dedicated checkout and order loading for customers who order online and come to pick up their orders in the store. We also mentioned how Best Buy had recently acquired a healthcare service provider and was helping aging seniors install devices at home to monitor their daily living.

Our goal was to make sure B2B participants paid attention to and subsequently remembered the main message for the digital transformation solution in the presentation, which was, "Customer first, technology second." The elaboration—the "more"—positively impacted attention and subsequent precision memory. In another version of the study, we took the design a step further and amplified it with aesthetic elements to intensify the contrast, unity, and dominance of specific concepts. The memory of the most important messages was even more precise and detailed in the second version.

The aesthetic elements that stemmed from more intense visuals, sharper contrast, visual unity, and dominance of specific messages rendered better memory performance.

Take a look at the detailed responses from participants in the study who were asked 48 hours after exposure to the presentation what they remembered regarding digital transformation.

Most reported memories came from the second half of the deck, where the content was elaborated. Note how participants remembered the *same* slides and concepts; they did not remember things randomly. An additional

I remember specific examples from Home Depot, and Target. Starbucks and Best Buy all thinking about customer needs first and technology second. I also remember the message that rushing to put everything into the cloud can cause issues rather than solve them.

Many companies such as Target, Starbucks, Home Depot, and Best Buy put customer experience first and technology second. Yet, they still need cloud, AI technology, and security tools.

The two [concepts] I remember the most would be how Best Buy uses a healthcare service to monitor seniors at home, and Home Depot does parking.

I remember Starbucks, Best Buy, Home Depot, and Target did this. It is more about the long-term journey and less about quick wins in implementing cloud, security, and AI tech strategies."

benefit of elaboration is enabling your audiences to walk away with *uniform* attention and memory. When attention and memory are uniform, decision-making may be easier and faster because customers are more likely to move forward when they all bring to mind the same concepts.

Analyze your communication materials, and look for ways to make room for elaboration because they will enable the brain to see the essentials and remember them later. The key word is "see." The brain needs to see to acquire knowledge of the world. Survival is impossible unless we know the world around us at this moment and the next moment. In its quest to know the world, the brain is looking for essential properties to remember to characterize other objects and situations in the future. It would be exhausting if we constantly had to process everything as new. However, the information around us is never constant, so vision is an active process. People look at constantly changing things and extract what is necessary to identify what might have enduring properties and discount what is unnecessary.

Where your business content is concerned, it is important to ask: Am I helping the brain recognize what is essential and enduring? If you're helping your audiences identify what is essential in your materials, you will make complexity manageable, and in the process, capture attention and be memorable.

How do you help the brain see the essentials? To answer this, we turn to the study of fractals.

Make Friends with Fractals

A fractal is a pattern that repeats itself at every level of magnification. Think: nested Russian dolls, broccoli, or snowflakes. Regardless of scale, each reduced part looks like the whole. For instance, the smaller branches of a tree look like the parent trunk.

Fractals are all around you, from landscapes to cloud formations to your body. Our retinal vessels have the characteristics of fractals, and so do the EEG patterns in the brain. Jackson Pollock's poured patterns are also said to have fractal properties, which might explain the long-term appeal of his work. Fractals are helpful to study and understand because they offer perceived regularities in a complex system—in short, what is essential. In addition, they naturally optimize, which is what you want to aim for when things are complex. For example, the surface of the lining of the lungs has a fractal pattern that allows for more oxygen to be absorbed. A wireless antenna has a fractal structure and can capture signals over a broader range of bands compared to a simple antenna. In the same way, you can use fractals to optimize complexity and attract attention to what is essential and enduring.

Here is how I know that understanding and using fractals will be commercially valuable to you.

We defined fractals as patterns that repeat at any level of magnification. This special quality of the scale invariance of fractals can be identified and quantified by a parameter called the fractal dimension, FD. Fractals help us understand complex structures in space, and even though brain processes happen across time, we can also look for fractal properties as they apply to a time series. Given that EEG is a great indicator of cortical arousal, we can analyze the fractal properties of EEG signals across a discrete time sequence (e.g., someone watching a business video over several minutes).

To study the fractal properties of EEG signals across time, we can use Higuchi's fractal dimension (HFD), which is an efficient algorithm for measuring fractal dimension (FD) across discrete time sequences. Studies that have used HFD have found that a higher HFD value is associated with better memory and learning. In our neuroscience studies, we often analyze EEG data from participants exposed to a stimulus (e.g., a business video)

to identify moments with a high HFD value and correlate this metric with techniques used in that stimulus.

In one neuroscience study I conducted, we monitored the brain's reaction to video content. During this study, I asked the question: Which video style (cartoon or real people) and effects have a more substantial impact on variables such as attention, working memory, valence, arousal, and motivation to act on the content? We showed participants two video types that addressed information pertinent to teams of sales reps. Video 1 (cartoon style) explained several sales compensation plans, and Video 2 contained similar content addressed to sellers, but expressed through real footage.

Anytime we include participants in a neuroscience study, we want to capture a baseline of their brains when they are not stimulated. The data showed a higher HFD value and more activity in the brain during their baseline than while watching the cartoon-based video. This suggests that when understimulated, the brain retreats inward, where there is much more going on. The brain activity during the cartoon video resembled more the

These contrasting examples revealed that the brain processes content more deeply in realistic scenes compared to simplified and abstract scenes.

state of understimulation to external items, which led to less attention and memory. In contrast, watching Video 2 significantly increased attention, valence, motivation, and memory scores. This reinforces a guideline emphasized earlier: Keep your complex content. Don't simplify it. In this case, complexity was created by adding realistic scenery, including actual people (not cartoons), and avoiding overly simplistic and abstract designs. For example, in the picture included on the page to the left, it's likely that the real cat has a stronger impact than the cat drawing.

We also noted significantly higher HFD values in the temporal and parietal lobes for participants who watched Video 2. These areas in the brain are associated with memory and object association. These aspects indicate that the real-life footage included in Video 2 contributed to more memory and learning. In contrast, the cartoon-based design in Video 1 showed a visual increase in alpha, often an indicator of sleepiness or drowsiness. This may have resulted from a design that was too simplistic and may not have been taken seriously. People often associate cartoons with humor. Cartoon-based design may be cheaper, but the real-life footage offered a worthwhile ROI: memory and learning. If budget is an issue and motion graphics (cartoon-based) approaches still need to be used, consider a combination of illustrations and real-life photos. When you preserve some realism, you add complexity, and the brain synchronizes better with a complex signal.

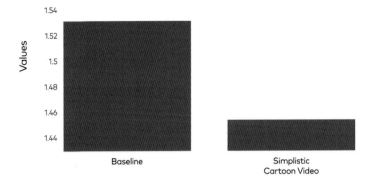

We noted more activity in the brain while staring at a beige wall (Baseline) than while watching a simplistic cartoon video.

HFD Brain Region

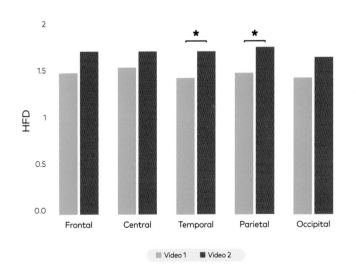

We noted significantly higher HFD values in the temporal and parietal lobes for participants who watched Video 2 (the natural scene video). These areas in the brain are responsible for memory and object association.

In other studies investigating the fractal properties of EEG signals across time using the brain's exposure to successful movies, findings show that more shots and *more complex shots* synchronized better with brain fractality. In fact, most current movies are made to have this type of synchronization, and many movie producers know to frequently switch between simple and complex shots and create scenes with enough complexity to sustain interest and motivation to watch. Reflecting on your content, if you're ever tempted by too much simple, Zen-like design, *reconsider minimalism* as it may not allow the brain to create object associations essential for attention, memory, and learning.

Instead of minimalist approaches to content and design, keep your complexity and wrap it in a swirling similarity of patterns or a repeated set of "equations" or rules, which is how fractals operate. For example, this corporate deck shows how the concepts expressed in the black slide repeat themselves frequently, indicating something is essential, but they are also alluded to at a smaller level of magnification in the white slides. Because each slide is a "copy" of just a few essential messages or "rules" at different scales, it draws attention to what is essential.

In this sequence, the same pattern (dark slide) repeats itself, and elements related to those items are present at smaller levels of magnification in other slides.

Provide Profluence

Earlier I mentioned Jackson Pollock, the artist who pioneered the drip technique: splashing liquid household paint onto a horizontal canvas. When he created his works of art, painting upright was customary, and Pollock stood out (ha!) because he laid his canvas on the floor, attacking it from all four sides and using his body to drizzle, splatter, and pour the paint. The technique was undeniably successful. In 2006, Pollock's *No. 5, 1948* sold for $140 million, one of the highest prices ever paid for a painting.

I remember exactly where I was when I learned more about the artist and his story. It started with a cookbook I found on a sale rack at a store. The book mentioned Pollock, which made me ask instantly, "What does Pollock have to do with a cookbook?" Apparently, not only was he an artist, but he was also a talented chef and gardener. The book idyllically portrayed Pollock and his wife, painter Lee Krasner, cooking humble but delicious meals for their friends at their farmhouse in Long Island, New York. "Humble" because this was shortly after World War II, and they were growing most of the ingredients themselves, experimenting with different combinations and approaches, as artists do.

The book juxtaposed pictures of delightful dishes with Pollock's intense paintings, offering a feast for the senses. While browsing through recipes for creamy onion soup and chili con carne, with brief descriptions of the artists cooking together, a few phrases related to details about the painter's personal life caught my attention and kept it for a while. What started as attention to a recipe for delicious quiche with forest mushrooms quickly morphed into other details that had put the painter's life on the rocks. I had intended to spend just a few seconds with the book, and 30 minutes later I was still learning about the painter's story because each level of detail elicited a response stronger than the previous one and moved the story forward.

This notion of moving a story forward and giving your audience the feeling that things are going somewhere is called *profluence*. As you progress from one segment to the next (e.g., slides in a presentation or pages in a book), give your audience the sense that progress is being made toward a worthwhile point.

So, where are *we* going after this?

Let's consider one final aspect about attention: the notion that people hardly ever pay attention alone. What influences collective attention?

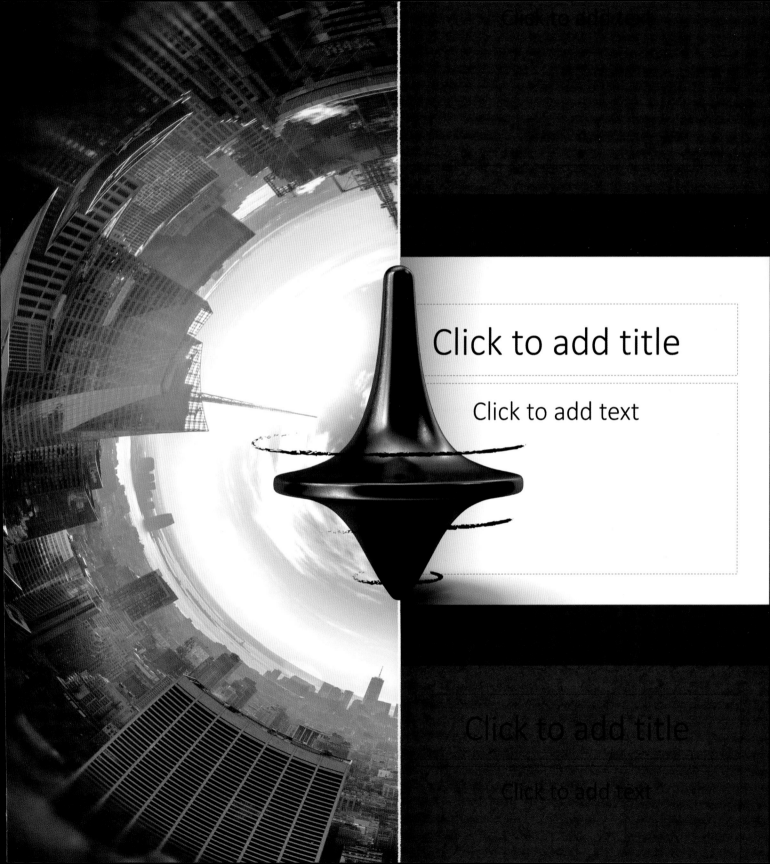

Click to add title

Click to add text

Collaborative attention and remembering can get us

in trouble with the truth

CHAPTER 12

The Risks and Rewards of Collective Attention

Think of the sum total of what you know in order to do your job well. How much of it has come from paying attention of your own accord while learning what you need directly versus consuming what others have told you, verbally or in writing? Some psychologists believe that as much as 90 percent of what we know is secondhand. This is a large percentage, reminding us that we regularly rely on other people's attention and memory to succeed. Attention is not just an individual process; it is collective because human behavior is inherently social. We often need others to pay attention, remember, and make decisions. Paying attention can be a social act.

In this chapter, we ask: Who is influencing *your* attention? So far, we've looked at how you attract others' attention. Where do others prompt *you* to look? How do you know if—as you're allowing others to influence your attention—you're still staying true to your cause? And how do you balance the advantages and pitfalls of collective attention? You can apply the guidelines in this chapter in two ways: to ponder who is influencing your attention and to keep in mind that when you impact others' attention, they are likely collaborating with other people.

I grew up in Communist Romania, and many things from back then became active in my mind and got my attention only when my friends and family prompted me to look and reflect.

Dad: Remember when we could drive on weekends based on the last digit of our license plate number? Odd number one weekend, even number the next. At least there was less stress with such little traffic.

Mom: Remember when we ate our first Mars chocolate bar? We got it from our neighbor, who had some connections at the border. I sliced off a small piece and packed the rest in the fridge; we stretched it to eat over four days. What's happening to our willpower these days?

Iris, my friend from high school: Remember when we could not wear bangs at school and had to keep the hair out of our faces with that stupid white elastic band? That sucks when you're a teenager trying to make an impression. I wonder if we still carry some of that trauma today.

Without their prompts, none of these memories would have been activated. And how they talked about these experiences mattered. There is a difference between *collected* attention and memory (just a list of facts) versus *collective* attention and memory, which implies shared sense-making. It probably happens in your family, too. Every time you activate shared experiences, the activity is less about what actually happened or what we paid attention to but rather about the meaning we derived from them.

The bright side of collective attention and memory is long-lasting meaning. But there is a dark side, too. When we talk to others about our shared experiences, our memories of those events become malleable. There is a point where we influence each other's attention and memory so much that uniformity settles among group members, and this can have negative consequences too. According to cognitive scientists, when we have a shared experience, initially, there are differences in our memories. This is because we may pay attention to various stimuli differently, and our ability to recall what we experience is different too. However, when we regroup later, we can influence one another to the point where our past attention and memories become similar. The advantage is social harmony. The disadvantage is that someone may put in our minds something inaccurate.

Attention and memory conformity can have positive and negative aspects. I study unified attention, meaning multiple people paying attention to the same things, with neuroscience tools and algorithms. For instance, in the hyperscanning studies I conduct (when we scan more than one person at a time), I observe when people's brains synchronize. Why is it essential that people's brains synchronize? Interbrain synchrony has been associated with shared understanding and better collaboration and cooperation. In addition, interbrain synchrony is also more likely to occur when participants are engaged in a task, which is likely enabled by similar attention mechanisms. Shared understanding, collaboration, cooperation, engagement, and unified attention are desirable dimensions of persuasive business content, so it is useful to monitor brain synchronization.

In one neuroscience study I conducted, we paired people and divided them into four groups while they watched a high-level sales presentation on a tech solution.

The pairs in Group 1 were in the same room, face-to-face with the presenter. The pairs in Group 2 watched the presentation via Zoom. The pairs in Group 3 joined the presenter via phone, simulating a traditional conference call. And the pairs in Group 4 had a hybrid experience, in which one person in each pair joined the presenter face-to-face, while the other joined remotely. To better understand the similarity among people's experiences within each group and across modalities, we computed a complex correlation matrix and compared every participant's neural signals with those of all other participants. This afforded us the possibility to interpret potential scenarios that were not physically part of the experiment but could be carried through computationally, such as one participant being on Zoom and the other joining via the phone (which often happens as some people may join virtual calls from their cars).

The results indicated that participants who experienced the sales presentation in an entirely virtual setting (not hybrid or face-to-face) also registered the most similarity in terms of engaging with the content, meaning they paid attention to the same things. This indicates that you can be successful with an entirely virtual presentation for a high-level overview of your solution. But the more significant point is that now, we have scientific approaches to studying collective attention, and the rest of this chapter turns these into guidelines for your business content.

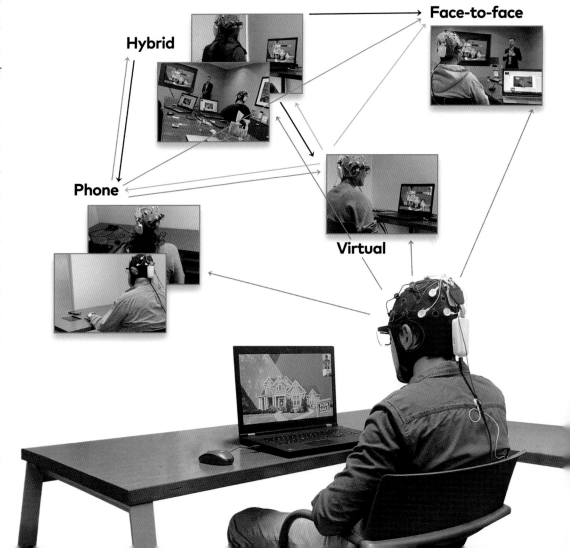

the pressure of **seeing and believing**

Credibility and Confidence Can Undermine Attention and Memory

When you want to make decisions, which are typically social, how do you select what to focus on? Credibility is often an important factor. Imagine you were tasked with buying a software platform for your team, but software is not your forte. So, you identify an expert with the credibility you're missing and look where they are looking and remember what they tell you is important. But is this situation optimal?

Our degree of confidence in our own attention and memory influences our inclination to conform. If we *believe* we lack accuracy when discussing a shared event with others, we are more likely *not* to report what we paid attention to and recall and are inclined to agree with other people's recollections. For example, in one experiment, each participant was assigned a partner and then separately shown a set of 21 slides depicting a criminal event; some participants saw a different version of the slides, in which there was an accomplice. When the pairs got back together to discuss the event, it was evident that memory was influenced, because, in the subsequent independent recall test, people reported seeing what they had *not* been shown. Members of the pair tended to conform to the most confident participant's observations.

Do we tend to conform to other people's attention and memory, even though we know they are *never* accurate?

In one experiment, people were paired up to look at household settings (e.g., bathroom, kitchen, bedroom, closet). Some had typical objects and some atypical objects. The researcher planted one of the pair to influence the other person's attention—and therefore memory—with different degrees of inaccuracy. The rate at which the fake participant misreported objects during group recall ranged from: 0 percent, 33 percent, 66 percent, and 100 percent. Researchers wanted to determine whether the other person would be influenced in their later recall by someone who misreported everything while in groups. During the individual recall test, participants were prone to conformity. They reported they remembered items in the scene that their partner had mentioned, regardless of whether the fake partner was somewhat inaccurate (33 percent) or completely inaccurate (100 percent).

As you reflect on your own conversations with others, where the intent is to pay attention to and extract the information you can use later, it is useful to ask: How often do you consider others more credible or more confident than you? Respect what they share, but check the validity from other sources, even if you believe you looked at the same things together. Or in the words of the Russian proverb popularized by President Ronald Reagan during the Cold War, "Trust but verify."

Collaborative attention inhibits individual memory

Guard Against Time and Order Conformity

We are susceptible to attention and memory conformity when we know others have been exposed to the information for longer. In one study, researchers paired up participants and then exposed each partner separately to four pictures, in which some details stayed the same and some were changed. For example, one member saw a kitchen scene, showing two cups and a plate near a sink and a tree visible through the kitchen window; the other saw two cups and a *teapot* near the sink and a *house* visible through the kitchen window. Researchers also told participants that they saw the pictures half or twice as long as their partners. In reality, the exposure to information was the same for all participants. When participants reunited in pairs and answered a recall test, those who were led to believe they had seen a picture for half the time compared to their partner were more likely to report images they had not seen and were less accurate in reporting pictures they had seen.

The order in which people speak influences our attention and subsequent memory. In a social setting, we tend to agree more with someone speaking first. There are several explanations for this effect. Those who speak first are less exposed to potential misinformation and may also be perceived as having more confidence since they were courageous enough to speak first. In another study, participants were paired up and exposed to different versions of an event: One member saw someone steal a wallet, while the other saw him putting it back where he found it. Later, the pairs got together to discuss what they had seen. People who spoke second were nine times more likely to be exposed to misinformation than those who spoke first. They were also six times more likely to be misled. These findings applied whether people *observed* a conversation or were *actively part* of the conversation.

Sometimes conformity occurs because of a phenomenon called *social loafing*. According to this theory, as soon as a group member contributes to something, the rest of the group exerts less cognitive effort. So, if a group member speaks first, the rest may not spend that much effort recalling their own memories, therefore conforming to what's already been said. We conform because the alternative implies further mental effort. We save energy by going along with the crowd.

Reflecting on your own content, when you are confident about what you have to say, it helps if you *speak first*. In addition, it may be helpful to meet with influential, powerful people one-on-one before joining a group. It is beneficial to attend meetings or other collective events when you are well rested and have enough energy to make your own contributions—this will help you avoid the temptation to just go along with the crowd. In the same vein, be cautious about being influenced by people who operate under a lot of stress and lack of sleep. The information they share with you may have been impacted by other social circles and may not be accurate because there was insufficient energy for debate or dispute.

The more time elapses after an event, the more inclined you are to conform to someone else's attention and memory because precision for having seen details turns into familiarity. Conversely, the longer the time lapse, the more fake memories may prevail. Let's say you attend an event with a few other people. A few hours later, you get together to reflect on it. Someone mentions something that contradicts what you remember. Because that false memory is so distinguished from everything else, it attracts more attention and engagement. Research shows that once a false memory that stood out from the rest of the memories is discussed weeks later, it tends to be addressed as a real memory just because it is the most vivid and comes to mind very quickly—therefore, "it must be true."

When you speak to others, and your memories are contradictory, and no decisions have been made on an issue, it is helpful to write down essential thoughts before revisiting them later. This way, you eliminate the danger of false memories.

We Must Counterbalance Our Tendency to Conform with People Who Are Like Us

We conform more to friends' memory than strangers' and to the memory of those who share our beliefs than those who do not. For example, pretend you are part of an experiment where you meet two virtual partners, and one of them agrees with you on a topic 75 percent of the time, and the other disagrees with you 75 percent of the time. After a few encounters where you determine who shares your beliefs, you have the opportunity to view some pictures with these partners. Later, you engage in a collaborative memory test. You don't remember everything. Who do you trust more with their attention and memories?

We tend to conform more to *agreeable* partners and adopt more information about the past from in-groups than out-groups. It is adaptive to act this way because this is how we maintain relationships and sustain trust. It is also a good reminder that those who share our beliefs may be wrong. It is helpful to verify important information with other sources to counterbalance our bias for conforming with those we like and who are like us.

Social Contagion and Collective Attention

Some attention and memory conformity is normative, meaning it derives from our need for social acceptance and the realization that there may be costs for disagreeing in social situations. In these cases, harmony trumps accuracy because the need to belong is an innate, evolutionarily adaptive motive. Humans constantly monitor their state in relation to a desired end state, and because social belonging is often considered a desirable end state,

Challenge the habit of bonding with the crowd

What are
your
motivations
to conform?

we continuously monitor our social acceptance. Some researchers go as far as concluding that self-esteem is a function of our social acceptance. And just as our physical hunger directs attention and biases memory for food, our social hunger directs attention and biases memory for social cues.

Do you conform to sustain social harmony, even when you realize that others don't have much credibility and you know firsthand that they are often distracted and have *poor* memory? In one study, prior to the actual experiment, each subject was assigned a fake partner (someone planted by the researcher), and the pairs were exposed to a general memory test. In the high credibility condition, the fake partner remembered 13 out of 15 words correctly. Only 3 out of 15 words were remembered correctly in the low credibility condition. During the experiment, the pairs were shown a household scene. Even in this situation, low credibility had an impact. Participants still adopted false memories even though they explicitly categorized their partner as having poor memory on the previous test. The study suggested that people do not spontaneously differentiate between accurate and inaccurate partners in social memory events. Our inclination is to *follow the habit of bonding with the crowd.* Only when participants were reminded at test time of their partners' poor memory—and this information was active in someone's attention—were they able to suppress the social contagion effect.

Our relationships with others are so critical that some scientists have popularized a *social brain* hypothesis, which maintains that the leading factor in the increase in brain size in primates over the years, keeping proportionate with body size, was to keep track of the number of relationships. If we are to survive in larger groups, we must keep track not only of our relationships with others but also their relationships with other people. As Sigmund Freud famously said, all psychology is social.

fMRI studies confirm that various brain networks keep track of our *social load.* It turns out that even our working memory, which helps us keep in mind words, numbers, objects, or locations to accomplish a task, is not just a purely cognitive and perceptual process. Working memory has a social component, too, concerned with traits, beliefs, and relationships. Working memory is shown to recruit brain networks related to thinking about how others are thinking. We don't just pay attention; we think about how others pay attention.

The surprising findings from neuroscience studies are that the network preoccupied with social processing overlaps with the default network, which is active when the brain is at rest. Typically, the more cognitive effort we go through, the less activity there is in the default network. However, fMRI studies confirm that even in the default network, there is *some* activation when we think about the mental states, traits, and beliefs of others.

The satiation level of belongingness also impacts attention and subsequent memory. Your social monitoring system has an adaptive role. When social needs are unmet (e.g., when you feel rejected), socially relevant information receives preferential attention, resulting in stronger recall. Studies show this is the case for both large and small groups, including the smallest groups of all: a group of two.

When you create content, it is helpful to *take a log of your current social needs.* How much do you tend to agree with others and trust what they say based on your current social needs? Are you giving preferential attention to some elements because you want to agree with others, because you want to make a positive impression, or because you appreciate harmony more than accuracy? There is no right or wrong answer. There is just the realization that you may make some attention and memory trade-offs depending on your social needs at a given moment.

Beware of Creating Content with Narcissists

If some of the content you create and, in turn, share with others comes from narcissists, there is yet one more reason to be cautious about how *they* pay attention, recall information, and share it with you. Narcissists tend to have selective attention and recall and view past events through the lens of shaky self-esteem.

Narcissists are marked by self-importance, requiring attention and admiration from others ("He's never met a reflective surface he didn't like," goes a Jane Austen quote), and responding to ego-threatening feedback with rage, shame, or humiliation. When their ego is threatened, narcissists are also prone to distorting reality. These attention and memory distortions serve to protect or enhance their ego. They may also remember more positive aspects from the past to reduce current negative feelings. Narcissists are also prone to recalling more negative information about others.

Narcissists' attention and memory distortions are understandable because mood influences recall, and these individuals are more emotionally reactive, especially in their quest to protect and enhance their self-esteem.

In one study, male participants were led to believe they were interviewed by a woman responding to a dating ad and evaluating them as potential dates. The woman's lines were scripted to ensure that the interview was the same for everyone. Afterward, each participant was asked what he thought about the woman and what he believed the woman might have thought about him. Participants were also asked to give details about their dating history. A week later, each participant was contacted again and was told that the woman had either considered or rejected them as a date. Then they were asked the same questions as before about their thoughts regarding the conversation and their prior dating history. The researchers reported that "narcissistic participants

Narcissists are prone to **attention** and **memory distortions**

thought the woman enjoyed talking to them more, liked them more, and found their personality more attractive" compared to their considerations a week earlier. This was surprising because the woman's scripted instructions were vague and did not include any compliments or ego-enhancing words.

Researchers concluded that narcissists are much more likely to draw positive conclusions even based on vague social feedback. When the narcissistic participants were asked to describe their past dating history again after being told they were considered a potential date by the woman, they tended to describe the past as more successful than the first time. The intriguing finding was that the narcissists who were told they had been selected as potential dates, when asked about their dating history again, were less likely to say they had dated more than one woman at a time and described themselves as faithful mates, even though this was not their original description. In light of new information, their story changed to one that portrayed them as worthy partners.

Reporting these results is intended to help you *consider the validity of your information sources*. If you collaborate with narcissists often, take extra care in sifting through what they share with you, and balance it with information from other sources that may not be so prone to attention and memory distortions. (Quadrant II presented additional information on vetting sources to ensure attention is directed at the truth.)

Counteract Conformity with Personal Experiences

One of the best ways to correct imprecise attention and memories is to start with what you know. In his book *Alone*, Admiral Richard Byrd describes his adventures during the five months he spent solo at a weather station hut in Antarctica. He was buried under ice shelves and, at times, endured temperatures between –58° and –76°F (–50° and –60°C). "The slightest move," he notes, "disturbing the nice temperature balance in the sleeping bag, sends a blast of frosty air down my back or stomach. . . . Needless to say, I dress faster than a fireman." He can quickly come up with those vivid details because he was there and had firsthand experience, which heightens attention and sharpens memories.

The band Imagine Dragons credits their success to having a wide range of experiences. "I'm on top of the world," they say in one of their hit songs, "Waiting on this for a while now / Paying my dues to the dirt / I've been waiting to smile." The source of these lyrics is deeply personal, says Dan Reynolds, the band's front man. The band paid its dues, playing small clubs and minor gigs, while perfecting its craft. Dan recalls arriving on foot at a Katy Perry after-party when other guests were rolling up in limos and pricey sports cars. When he writes lyrics, he describes his challenges creating his own path, coming from a conservative Mormon background, his struggles with faith and confusion, his purpose, and finally growing up and finding joy. Watch them in concert, and you immediately understand how the firsthand feelings and experiences captured in the lyrics have an immediate hold on the audience's attention.

Consider your own examples and the times you "paid your dues to the dirt." Relate those experiences to others, and you decrease the likelihood of attention and memory conformity.

Nostalgia, Attention, and Memory Conformity

The concept of collective attention and memory is incomplete without addressing nostalgia. Even though we can get nostalgic on our own, nostalgia also occurs when we get together with others and reminisce about the past. There are advantages and disadvantages when other people use nostalgia to impact our attention and memory. To distinguish between the two, you must ask: Why do others want to bring our attention to the past?

Scientists remark that we collectively return to the past as a source of self-esteem, mental stability, and revival of essential values and meaning. For example, group memories tied to graduation, family events, and career success help us to create a coherent self-identity and give us satisfaction. From this angle, nostalgia is seen as a social emotion that connects us with others and fortifies a sense of belonging, safety, and general well-being. When we return to the past with positive emotions, we tend to filter out the negative and retrieve idealized images. A lot of older people in Romania, for instance, mentally reactivate images from the Communist era by suppressing the negative and retrieving memories through rose-tinted glasses.

Nostalgia-based approaches to business, particularly in marketing, are increasing. The revival of the Mini Cooper automobile by BMW has been successful. State Farm Insurance has used Elvis impersonators to sing its jingle, "State Farm is there." Jack Daniels created a special edition of its whiskey to celebrate Frank Sinatra's hundredth birthday. The campaign launched at the Las Vegas airport, and people were invited to taste the product and listen to Frank Sinatra. The initiative expanded to 200 airports and helped Jack Daniels increase its Brand Power Index (BPI) score by 27 percent in the first quarter. BPI ranks the most popular brands each quarter, as evidenced by consumers' engagement with social media and online searches. Old Navy, Microsoft, Arby's, and Sony are seeing a rise in their BPI index after using nostalgia-based marketing materials.

The difference between nostalgia and simply recollecting facts from the past is that nostalgia is an emotion, a particularly complex one. Some scientists study it as a positive emotion because many people tend to look

Some attention
might take
you on dark
memory lanes.

You don't
have to go.

to the past with warmth, joy, and overall satisfaction. Other scientists study the negative side of nostalgia because some people retrieve the past with regret, sadness, and the feeling that something has been lost irredeemably. There is also a middle ground where some people have a bittersweet attitude toward the past, which helps them redeem positive emotions but consider the past a "lost paradise."

What are some practical applications of knowing that others may be prompting you to pay attention by taking you down memory lane? Look at nostalgia as a mixed emotion. When people pay attention to the past with positive emotions, you can join them—but question memory accuracy and verify memories with other sources of information because they may be retrieving what happened through rose-tinted glasses. You can then decide whether you pay attention more to veracity, connection-building, or sense-making. Even for nostalgic commemorative events, such as Ike and Tina Turner, some biographers may not be so much concerned about what really happened (collected memory) as they are with the revelations of profound events (collective memory), related to abuse, discrimination, mental health, and, ultimately, prevailing resilience.

If those in your social circles habitually return to the past with negative emotions, resist going. Bring the conversation to the present and redirect attention to potential sources of future rewards.

What Do You Choose to Pay Social Attention To?

What you choose to pay attention to, remember, and forget shapes your identity as a family, team, company, or nation. Without collective attention and memory, we would not appreciate libraries, photo albums, collections, textbooks, commemorative parades, or the various Halls of Fame.

Some anthropologists use the phrase "corporate museums" to symbolize the framework of collective attention and memory we have in our professional lives, which include shared meanings, routines, and artifacts from the past that help with making collective decisions in the future. It does not mean that this content is always accurate or legend-free. As long as you have the proper proportions between accuracy and shared sense-making, collective attention is on your side.

What do you choose to keep in your collective attention?

What do you
choose to keep in your

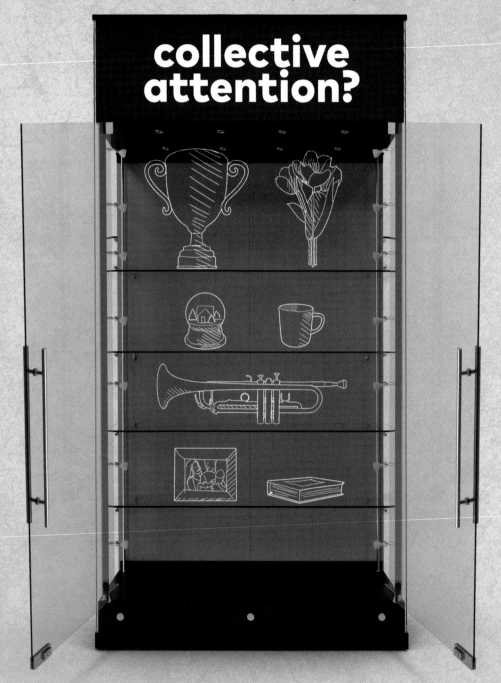

collective attention?

Practical Guidelines from Quadrant IV: Visual Search

1. Offer intermittent rewards to your audiences because they will sustain behavior when they cannot predict rewards.

2. Trigger the buyer's brain with cues that lead to wanting, such as food, discreet/sophisticated sexual connotations, and aesthetically appealing design.

3. Develop content that impacts a group (not just for one individual). Clarify how content will help your audience gain social rewards because social motives are attention worthy.

4. Speed up the perception of time by offering multiple rewards quickly (e.g., high-intensity slides). Conversely, offer an element of surprise to slow down time perception and invite your audiences to linger longer.

5. Avoid presenting oversimplified content because the business brain learns and understands complex content better. Complex content also leads to less mind wandering. You can manage complexity well by displaying details gradually, maintaining a balance between concrete and abstract concepts, and offering unconventional ideas.

6. You can also manage complexity by clarifying to a business audience what is essential. One way to clarify essentials is to identify patterns that can repeat themselves at any level of magnification (get inspiration from fractals).

7. Ensure that even though your content is complex, it is marked by profluence, meaning it gives the impression that the story is moving toward a worthwhile point.

8. Consider speaking first to instill confidence in your audience, set the bar high for others who may speak about the same topic, and potentially discontinue additional mental effort when others look at the competition.

9. Watch out for ways in which your own attention is being influenced by assessing your current social needs. Your attention is likely to be impacted when you want to make a positive impression and are seeking harmony more than accuracy.

Become a Choreographer of Attention

I recently saw a university commercial announcing that they were "redefining possible." The first time a company used this marketing phrase may have made us look. The fifteenth time somebody said it, it may have seemed familiar. By the 5,079th time, however, it is a cliché. While it may attract attention through images or motion, it is short-lived and non-actionable. Besides, anyone in any field could use this message.

Creating an attention-grabbing message with consequences often requires a distinctive approach, which takes work. Ultimately, it's not that hard to be distinctive, but it is hard to be distinctive *and* better.

What would prevent someone from creating distinctively better messages that make us look? I have heard a list of excuses: "I don't know where to begin," "I am busy with other things," "I tried it once, and it didn't work," "It's too expensive," "It's too hard to change," and "Other departments in my company create the content."

It's not surprising that we have excuses. After all, business professionals are overworked yet compulsively schedule even more things to do during their workday. As technology accelerates rapidly, there is also the pressure to keep up with increasingly complicated markets.

Do you have any excuses or defenses that may impact how others pay attention? If you do, here are ways to tackle them.

Content **gets better** when you **get better.**

Rush Slowly

Many business communicators we work with live their days at a hectic pace and constantly seem frazzled and guilty that they can't do it all. Some believe that maintaining this type of schedule enables them to do more. However, waking up an hour earlier and working an hour later does more damage than good. Frankly, we'd be better served by more sleep.

Business professionals often respond to a lack of time by multitasking. In one of my seminars, someone said: "This morning, while I was eating a bagel, blow-drying my hair, and putting on makeup, I reached over and flushed the toilet with my foot." Speed is not the only standard for measuring the quality of your content.

When people operate on compressed time, the quality of their content suffers. You do not have time to descend into depth when you're in a rush. And developing content too quickly is like vacuuming too quickly: You miss stuff. What is the fix? I like the Latin saying: *Festina lente*, which means to "rush slowly." I like it because it reminds us to maintain a sense of urgency yet take the time to contemplate. It's the unhurried experiences that offer inspiration for attention-grabbing content.

Request Feedback

To get to depth and more attention-grabbing concepts, ask for feedback regularly, which helps you cut through self-deceit and reveals blind spots in your thinking. Here is how I improved the attention power of some slides in a presentation I delivered on the merits of neuroscience. The collection shows the progression of one slide, and each version improved because of feedback.

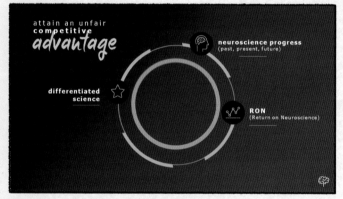

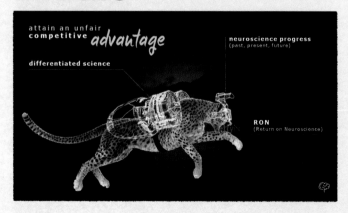

Create Your Own "Salon des Refusés"

In the 1800s in Paris, the ultimate authority in critiquing art and artists was "the Academy" (Académie *des Beaux-Arts*). They would host an official show, the Salon, in Paris to showcase French art each year. The Academy jury preferred representational art and praised polished work that bore no trace of a visible brushstroke. A rejected painting was terrible news for innovative artists since the Salon show provided the only opportunity to display their works to art collectors, dealers, critics, and writers. The chosen art came from reputable, conservative artists, who were typically members of the Academy. Unconventional work was usually rejected.

In 1863, the Salon selection jury rejected more than half the submissions it received, and because so many artists protested, Emperor Napoleon III, sensitive to public opinion, ordered a new exhibition called the *Salon des Refusés* ("Exhibition of Rejected Art"). This approach would allow the public to judge the merits of the rejected works. The Salon des Refusés drew vast crowds of more than a thousand per day, many of whom were particularly affronted, for example, by the scandalous nudity in Manet's oil painting *Le Dejeuner sur l'herbe* ("The Luncheon on the Grass"), which portrayed a naked woman having a picnic with two fully dressed men. Other artists who produced "sketchy and unfinished work" compared

to the expected academic refinement were part of the new movement, such as Paul Gauguin, Henri Matisse, and Vincent van Gogh. The Salon of the Rejected was essential because it prevented highly conservative academic bodies from dominating aesthetics and public taste in art. It also welcomed emerging forms of avant-garde art and surprising styles like Impressionism.

I mention this because each time you create content you think is impactful and makes someone look, it may be rejected by others in your organization. But each rejected sample paves the way toward new ways of thinking. Each time you feel stuck searching for attention-grabbing concepts, revisit your own Salon des Refusés, your rejected collection. It may spark a new idea. I know this from experience.

Here are some excerpts from my own Salon des Refusés. I remember advising a client who wanted to visualize the idea of "companies being stuck" with an executive chair chained to its surroundings. As the presentation progressed, we removed two wheels from the chair to dramatize being even more stuck. We then switched to a positive tone and showed how you can become agile when you use a specific solution and visualized this by removing the chains. Initially, the client liked the design, but then one person (one person!) from the client team had a "visceral reaction to the chained chair," as they put it, and the entire approach was replaced with something totally safe: First showing a person with his head in his hands, who then, on an on-click animation, becomes a happy person. Definitely not something that would make you look more closely.

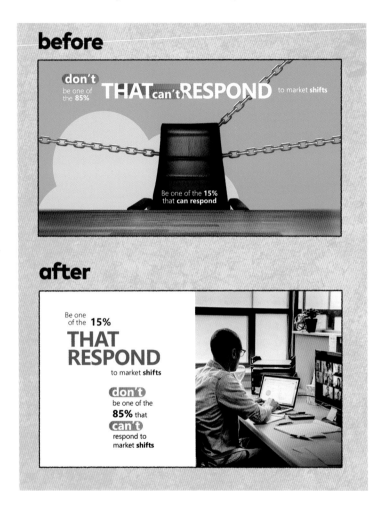

In this next example, the purpose of the presentation was to show executive decision makers how to motivate their employees with a new approach to information sharing that improves productivity and performance. This path to motivation was to be achieved through gaming; therefore, the title "Let the games begin." We aimed to create a title slide introducing the idea that employees could motivate themselves. And, if allowed autonomy, creativity, and mastery of skills (which gaming would ensure), they would thrive and soar (the subtle Superman suit would give the viewer an aha moment). The client liked the text but was not daring enough to use it and replaced it with a predictable stock photo image.

Trust me, it will feel better to be rejected because of an audacious idea than to be approved for a cliché.

I often reject initially somewhat good ideas because I know initial rejection can get us to even more attention-grabbing and memorable pieces. Here are some examples from my own presentations, where I was looking to improve the initial design by building and breaking consistencies.

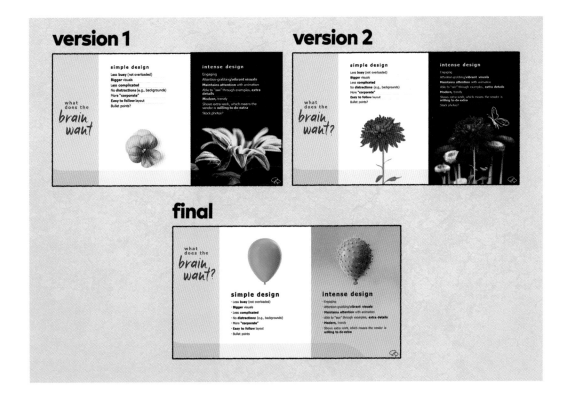

Click to add title

Click to add text

Rejections can propel you, so be prepared to break that wall and push boundaries. The brain has a contradictory need for both consistency and flexibility so that you can write on it in multiple ways. And sure, producing multiple versions to make people look can be expensive—but developing content that is ignored costs a fortune.

Bring Yourself to the Content

I remember reading about Manolo Blahnik, the famous Spanish shoemaker whose first name is now a noun for women who love to adorn their feet with sophisticated beauty. Early in his career, when he was starting to make a name for himself, he was invited to appear on the cover of *Vogue*, an honor and a massive opportunity for anyone aspiring to be a fashion icon. Manolo had already achieved a modicum of fame and could easily have shown up with the expectation that the *Vogue* staff would dress him for the photo shoot. Instead, Manolo brought his own clothes and his own shoes. In other words, he brought his own "content."

Some business content is not attention-grabbing because it feels detached, as if created on a production line. In the name of efficiency and standardization, organizations often offer impersonal content. For instance, when building a corporate deck, marketing teams could consider a template slide that says, "Insert yourself and your way of seeing here." When you bring yourself to the content, you will instantly have attention-grabbing power because, by default, you offer something unique.

Sometimes, to make your contribution, you have to *experience* that contribution. I believe in self-experimentation because it offers you the foundation of science: observation. Developing distinct and better ideas is difficult, but by exploring what works for you, you're already on your way to finding something new or unexpected. I am impressed when scientists, for instance, self-experiment. Barry Marshall, an Australian gastroenterologist, took two weeks to confirm that *Helicobacter pylori* bacteria cause ulcers because he drank it himself. Michel Siffre, a French explorer, lived in a cave for two months without time-of-the-day information to investigate variables such as sleep. British engineer Kevin Warwick worked on linking the nervous system with the internet, so he had an array of 100 electrodes fired into the median nerve fibers of his left arm for three months. Of course, you don't have to go to these lengths, but you can see how your observations and experiences can create a foundation for fresh content that makes people look.

Seek Solitude and Silence

Silence allows the mind and body to regroup. Unfortunately, knowing how to relax and refresh is becoming an increasingly rare skill. At the beginning of the neuroscience studies I conduct, I record a baseline of the brain by asking participants to relax and focus on a simple stimulus. I want to know what their brains are like in an unstimulated state so I can compare it with what their brains are like—or should be like—in a stimulated state. I am noticing more and more how difficult it is for people to slow down and unwind. The more time you spend in silence and reflection, the more you increase your chances of creating attention-grabbing content.

Solitary time also gives you a chance to practice conveying your message. The guideline "just show up and be yourself" does not work if you want to be in charge of what people look at in your content. Others may remind you, "Have a conversation with the audience." A free-flowing conversation does not guarantee that people will pay attention to what is important. If you ever want to test that theory, sit in a coffee shop and listen to a conversation at a table near you. It will often be one of the most boring conversations you've heard. This is because a message takes time and skill to structure and convey in a way that makes people look.

In that spirit, let's put this book down and have a cup of tea.

CHECKLIST FOR CREATING CONTENT THAT CAPTURES ATTENTION

This checklist encapsulates key neuroscience concepts that align with how customers pay attention, think, and decide. The best news: The guidelines are within your control when attracting people's attention. To use the checklist successfully, identify three to four guidelines relevant to your content (e.g., sales presentation, marketing campaign, or training) from each quadrant included in the book. Rate each on a scale from 1 to 5, where 5 indicates the strongest implementation of that principle. This approach helps you apply the guidelines in the most impactful way to create meaningful commercial interactions.

For an electronic version of the checklist, email your request to info@carmensimon.com.

	Description	1	2	3	4	5
	Automatic Triggers					
1	Use perceptual, affective, semantic, and repetition priming to prepare the brain to pay attention to what is important.					
2	If you prime the brain with negative images or text, neutralize the negative and then move on to positive priming before you present your solution so your buyer's brain is more likely to be in a state of cognitive flexibility.					
3	Engage your audience with physical movement when your content permits, such as asking them to take notes or draw along with you, if you're using a whiteboard.					

(continues)

	Description	1	2	3	4	5
	Automatic Triggers *(continued)*					
4	If you cannot involve your audiences physically, offer the perception of movement through animations, using words that symbolize movement, and sharing stories with action that "moves" across a timeline.					
5	Use provocative content to attract attention and impact memory and decisions. You can create provocative content by challenging the status quo, proposing something counterintuitive, exposing assumptions, viewing an issue from an unexpected perspective, and offering exaggeration.					
6	You can also provoke with design by creating materials that are not expected or popular in your field (such as custom, hand-drawn illustrations on top of stock photography or avoiding photos with straight edges).					
7	Perspective-taking also impacts provocative content and can be achieved by asking whether you can change something in your content in terms of its meaning, context, humor, components (can you interchange elements), finding a silver lining, or even looking at it backward.					
	Guided Action					
1	Offer a variety of stimulation types (such as stories, stats, customer examples, abstract conclusions) to avoid habituation and challenge people's cognitive abilities by accelerating the pace of your message or providing deeper, more complex, or creative messages.					
2	Offer more content choices to new customers and fewer choices to existing customers. Invite your audience to select the type of content they prefer to receive from you, the process of working with you, and/or the environment in which they meet with you.					
3	Present your solutions in terms of probabilities, and offer your audience specific approaches on how to handle low-probability events.					
4	Gather enough evidence to substantiate your claims. It's better to present fewer claims with more evidence than more claims with superficial evidence.					

	Description	1	2	3	4	5
	Guided Action					
5	Define your key terms to discover if you have any knowledge gaps in what you present and get to the essence of the truth.					
6	To the extent you can, offer your audience information based on experimental studies that follow the scientific method to show how one variable causes another.					
7	Base the claim of value you make on generally agreed-upon criteria in your field.					
8	If you're making claims of policy (telling your audience to do something differently), prepare to offer information or guidelines at a time when people's routines are already disrupted (such as during a leadership change or transition to other software, going global, or taking on a new role).					
9	Consider whether there are some experiences that only you, an expert, might have and understand fully. Then link this experience through a metaphor to an abstract concept you want to help others see and feel in the same way you see and feel it.					
10	Use metaphors to link the abstract to the concrete and to protect the brain from cognitive workload.					
11	Pair a common concept with a unique metaphor.					
12	If your content lends itself to metaphors, use *multiple* and *original* ones, as people remember the content better without experiencing a heavy cognitive workload.					
13	Avoid clichéd metaphors because they increase fatigue and decrease recall.					
	Introspection					
1	Tax the perceptive and cognitive workload within reasonable limits to engage all attentional capacities and prevent distractions.					
2	Link content to your audience's future goals because the brain tends to mind wander to a future state and unfulfilled ambitions.					

(continues)

	Description	1	2	3	4	5
	Introspection *(continued)*					
3	Make allowances for *some* mind wandering, which is often associated with problem solving and imagining creative solutions.					
4	Help the brain plan for action by offering a set of organized steps, showing how your experiences map to the steps you're advising, and building anticipation for the future.					
5	Use temporal transitions to describe a process or to order arguments in your discourse, which is how persuasion is born.					
6	Include additive transitions to link ideas together and adversative transitions to contrast ideas and offer arguments contrary to expectations.					
7	Use causative transitions to help the brain draw meaning and remove the possibility of misinterpretation.					
8	Develop a storyboard to plan transitions, and implement them well.					
9	Integrate text and images to help the brain build better associations between them.					
10	Use transitions for cognitive closure, giving the buyer's brain clear, unambiguous knowledge.					
	Visual Search					
1	Offer intermittent rewards to your audiences because they will sustain behavior when they cannot predict rewards.					
2	Trigger the buyer's brain with cues that lead to wanting, such as food, discreet/sophisticated sexual connotations, and aesthetically appealing design.					
3	Develop content that impacts a group (not just for one individual). Clarify how content will help your audience gain social rewards because social motives are attention worthy.					

	Description	1	2	3	4	5
	Visual Search					
4	Speed up the perception of time by offering multiple rewards quickly (e.g., high-intensity slides). Conversely, offer an element of surprise to slow down time perception and invite your audiences to linger longer.					
5	Avoid presenting oversimplified content because the business brain learns and understands complex content better. Complex content also leads to less mind wandering. You can manage complexity well by displaying details gradually, maintaining a balance between concrete and abstract concepts, and offering unconventional ideas.					
6	You can also manage complexity by clarifying to a business audience what is essential. One way to clarify essentials is to identify patterns that can repeat themselves at any level of magnification (get inspiration from fractals).					
7	Ensure that even though your content is complex, it is marked by profluence, meaning it gives the impression that the story is moving toward a worthwhile point.					
8	Consider speaking first to instill confidence in your audience, set the bar high for others who may speak about the same topic, and potentially discontinue additional mental effort when others look at the competition.					
9	Watch out for ways in which your own attention is being influenced by assessing your current social needs. Your attention is likely to be impacted when you want to make a positive impression and are seeking harmony more than accuracy.					

ACKNOWLEDGMENTS

The words in this book are the result of the help, love, and support of many. Thank you so much for believing in me and for contributing to this project when it was just an idea. Thank you to all those who have produced the photos and visual compositions that enhance the ideas in the book. I am grateful to: Erik Peterson, Tim Riesterer, Casey Ebro, David Wallace, Jeff Faller, Maíra Vannucci, Iriny Amerssonis, Caio Caetano, Patricia Pontual, Gustavo Gusmão, Jessica Zimmerman, Vivian Brandini, Luiz Pellegrini, Nayara Gonzales, Debora Elvas, James Luyirika-Sewagudde Jr., Abby Kerr, Nicci Hammerel, Bobby Jenkins, Leslie Talbot, Kameron Hobbs, Anton Rius, Marioara Taran, Constantin Taran, Matt Vassar, Aureli Soria-Frisch, Eleni Kroupi, Paulina Clara Dagnino, Claire Braboszcz, Karan Chugani, Bernard Broyard, Tue Haas Petersen, Cazmon Suri, Shri Nandan, Mitzi Nandan, David Nason, Diana Andone, Neil Ramsey, David Studebaker, Erich Gerber, Erwan Rivet, Raj Verma, Domenic Ravita, Erik Charles, Jayant Umrani, Apurva Chandra, Saumya Chandra, Arushi Chandra, Cindy Turner, Joanna Yoo, Laurie Harrison, Lenny Firmin, Patricia Simon, Caesar Simon, and Sydney.

REFERENCES

Introduction

Anderson, B. (2011). There is no such thing as attention. *Frontiers in Psychology, 2,* 1–8. https://doi.org/10.3389/fpsyg.2011.00246.

Basso, M. A., & May, P. J. (2017). Circuits for action and cognition: A view from the superior colliculus. *Annual Review of Vision Science, 3,* 197–226.

Bekkering, H., & Neggers, S. F. W. (2002). Visual search is modulated by action intentions. *Psychological Science, 13,* 370–374.

Bernhard, H., Chapman, C. S., Cisek, P., Neyedli, H. F., Song, J. H., & Welsh, T. N. (2019). No one knows what attention is. *Attention, Perception, & Psychophysics, 81,* 2288–2303. https://doi.org/10.3758/s13414-019-01846-w.

Bonifacci, P., Viroli, C., Vassura, C., Colombini, E., & Desideri, L. (2022). The relationship between mind wandering and reading comprehension: A meta-analysis. *Psychonomic Bulletin and Review, 1,* 1–20. https://doi.org/10.3758/s13423-022-02141-w.

Bos, D. O. (2006). EEG-based emotion recognition. *The Influence of Visual and Auditory Stimuli, 4,* 1–17.

Buckner, R. L., & Schacter, D. L. (2004). Neural correlates of memory's successes and sins. In M. S. Gazzaniga (Ed.), *The Cognitive Neurosciences III,* 3rd ed. (pp. 739–752). Cambridge, MA: MIT Press.

Bundesen, C., Habekost, T., & Kyllingsbæk, S. (2005). A neural theory of visual attention: Bridging cognition and neurophysiology. *Psychological Review, 112*(2), 291–328. http://doi.org/10.1037/0033-295X.112.2.291.

Buneo, C. A., Jarvis, M. R., Batista, A. P., & Andersen, R. A. (2002). Direct visuomotor transformations for reaching. *Nature, 416,* 632–636.

Carlisle, N. B., & Woodman, G. F. (2011). When memory is not enough: Electrophysiological evidence for goal-dependent use of working memory representations in guiding visual attention. *Journal of Cognitive Neuroscience, 23*(10), 2650–2664. http://doi.org/10.1162/jocn.2011.21602.

Chai, W. J., Abd Hamid, A. I., & Abdullah, J. M. (2018). Working memory from the psychological and neurosciences perspectives: A review. *Frontiers in Psychology, 9,* 401.

Chanel, G., Kronegg, J., Grandjean, D., & Pun, T. (2006). Emotion assessment: Arousal evaluation using EEG's and peripheral physiological signals. *Multimedia Content Representation, Classification and Security, 4105,* 530–537. doi: 10.1007/11848035_70.

Christoforou, C., Papadopoulos, T. C., Constantinidou, F., & Theodorou, M. (2017). Your brain on the movies: A computational approach for predicting box-office performance from viewer's brain responses to movie trailers. *Frontiers in Neuroinformatics, 11,* 72–79.

Cisek, S., Sedikides, C., Hart, C., Godwin, H., Benson, V., & Liversedge, S. (2014). Narcissism and consumer behaviour: A review and preliminary findings. *Frontiers in Psychology, 5,* 232. 10.3389/fpsyg.2014.00232.

Cowan, J. A., & Allen, J. J. B. (2004). Frontal EEG asymmetry as a moderator and mediator of emotion. *Biological Psychology, 67*(1–2), 7–50.

Dalvit, S., & Eimer, M. (2011). Memory-driven attentional capture is modulated by temporal task demands. *Visual Cognition, 19*(2), 145–153. http://doi.org/10.1080/13506285.2010.543441.

Daly, I., Williams, D., Hwang, F., Kirke, A., Miranda, E. R., & Nasuto, S. J. (2019). Electroencephalography reflects the activity of sub-cortical brain regions during approach-withdrawal behaviour while listening to music. *Scientific Reports, 9*(1), 9415.

Davidson, R. J. (1992). Anterior cerebral asymmetry and the nature of emotion. *Brain and Cognition, 20*(1), 125–151.

Deubel, H., & Schneider, W. X. (1996). Saccade target selection and object recognition: Evidence for a common attentional mechanism. *Vision Research, 36,* 1827–1837.

Dixon, P., & Li, H. (2013). Mind wandering in text comprehension under dual-task. *Frontiers in Psychology, 4,* 1–14. doi: 10.3389/fpsyg.2013.00682.

Ernst, M., & Paulus, M. P. (2005). Neurobiology of decision making: A selective review from a neurocognitive and clinical perspective. *Biol Psychiatry, 58,* 597–604. doi: 10.1016/j.biopsych.2005.06.004.

Fagioli, S., Hommel, B., & Schubotz, R. I. (2007). Intentional control of attention: Action planning primes action related stimulus dimensions. *Psychological Research, 71,* 22–29.

Fecteau, J. H., & Munoz, D. P. (2006). Salience, relevance, and firing: A priority map for target selection. *Trends in Cognitive Science, 10,* 382–390. https://doi.org/10.1016/j.tics.2006.06.011.

Frantzidis, C., Bratsas, C., Papadelis, C., Konstantinidis, E., Pappas, C., & Bamidis, P. (2010). Toward emotion aware computing: An integrated approach using multichannel neurophysiological recordings and affective visual stimuli. *IEEE Transactions on Information Technology in Biomedicine, 14,* 589–597.

Gottlieb, J. (2012). Attention, learning, and the value of information. *Neuron, 76,* 281–295.

Klimesch, W., Sauseng, P., & Hanslmayr, S. (2007). EEG alpha oscillations: The inhibition-timing hypothesis. *Brain Research Reviews, 53,* 63–88.

Pylyshyn, Z. W. (2003). Return of the mental image: Are there really pictures in the brain? *Trends in Cognitive Sciences, 7*(3), 113–118.

Richardson, D. C., & Dale, R. (2005). Looking to understand: The coupling between speakers' and listeners' eye movements and its relationship to discourse comprehension. *Cognitive Science, 29,* 1045–1060.

Sankur (Eds.), *Multimedia Content Representation, Classification and Security* (Vol. 4105, pp. 530–537). Springer Berlin Heidelberg.

Shenhav, A., Botvinick, M. M., & Cohen, J. D. (2013). The expected value of control: An integrative theory of anterior cingulate cortex function. *Neuron, 79,* 217–240.

Treisman, A. M., & Gelade, G. (1980). A feature-integration theory of attention. *Cognitive Psychology, 12,* 97–136.

Tsujimoto, S., Genovesio, A., & Wise, S. P. (2010). Evaluating self-generated decisions in frontal pole cortex of monkeys. *Nature Neuroscience, 13,* 120–126.

Van der Stoep, N., Van der Stigchel, S., & Nijboer, T. C. W. (2015). Exogenous orienting of crossmodal attention in 3D space: Support for a depth-aware crossmodal attentional system. *PLoS ONE, 10,* e0116782.

Walker, R., Deubel, H., Schneider, W. X., & Findlay, J. M. (1997). Effect of remote distractors on saccade programming: Evidence for an extended fixation zone. *Journal of Neurophysiology, 78,* 1108–1119.

Wallis, J. D. (2007). Orbitofrontal cortex and its contribution to decision-making. *Annual Review of Neuroscience, 30,* 31–56.

Yeo, B. T., Krienen, F. M., Sepulcre, J., Sabuncu, M. R., Lashkari, D., Hollinshead, M., et al. (2011). The organization of the human cerebral cortex estimated by intrinsic functional connectivity. *Journal of Neurophysiology, 106,* 1125–1165.

Zhao, G., Ge, Y., Shen, B., Wei, X., Wang, K., Zhang, X., & Qiu, S. (2019). Evaluation of emotional states based on the synchronization of physiological signals: An fMRI study. *Frontiers in Neuroscience, 13.*

Chapter 1. Priming the Brain for Attention

Altarriba, J., & Bauer, L. M. (2004). The distinctiveness of emotion concepts: A comparison between emotion, abstract, and concrete words. *American Journal of Psychology, 117*(3), 389–410. doi: http://dx.doi.org/10.2307/4149007.

Ayrolles, A., Brun, F., Chen, P., Djalovski, A., Beauxis, Y., Delorme, R., Bourgeron, T., Dikker, S., & Dumas, G. (2021). HyPyP: A Hyperscanning Python Pipeline for inter-brain connectivity analysis. *Social Cognitive and Affective Neuroscience, 16*(1–2), 72–83. doi: 10.1093/scan/nsaa141. PMID: 33031496; PMCID: PMC7812632.

Barutchu, A., Spence, C., & Humphreys, G. W. (2018). Multisensory enhancement elicited by unconscious visual stimuli. *Experimental Brain Research, 236,* 409–417.

Berka, C., Levendowski, D., Lumicao, M., & Yau, A. (2007). EEG correlates of task engagement and mental workload in vigilance, learning, and memory tasks. *Aviation, Space, and Environmental Medicine.*

Chai, W. J., Hamid, A. I. A., & Abdullah, J. M. (2018). Working memory from the psychological and neurosciences perspectives: A review. *Frontiers in Psychology.*

Cowan, N. (2008). What are the differences between long-term, short-term, and working memory? Progress in Brain Research, 169, 323–338.

Ellis, H., & Ellis, A. (1998). Why we study . . . repetition priming. *Psychologist, 11*(10), 492.

Feldmann-Wüstefeld, T., & Schubö, A. (2013). Textures shape the attentional focus: Evidence from exogenous and endogenous cueing. *Attention, Perception, & Psychophysics, 75,* 1644–1666. doi: 10.3758/s13414-013-0508-z.

Hamburger, M., & Slowiaczek, L. M. (1998). Repetition priming and experimental context effects. *American Journal of Psychology, 111*(1), 1.

Harris, I. M., & Little, M. J. J. (2010). Priming the semantic neighbourhood during the attentional blink. *PLoS ONE 5*(9): e12645. doi: 10.1371/journal.pone.0012645.

Henson, R. N., Rylands, A. J., Ross, E., Vuilleumeir, P., & Rugg, M. D. (2004). The effect of repetition lag on electrophysiological and haemodynamic correlates of visual object priming. *NeuroImage, 21,* 1674–1689.

Hermans, D., De Houwer, J., & Eelen, P. (1994). The affective priming effect: Automatic activation of evaluative information in memory. *Cognition and Emotion, 8,* 515–533.

Hu, Y., Li, X., Pan, Y., & Cheng, X. (2017). Brain-to-brain synchronization across two persons predicts mutual prosociality. *Social Cognitive and Affective Neuroscience*, 1835–1844.

Hyman, I. E., Boss, S., Wise, B. M., McKenzie, K., & Caggiano, J. (2009). Did you see the unicycling clown? Inattentional blindness while walking and talking on a cell phone. *Applied Cognitive Psychology*, 24, 597–607.

Leggett, J. M. I., Burt, J. S., & Ceccato, J-M. (2019). Repetition priming and repetition blindness: Effects of an intervening distractor word. *Canadian Journal of Experimental Psychology, 73*(2), 105–117. http://dx.doi.org/10.1037/cep0000164.

Liu, Q. (2018). Graphic creative design based on subconsciousness theory. *NeuroQuantology, 16*(6), 471–477. doi: 10.14704/nq.2018.16.6.1646.

Long, A. (2016). La Mer: The dream cream. *Elle*, August 24, 2016, https://www.elle.com/beauty/makeup-skin-care/a37936/la-mer-the-dream-cream/.

Mohan, D. M., Kumar, P., Mahmood, F., Wong, K. F., Agrawal, A., El-gendi, M., et al. (2016). Effect of subliminal lexical priming on the subjective perception of images: A machine learning approach. *PLoS ONE 11*(2): e0148332. doi: 10.1371/journal.pone.0148332.

Montague, P. R., Berns, G. S., Cohen, J. D., et al. (2002). Hyperscanning: Simultaneous fMRI during linked social interactions. *Neuroimage, 16*, 1159–1164.

Pesciarelli, F., Kutas, M., Dell'Acqua, R., Peressotti, F., Job, R., et al. (2007) Semantic and repetition priming within the attentional blink: An event-related brain potential (ERP) investigation study. *Biological Psychology, 76*, 21–30.

Reinero, D. A., Dikker, S., & Van Bavel, J. J. (2021). Inter-brain synchrony in teams predicts collective performance. *Social Cognitive and Affective Neuroscience, 6*(1–2), 43–57. doi: 10.1093/scan/nsaa135.

Rensink, R. A. (2013). Perception and attention. In D. Reisberg (Ed.), *Oxford Handbook of Cognitive Psychology* (pp. 97–116). Oxford, UK: Oxford University Press.

Rogers, T. T., & McClelland, J. (2004). *Semantic Cognition: A Parallel Distributed Processing Approach*. MIT Press.

Rotteveel, M., & Phaf, R. H. (2004). Loading working memory enhances affective priming. *Psychonomic Bulletin & Review, 11*(2), 326–331.

Scott, D. (2018, March 11). Dolly the sheep: The first clone was almost kidnapped. Express. https://www.express.co.uk/news/uk/930279/dolly-the-sheep-clone-roslin-institute-kidnapping-mark-lynas#.

So, W. K. Y., Wong, S. H., Mak, J. N., & Chan, R. H. M. (2017). An evaluation of mental workload with frontal EEG. *PLOS ONE, 12*(4), e0174949. https://doi.org/10.1371/journal.pone.0174949.

Spruyt, A., Hermans, D., De Houwer, J., & Eelen, P. (2004). Automatic non-associative semantic priming: Episodic affective priming of naming responses. *Acta Psychologica, 116*, 39–54.

Valencia, A. L., & Froese, T. (2020). What binds us? Inter-brain neural synchronization and its implications for theories of human consciousness. *Neuroscience of Consciousness, 6*(1): niaa010.

Chapter 2. Embodied Cognition: Setting the Mind in Motion

Adeniyi, A. A., Ajieroh, V., Sofola, O. O., Asiyanbi, O., & Oyapero, A. (2017). A pilot test of an oral health education module for community health workers in Ikeja LGA, Lagos State. *African Journal of Oral Health, 7*(1), 8–16. https://doi.org/10.4314/ajoh.v7i1.162231.

Bartsch, R. A., & Cobern, K. M. (2003). Effectiveness of PowerPoint presentations in lectures. *Computers & Education, 41*(1), 77–86.

Broom, G. M., & Smith, G. D. (1979). Testing the practitioners' impact on clients. *Public Relations Review, 5*(3), 47–59.

Cutting, J. E. (2016). The evolution of pace in popular movies. *Cutting Cognitive Research: Principles and Implications, 1*, 30. doi: 10.1186/s41235-016-0029-0.

Dijk, J., Kerkhofs, R., Rooij, I., & Haselager, P. (2008). Special section: Can there be such a thing as embodied embedded cognitive neuroscience? *Theory & Psychology, 18*, 297–316. 10.1177/0959354308089787.

Fischer, R., & Liepelt, R. (2020). Embodied cognition in multitasking: Increased hand-specific task shielding when stimuli are presented near the hand. *Psychological Research, 84*(6), 1668–1682. doi: 10.1007/s00426-019-01174-6.

He, C., Chikara, R. K., Yeh, C. L., & Ko, L. W. (2021). Neural dynamics of target detection via wireless EEG in embodied cognition. *Sensors (Basel), 21*(15), 5213. doi: 10.3390/s21155213.

Hoenig, K., Müller, C., Herrnberger, B., Sim, E. J., Spitzer, M., Ehret, G., & Kiefer, M. (2011). Neuroplasticity of semantic maps for musical instruments in professional musicians. *NeuroImage, 56*, 1714–1725.

Kelly, S. D., Manning, S. M., & Rodak, S. (2008). Gesture gives a hand to language and learning: Perspectives from cognitive neuroscience, developmental psychology and education. *Language and Linguistics Compass, 2*, 569–588.

Longcamp, M., Lagarrigue, A., Nazarian, B., Roth, M., Anton, J. L., Alario, F. X., & Velay, J. L. (2014). Functional specificity in the motor system: Evidence from coupled fMRI and kinematic recordings during letter and digit writing. *Human Brain Mapping, 35*.

Merel, S. W., McKinney, C. M., Ufkes, P., Kwan, A. C., & White, A. A. (2016). Sitting at patients' bedsides may improve patients' perceptions of physician communication skills. *Journal of Hospital Medicine, 11*(12), 865–868.

Mouatt, B., Smith, A., Mellow, M., Parfitt, G., Smith, R., & Stanton, T. (2020). The use of virtual reality to influence motivation, affect, enjoyment, and engagement during exercise: A scoping review. *Frontiers in Virtual Reality, 1*.

Shuman, L. J., Besterfield-Sacre, M., & McGourty, J. (2005). The ABET professional skills—can they be taught? Can they be assessed? *Journal of English Education, 94*, 41–55.

Smoker, T., Murphy, C., & Rockwell, A. (2009). Comparing memory for handwriting versus typing. *Human Factors and Ergonomics Society Annual Meeting Proceedings, 53*.

Soni, N., Darrow, A., Luc, A., Gleaves, S., Schuman, C., Neff, H., Chang, P., Kirkland, B., Alexandre, J., Morales, A., Stofer, K. A., & Anthony, L. (2021). Affording embodied cognition through touchscreen and above-the-surface gestures during collaborative tabletop science learning. *International Journal of Computer-Supported Collaborative Learning, 16*(1), 105–144.

Taufik, A. (2010). The use of smartboard technology as an instructional tool. *Al-Bayan, 22*, 77–68.

Tench, R., Verčič, D., Zerfass, A., Moreno, A., & Verhoeven, P. (2017). *Communication Excellence: How to Develop, Manage and Lead Exceptional Communications*. New York, NY: Palgrave MacMillan.

Tsang, A. (2020). Enhancing learners' awareness of oral presentation (delivery) skills in the context of self-regulated learning. *Active Learning in Higher Education, 21*(1), 39–50.

Wilson, A. D., & Golonka, S. (2013). Embodied cognition is not what you think it is. *Frontiers in Psychology, 4*(58). doi: 10.3389/fpsyg.2013.00058.

Worthington, D. L., & Levasseur, D. G. (2015). To provide or not to provide course PowerPoint slides? The impact of instructor-provided slides upon student attendance and performance. *Computers & Education, 85*, 14–22.

Chapter 3. The Right Amount of Wrong: Handling Provocative Content

Albouy, J. (2017). Emotions and prosocial behaviours: A study of the effectiveness of shocking charity campaigns. *Recherche et Applications en Marketing* (English edition), *32*. https://doi.org/10.1177/2051570716689241.

Anabila, P., Tagoe, C., & Asare, S. (2016). Consumer perception of sex appeal advertising: A high context cultural perspective. *IUP Journal of Marketing Management, XIV*(4), 34–55.

Belke, B., Leder, H., & Carbon, C. C. (2015). When challenging art gets liked: Evidences for a dual preference formation process for fluent and non-fluent portraits. *PLoS ONE, 10*(8), e0131796. https://doi.org/10.1371/journal.pone.0131796.

Bölte, J., Hösker, T., Hirschfeld, G., & Thielsch, M. (2017). Electrophysiological correlates of aesthetic processing of webpages: A comparison of experts and laypersons. *PeerJ, 5*.

Buetti, S., Xu, J., & Lleras, A. (2019). Predicting how color and shape combine in the human visual system to direct attention. *Scientific Reports, 9*, 20258.

Dobele, A., Toleman, D., & Beverland, M. (2005). Controlled infection! Spreading the brand message through viral marketing. *Business Horizons, 48*, 143–149. https://doi.org/10.1016/j.bushor.2004.10.011.

Hsu, W.-C., Tseng, C.-M., & Kang, S.-C. (2018). Using exaggerated feedback in a virtual reality environment to enhance behavior intention of water-conservation. *Educational Technology and Society, 21*, 187–203.

Kawabata, H., & Zeki, S. (2004). Neural correlates of beauty. *Journal of Neurophysiology, 91*, 1699–1705.

Lange, F., & Dahlen, M. (2003). Let's be strange: Brand familiarity and ad-brand incongruency. *Journal of Product & Brand Management, 12*, 449–461. doi: 10.1108/10610420310506010.

Myers, S., Deitz, G., Huhmann, B., Jha, S., & Tatara, J. (2019). An eye-tracking study of attention to brand-identifying content and recall of taboo advertising. *Journal of Business Research, 111*. https://doi.org/10.1016/j.jbusres.2019.08.009.

Norman, D. A. (2004). *Emotional Design: Why We Love (or Hate) Everyday Things*. New York, NY: Basic Books.

Ozkaramanli, D., & Desmet, P. (2016). Provocative design for unprovocative designers: Strategies for triggering personal dilemmas. https://doi.org/10.21606/drs.2016.165.

Schultz, W., & Dickinson, A. (2000). Neuronal coding of prediction errors. *Annual Review of Neuroscience, 23*, 473–500.

Silveira, S., Fehse, K., Vedder, A., Elvers, K., & Hennig-Fast, K. (2015). Is it the picture or is it the frame? An fMRI study on the neurobiology of framing effects. *Frontiers in Human Neuroscience, 9*. https://doi.org/10.3389/fnhum.2015.00528.

Yüksel, A., & Yüksel, F. (2001). The expectancy-disconfirmation paradigm: A critique. *Journal of Hospitality & Tourism Research, 25*(2), 107–131. https://doi.org/10.1177/109634800102500201.

Chapter 4. The Psychology of Boredom: Engaging the Brain on a Level Beyond Flash

Asseburg, R., & Frey, A. (2013). Too hard, too easy, or just right? The relationship between effort or boredom and ability-difficulty fit. *Psychological Test and Assessment Modeling, 55*(1), 92–104.

Azevedo, R., & Strain, A. C. (2011). Integrating cognitive, metacognitive, and affective regulatory processes with MetaTutor. In R. Calvo & S. D'Mello (Eds.), *Explorations in the Learning Sciences, Instructional Systems and Performance Technologies*. New York: Springer.

Barbalet, J. (2000). Boredom and social meaning. *Journal of Sociology, 50*, 631–646.

Binnema, D. (2004). Interrelations of psychiatric patient experiences of boredom and mental health. *Issues in Mental Health Nursing, 25*, 833–842.

Brodsky, J. (1984). [Commencement address]. Dartmouth College, Hanover, NH.

Capra, F. (2002). *The Hidden Connections: Integrating the Biological, Cognitive, and Social Dimensions of Life into a Science of Sustainability*. New York: Doubleday.

Carriere, J. S. A., Cheyne, J. A., &Smilek, D. (2008). Everyday attention lapses and memory failures: The affective consequences of mindlessness. *Consciousness and Cognition, 17*, 835–847.

Chanel, G., Rebetez, C., Betrancourt, M., & Pun, T. (2008). Boredom, engagement and anxiety as indicators for adaptation to difficulty in games. *Mindtrek* (pp. 13–17). doi: 10.1145/1457199.1457203.

Cheyne, J. A., Carriere, J. S. A., & Smilek, D. (2006). Absent-mindedness: Lapses in conscious awareness and everyday cognitive failures. *Consciousness and Cognition 15* (3): 578–592.

Epstein, J. (2011, June). Duh, boring. Commentary. https://www.commentary.org/articles/joseph-epstein/duh-boring/.

Fahlman, S. A., Mercer, K. B., Gaskovski, P., Eastwood, A. E., & Eastwood, J. D. (2009). Does a lack of life meaning cause boredom? Results from psychometric, longitudinal, and experimental analyses. *Journal of Social and Clinical Psychology, 28*(3). 307–340.

Johnson, S. (2001). *Emergence: The Connected Lives of Ants, Brains, Cities, and Software*. New York: Scribner.

Joussemet, M., Koestner, R., Lekes, N., & Houlfort, N. (2004). Introducing uninteresting tasks to children: A comparison of the effects of rewards and autonomy support. *Journal of Personality, 72* (1), 139–166.

Kalyuga, S. (2011). Cognitive load theory: Implications for affective computing. In P. M. McCarthy & R. C. Murray (Eds.). *Proceedings of the 24th International Florida Artificial Intelligence Research Society Conference* (pp. 105–110). Menlo Park, CA: Association for the Advancement of Artificial Intelligence (AAAI).

Kanevsky, L., & Keighley, T. (2003). To produce or not to produce? Understanding boredom and the honor in underachievement. *Roeper Review, 26*(1), 20–29.

Khan, M. M. R. (1986). Introduction. In D. W. Winnicott, *Holding and Interpretation* (pp. 1–18). London: Hogarth.

Kinchin, G. D., & O'Sullivan, M. (2003). Incidences of student support for and resistance to a curricular innovation in high school physical education. *Journal of Teaching in Physical Education, 22*(3), 245–260.

MacKenzie, G. (1998). *Orbiting the Giant Hairball: A Corporate Fool's Guide to Surviving with Grace*. New York: Viking.

Malkovsky, E., Merrifield, C., Goldberg, Y., & Danckert, J. (2012). Exploring the relationship between boredom and sustained attention. *Experimental Brain Research, 221*(1), 59–67.

Maltsberger, J. T. (2000). Case consultation: Mansur Zaskar: A man almost bored to death. *Suicide and Life-Threatening Behavior, 30*(1), 83–90.

Pekrun, R. (2006). The control-value theory of achievement motivations: Assumptions, corollaries, and implications for educational research and practice. *Educational Psychology Review, 18*, 315–341.

Posner, J., Russell, J. A., Gerber, A., Gorman, D., Colibazzi, T., Yu, S., et al. (2009). The neurophysiological bases of emotion: An fMRI study of the affective circumplex using emotion-denoting words. *Human Brain Mapping, 30*(3), 883–895.

Rad, C. (2015, June 13). 17x17x17 Rubik's Cube: The world's largest solved in 7.5 hours. IGN. https://sea.ign.com/rubiks-cube/85607/news/17x17x17-rubiks-cube-the-worlds-largest-solved-in-75-hours.

Taylor, M. (2001). *The Emergence of Complexity*. Chicago: University of Chicago Press.

Todman, M. (2007). Psychopathology and boredom: A neglected association. Paper presented at the International Conference on Psychology, Athens, Greece.

van Tilburg, W. A. P., & Igou, E. R. (2011). On boredom: Lack of challenge and meaning as distinct boredom experiences. *Motivation and Emotion, 35*(3).

Vodanovich, S. J. (2003). Psychometric measures of boredom: a review of the literature. *Journal of Psychology, 137*(6), 569–596.

Vogel-Walcutt, J. J., Fiorella, L., Carper, T., & Schatz, S. (2012). The definition, assessment, and mitigation of state boredom within educational settings: A comprehensive review. *Educational Psychology Review, 24*, 89–111.

Wallace, J. C., Kass, S. J., & Stanny, C. J. (2002). The cognitive failures questionnaire revisited: Dimensions and correlates. *Journal of General Psychology, 129*, 238–256.

Chapter 5. Give Them Something to Think About

Albrecht, K. (2007). *Practical Intelligence: The Art and Science of Common Sense*. San Francisco, CA: Jossey-Bass.

Alda, A. (2023) Things are either true or false. 2014: What Scientific Idea Is Ready for Retirement. Edge. https://www.edge.org/response-detail/25379.

Chaput, J.-P., Ferraro, Z. M., Prud'homme, D., & Sharma, A. M. (2014). Widespread misconceptions about obesity. *Canadian Family Physician, 60*(11), 973–975.

Echterhoff, G., Higgins, E. T., Kopietz, R., & Groll, S. (2008). How communication goals determine when audience tuning biases memory. *Journal of Experimental Psychology, 137*, 3–21.

French, L., Garry, M., & Mori, K. (2011). Relative—not absolute—judgments of credibility affect susceptibility to misinformation conveyed during discussion. *Acta Psychologica, 136*, 119–128.

Frith, C. D., & Frith, U. (2012). Mechanisms of social cognition. *Annual Review of Psychology, 63*, 287–313.

Gamst, G. (1982). Memory for conversations: Toward a grammar of dyadic conversation. *Discourse Processes, 5*(1), 33–51.

Lindley, D. (2002). Seeing and doing: The concept of causation. *International Statistical Review, 70*, 191–214.

Nadler, G., & Chandon, W. J. (2004). *Smart Questions: Learn to Ask the Right Questions for Powerful Results.* San Francisco, CA: Jossey-Bass.

Oeberst, A., & Seidemann, J. (2014). Will your words become mine? *Canadian Journal of Experimental Psychology, 68*(2), 84–96.

Pearl, J. (2009). *Causality: Models, Reasoning, and Inference* (2nd ed.). New York: Cambridge University Press.

Reysen, M. B. (2005). The effects of social pressure on group recall. *Memory & Cognition, 31*, 1163–1168.

Skagerberg, E. M., & Wright, D. B. (2009). Sibling differentials in power and memory conformity. *Scandinavian Journal of Psychology, 50*, 101–107.

Thomke, S. (2003). *Experimentation Matters: Unlocking the Potential of New Technologies for Innovation.* Boston, MA: Harvard Business School Press. Tweney, R. (2001). Scientific thinking: A cognitive-historical approach. In K. Crowley, C. D. Schunn, & T. Okada (Eds.), *Designing for Science: Implications from Everyday, Classroom, and Professional Settings* (pp. 141–173). Mahwah, NJ: Erlbaum.

van Eemeren, F. H., Grootendorst, R., Snoeck Henkemans, A. F., Blair, J. A., Willard, C. A., Plantin, C., Johnson, R. H. (1996). *Fundamentals of Argumentation Theory: A Handbook of Historical Backgrounds and Contemporary Developments.* (Routledge), 129–149.

Windschitl, M. (2004). Caught in the cycle of reproducing folk theories of "inquiry": How pre-service teachers continue the discourse and practices of an atheoretical scientific method. *Journal of Research in Science Teaching, 41*(5), 481–512.

Windschitl, M., & Thompson, J. (2006). Transcending simple forms of school science investigation: The impact of pre-service instruction on teachers' understandings of model-based inquiry. *American Educational Research Journal, 43*(4), 783–835.

Chapter 6. Mastering Metaphors

Barrett, L. F., & Russell, J. A. (1999). The structure of current affect: Controversies and emerging consensus. *Current Directions in Psychological Science, 8*(1), 10–14.

Berka, C., Levendowski, D. J., Lumicao, M. N., Yau, A., Davis, G., Zivkovic, V. T., Olmstead, R. E., Tremoulet, P. D., & Craven, P. L. (2007). EEG correlates of task engagement and mental workload in vigilance, learning, and memory tasks. *Aviation, Space, and Environmental Medicine, 78*(5), B231–B244.

Bos, D. O. (2006). EEG-based emotion recognition. *The Influence of Visual and Auditory Stimuli, 4*, 1-17.

Brandmeyer, T., & Delorme, A. (2018). Reduced mind wandering in experienced meditators and associated EEG correlates. *Experimental Brain Research, 236*(9), 2519–2528.

Chai, W. J., Abd Hamid, A. I., & Abdullah, J. M. (2018). Working memory from the psychological and neurosciences perspectives: A review. *Frontiers in Psychology, 9*, 401.

Chanel, G., Kronegg, J., Grandjean, D., & Pun, T. (2006). Emotion assessment: Arousal evaluation using EEG's and peripheral physiological signals. In B. Gunsel, A. K. Jain, A. M. Tekalp, & B. Sankur (Eds.), *Multimedia Content Representation, Classification and Security* (Vol. 4105, pp. 530–537). doi: 10.1007/11848035_70.

Cohen, S. S., Madsen, J., Touchan, G., Robles, D., Lima, S. F. A., Henin, S., et al. (2018). Neural engagement with online educational videos predicts learning performance for individual students. *Neurobiology of Learning and Memory, 155*, 60–64. doi: 10.1016/j.nlm.2018.06.011.

Fernández, P. R. (2007). Suppression in metaphor interpretation: Differences between meaning selection and meaning construction. *Journal of Semantics, 24*, 345–371.

García-Madariaga, J., Moya, I., Recuero, N., & Blasco, M. F. (2020). Revealing unconscious consumer reactions to advertisements that include visual metaphors. A neurophysiological experiment. *Frontiers in Psychology, 11*, 760.

Giora, R. (1997). Understanding figurative and literal language: The graded salience hypothesis. *Cognitive Linguistics, 8*, 183–206.

Glucksberg, S. (2003). The psycholinguistics of metaphor. *Trends in Cognitive Sciences, 7*, 92–96.

Glucksberg, S., Gildea, P., & Bookin, H. B. (1982). On understanding nonliteral speech: Can people ignore metaphors? *Journal of Verbal Learning and Verbal Behavior, 21*, 85–98.

Katz, A. N. (2018). On interpreting statements as metaphor or irony: Contextual heuristics and cognitive consequences. In J. S. Mio & A. N. Katz (Eds.), *Metaphor: Implications and Applications* (pp. 1–22). doi: 10.4324/9781315789316-1

Koelstra, S., Muhl, C., Soleymani, M., Jong-Seok Lee, Yazdani, A., Ebrahimi, T., Pun, T., Nijholt, A., & Patras, I. (2012). DEAP: A database for emotion analysis: Using physiological signals. *IEEE Transactions on Affective Computing, 3*(1), 18–31.

Kuppens, P., Tuerlinckx, F., Russell, J. A., & Barrett, L. F. (2013). The relation between valence and arousal in subjective experience. *Psychological Bulletin, 139*(4), 917–940.

Lai, H. L. (2008). Understanding and classifying two-part allegorical sayings: Metonymy, metaphor, and cultural constraints. *Journal of Pragmatics, 40*, 454–474.

Lai, V. T., Curran, T., & Menn, L. (2009). Comprehending conventional and novel metaphors: An ERP study. *Brain Research, 1284*, 145–155.

Lakoff, G., & Johnson, M. (1980). *Metaphors We Live By*. Chicago: University of Chicago Press.

Lal, S. K. L., & Craig, A. (2001). A critical review of the psychophysiology of driver fatigue. *Biological Psychology, 55*(3), 173–194.

Müller, M. M., Keil, A., Gruber, T., & Elbert, T. (1999). Processing of affective pictures modulates right-hemispheric gamma band EEG activity. *Clinical Neurophysiology, 110*(11), 1913–1920.

Russell, J. (1980). A circumplex model of affect. *Journal of Personality and Social Psychology, 39*, 1161–1178.

Stern, J. A., Boyer, D., & Schroeder, D. (1994). Blink rate: A possible measure of fatigue. *Human Factors: The Journal of the Human Factors and Ergonomics Society, 36*(2), 285–297.

Stewart, John. (2019). Afterword: A view from enaction. *Language Sciences, 71*, 68–73, ISSN 0388-0001, https://doi.org/10.1016/j.langsci.2018.06.004.

Tourangeau, R., & Sternberg, R. J. (1982). Understanding and appreciating metaphors. *Cognition, 11*, 203–244.

Wilson, D. (2011). Parallels and differences in the treatment of metaphor in relevance theory and cognitive linguistics. *Intercultural Pragmatics, 8*(2), 177–196. https://doi-org.stanford.idm.oclc.org/10.1515/IPRG.2011.009.

Chapter 7. Mind Wandering:
Help Them See When They Are Not Looking

Baird, B., Smallwood, J., Mrazek, M. D., Kam, J. W., Franklin, M. S., & Schooler, J. W. (2012). Inspired by distraction: Mind wandering facilitates creative incubation. *Psychological Science, 23*, 1117–1122.

Baldwin, C. L., Roberts, D. M., Barragan, D., Lee, J. D., Lerner, N., & Higgins, J. S. (2017). Detecting and quantifying mind wandering during simulated driving. *Frontiers in Human Neuroscience, 11*.

Bixler, R., D'Mello, S., & White, S. (2016). Automatic gaze-based user-independent detection of mind wandering during computerized reading. *User Modeling and User-Adapted Interaction, 26*. doi: 10.1007/s11257-015-9167-1.

Cavanagh, J. F., Cohen, M. X., & Allen, J. J. B. (2009). Prelude to and resolution of an error: EEG phase synchrony reveals cognitive control dynamics during action monitoring. *Journal of Neuroscience, 29*(1), 98–105.

Cavanagh, J. F., & Frank, M. J. (2014). Frontal theta as a mechanism for cognitive control. *Trends in Cognitive Sciences, 18*(8), 414–421.

Christoff, K., Irving, Z. C., Fox, K. C. R., Spreng, R. N., & Andrews-Hanna, J. R. (2016). Mind-wandering as spontaneous thought: a dynamic framework. *Nature Reviews Neuroscience, 17*(11), 718–731.

Compton, R., Gearinger, D., & Wild, H. (2019). The wandering mind oscillates: EEG alpha power is enhanced during moments of mind-wandering. *Cognitive, Affective, & Behavioral Neuroscience, 19*.

Ergenoglu, T., Demiralp, T., Bayraktaroglu, Z., Ergen, M., Beydagi, H., & Uresin, Y. (2004). Alpha rhythm of the EEG modulates visual detection performance in humans. *Cognitive Brain Research, 20*(3), 376–383.

Gonçalves, Ó. F., Rêgo, G., Conde, T., Leite, J., Carvalho, S., Lapenta, O. M., & Boggio, P. S. (2018). Mind wandering and task-focused attention: ERP correlates. *Scientific Reports, 8*, 7608.

Huijser, S., van Vugt, M. K., & Taatgen, N. A. (2018). The wandering self: Tracking distracting self-generated thought in a cognitively demanding context. *Consciousness and Cognition, 58*, 170–185.

Jin, C. Y., Borst, J. P., & van Vugt, M. K. (2019). Predicting task-general mind-wandering with EEG. *Cognitive, Affective, & Behavioral Neuroscience, 19*(4), 1059–1073.

Kam, J. W. Y., & Handy, T. C. (2013). The neurocognitive consequences of the wandering mind: a mechanistic account of sensory-motor decoupling. *Frontiers in Psychology, 4*, 725.

Kam, J. W. Y., Irving, Z. C., Mills, C., Patel, S., Gopnik, A., & Knight, R. T. (2021). Distinct electrophysiological signatures of task-unrelated and dynamic thoughts. *Proceedings of the National Academy of Sciences, 118*(4).

McVay, J. C., Kane, M. J., & Kwapil, T. R. (2009). Tracking the train of thought from the laboratory into everyday life: An experience-sampling study of mind-wandering across controlled and ecological contexts. *Psychonomic Bulletin & Review, 16*, 857–863.

Moreno, R., & Mayer, R. E. (2002). Verbal redundancy in multimedia learning: When reading helps listening. *Journal of Educational Psychology, 94*(1), 156–163.

Risko, E. F., Anderson, N., Sarwal, A., Engelhardt, M., & Kingstone, A. (2012). Everyday attention: Variation in mind wandering and memory in a lecture. *Applied Cognitive Psychology, 26*, 234–242.

Seli, P., Cheyne, J. A., & Smilek, D. (2012). Attention failures versus misplaced diligence: Separating attention lapses from speed–accuracy trade-offs. *Consciousness and Cognition, 21*, 277–291.

Smallwood, J., McSpadden, M., & Schooler, J. W. (2007). The lights are on, but no one's home: Meta-awareness and the decoupling of attention when the mind wanders. *Psychonomic Bulletin & Review, 14*, 527–533.

Thomson, D. R., Besner, D., & Smilek, D. (2013). In pursuit of off-task thought: Mind wandering-performance trade-offs while reading aloud and color naming. *Frontiers in Psychology, 4*, Article 360.

Verhoef, P. C. (2003). Understanding the effect of customer relationship management efforts on customer retention and customer share development. *Journal of Marketing, 67* (October), 30–45.

Wilson, T. D., Reinhard, D. A., Westgate, E. C., Gilbert, D. T., Ellerbeck, N., Hahn, C., & Shaked, A. (2014). Just think: The challenges of the disengaged mind. *Science, 345*, 75–77.

Zeithaml, V. A., Rust, R. T., & Lemon, K. N. (2001). The customer pyramid: creating and serving profitable customers. *California Management Review, 43* (4), 118–142.

Chapter 8. What Happens Next?
The Neuroscience of Predicting the Future

Addis, D. A., Wong, A. T., & Schacter, D. L. (2007). Remembering the past and imagining the future: Common and distinct neural substrates during event construction and elaboration. *Neuropsychologia, 45*, 1363–1377.

Bar, M. (2009). The proactive brain: Memory for predictions. *Philosophical Transactions of the Royal Society B: Biological Sciences, 364*, 1235–1243.

Baumeister, R. F., Hofmann, W., Summerville, A., Reiss, P. T., & Vohs, K. D. (2020). Everyday thoughts in time: Experience sampling studies of mental time travel. *Personality and Social Psychology Bulletin, 46*(12), 1631–1648. https://doi.org/10.1177/0146167220908411.

Berg, J. J., Gilmore, A. W., Shaffer, R. A., & McDermott, K. B. (2021). The stability of visual perspective and vividness during mental time travel. *Consciousness and Cognition, 92*, 103116. https://doi.org/10.1016/j.concog.2021.103116.

Blatstein, I. M. (2012). Strategic planning: Predicting or shaping the future? *Organization Development Journal, 30*, 31–38.

Clark, A. (2013). Whatever next? Predictive brains, situated agents, and the future of cognitive science. *Behavioural and Brain Sciences, 36*(3), 181–204. https://doi.org/10.1017/S0140525X12000477.

Debus, D. (2014). "Mental time travel": remembering the past, imagining the future, and the particularity of events. *Review of Philosophy and Psychology, 5*(3), 333–350.

Girardeau, J. C., Sperduti, M., Blondé, P., & Piolino, P. (2022). Where is my mind . . . ? The link between mind wandering and prospective memory. *Brain Sciences, 12*(9), 1139. https://doi.org/10.3390/brainsci12091139.

Michaelian, K., Klein, S., & Szpunar, K. (2016). The past, the present, and the future of future-oriented mental time travel: Editors' introduction. In K. Michaelian, S. B. Klein, & K. K. Szpunar (Eds.), *Seeing the Future: Theoretical Perspectives on Future-Oriented Mental Time Travel* (pp. 1–18). Oxford, UK: Oxford University Press. https://doi.org/10.1093/acprof:oso/9780190241537.003.0001.

Mullally, S. L., & Maguire, E. A. (2014). Memory, imagination, and predicting the future: A common brain mechanism? *Neuroscientist, 20*, 220–234.

Radüntz, T. (2020). The effect of planning, strategy learning, and working memory capacity on mental workload. *Scientific Reports, 10*.

Schacter, D. L., & Addis, D. R. (2007). The cognitive neuroscience of constructive memory: Remembering the past and imagining the future. *Philosophical Transactions of the Royal Society B: Biological Sciences, 362*, 773–786.

Seligman, M. E. P., Railton, P., Baumeister, R. F., & Sripada, C. (2013). Navigating into the future or driven by the past. *Perspectives on Psychological Science, 8*(2), 119–141.

Smallwood, J., Schooler, J. W., Turk, D. J., Cunningham, S. J., Burns, P., & Macrae, C. N. (2011). Self-reflection and the temporal focus of the wandering mind. *Consciousness and Cognition, 20*(4), 1120–1126. https://doi.org/10.1016/j.concog.2010.12.017.

Szpunar, K., Spreng, R. N., & Schacter, D. (2016). Toward a taxonomy of future thinking. In K. Michaelian, S. B. Klein, & K. K. Szpunar (Eds.), Seeing the *Future: Theoretical Perspectives on Future-Oriented Mental Time Travel* (pp. 21–35). Oxford, UK: Oxford University Press.

Verschure, P. F. M. J., Pennartz, C. M. A., & Pezzulo, G. (2014). The why, what, where, when and how of goal-directed choice: Neuronal and computational principles. *Philosophical Transactions of the Royal Society, 369*, 20130483.

Chapter 9. Transitions:
Help Them See Your Message When You Aren't There

Ampa, A.T., Akib, E., & Sari, D. K. (2019). The use of transitional signals in essay writing by EFL students. *International Journal of English Language & Translation Studies, 7*(2), 33–38.

Cacioppo, J. T., & Petty, R. E. (1982). The need for cognition. *Journal of Personality and Social Psychology, 42*, 116–131.

Dechene, A., Stahl, C., Hansen, J., & Wanke, M. (2010). The truth about the truth: A meta-analytic review of the truth effect. *Personality and Social Psychology Review, 14*(2), 238–257.

Dijksterhuis, A. P., Van Knippenberg, A. D., Kruglanski, A. W., & Schaper, C. (1996). Motivated social cognition: Need for closure effects on memory and judgment. *Journal of Experimental Social Psychology, 32*, 254–270.

Eckstein, M. K., Guerra-Carrillo, B., Miller Singley, A. T., Bunge, S.A. (2017). Beyond eye gaze: What else can eyetracking reveal about cognition and cognitive development? *Developmental Cognitive Neuroscience, 25*, 69–91. doi: 10.1016/j.dcn.2016.11.001.

Hawkins, S. A., Hoch, S. J., & Meyers-Levy, J. (2001). Low-involvement learning: Repetition and coherence in familiarity and belief. *Journal of Consumer Psychology, 11*(1), 1–11.

Kruglanski, A. W., & Fishman, S. (2009). The need for cognitive closure. *Handbook of Individual Differences in Social Behavior*, 343–353.

Neuberg, S. L., Judice, T. N., & West, S. (1997). What the Need for Closure Scale measures and what it does not: Toward differentiating among related epistemic motives. *Journal of Personality and Social Psychology, 72*, 1396–1412.

Rankin, C. H., Abrams, T., Barry, R. J., Bhatnagar, S., Clayton, D.F., Colombo, J., Coppola, G., Geyer, M. A., Glanzman, D. L., Marsland, S., McSweeney, F. K., Wilson, D. A., Wu, C. F., Thompson, R. F. (2009). Habituation revisited: An updated and revised description of the behavioral characteristics of habituation. *Neurobiology of Learning and Memory, 92*(2),135–138.

Rensink, R. A. (2013). Perception and attention. In D. Reisberg (Ed.), *The Oxford Handbook of Cognitive Psychology* (pp. 97–116). Oxford, UK: Oxford University Press.

Webster, D. M., & Kruglanski, A. W. (1997). Cognitive and social consequences of the need for cognitive closure. *European Review of Social Psychology, 8*(1), 133–173.

Xiao, Y., Lopez, P., Wu, R., Wei, P.-H., Shan, Y.-Z., Weisholtz, D., Cosgrove, W., Madsen, J., Stone, S., Zhao, G.-G., & Kreiman, G. (2023). Integration of recognition, episodic, and associative memories during complex human behavior. (Preprint.) Retrieved from https://doi.org/10.1101/2023.03.27.534384.

Yoshihito, S. (2010). Enhancing students' fluency in writing: Learning to use transition words. *Open Journal of Modern Linguistics, 2*(1), 1–8. doi: 10.4236/ojml.2012.21003.

Chapter 10. The Decision to Look: Mixing Business with Pleasure

Arias-Carrion, O., & Poppel, E. (2007). Dopamine, learning, and reward-seeking behavior. *Acta Neurobiologiae Experimentalis, 67,* 481–488.

Bargh, J. A., Gollwitzer, P. M., Lee-Chai, A., Barndollar, K., & Trotschel, R. (2001). The automated will: Non-conscious activation and pursuit of behavioral goals. *Journal of Personality and Social Psychology, 81,* 1014–1027.

Berridge, K. C. (2003). Pleasures of the brain. *Brain and Cognition, 52,* 106–128.

Berridge, K. C. (2007). The debate over dopamine's role in reward: The case for incentive salience. *Psychopharmacology, 191,* 391–431.

Berridge, K. C., & Aldridge, J. W. (2009). Decision utility, incentive salience, and cue-triggered "wanting." *Oxford Series in Social Cognition and Social Neuroscience,* 509–533.

Bhanji, J. P., & Delgado, M. R. (2014). The social brain and reward: Social information processing in the human striatum. *Wiley Interdisciplinary Reviews: Cognitive Science, 5*(1), 61–73. doi: 10.1002/wcs.1266.

Chiew, K. S., & Braver, T. S. (2011). Positive affect versus reward: Emotional and motivational influences on cognitive control. *Frontiers in Psychology,* 1–10. doi: 10.3389/fpsyg.2011.00279.

Droit-Volet, S., & Gil, S. (2009). The time-emotion paradox. *Philosophical Transactions of the Royal Society B: Biological Sciences, 364*(1525), 1943–1953. doi: 10.1098/rstb.2009.0013.

Fayolle, S., Gil, S., & Droit-Volet, S. (2015). Fear and time: Fear speeds up the internal clock. *Behavioural Processes, 120,* 135–140. doi: 10.1016/j.beproc.2015.09.014.

Gardner, M. P. H., Schoenbaum, G., & Gershman, S. J. (2018). Rethinking dopamine as generalized prediction error. *Proceedings of the Royal Society B: Biological Sciences, 285,* 20181645. http://dx.doi.org/10.1098/rspb.2018.1645.

Guynn, M. J. (2003). A two-process model of strategic monitoring in event-based prospective memory: Activation/retrieval mode and checking. *International Journal of Psychology, 38* (4), 245–256.

Lieberman, D. Z., & Long, M. E. (2018). *The Molecule of More: How a Single Chemical in Your Brain Drives Love, Sex, and Creativity and Will Determine the Fate of the Human Race.* Dallas, TX: BenBella Books, Inc.

McDaniels, M. A., & Einstein, G. O. (2000). Strategic and automatic processes in prospective memory retrieval: A multiprocess framework. *Applied Cognitive Psychology, 14,* 127–S144. https://doi.org/10.1002/acp.775.

Ryan, R. M. (2012). *The Handbook of Human Motivation.* Oxford, UK: Oxford University Press.

Shohamy, D., & Adcock, R. A. (2010). Dopamine and adaptive memory. *Trends in Cognitive Sciences, 14*(10), 1–14.

Vivinetto, G. (2016, August 2). What hookup culture? Millennials having less sex than their parents. NBC News. Retrieved from https://www.nbcnews.com/health/sexual-health/what-hookup-culture-millennials-having-less-sex-their-parents-n621746.

Chapter 11. Harnessing Complexity

Allen, P. M. (2001). A complex systems approach to learning, adaptive networks. *International Journal of Innovation Management, 5*(2), 149–180.

Amlien, I. K., Sneve, M. H., Vidal-Piñeiro, D., Walhovd, K. B., & Fjell, A. M. (2019). Elaboration benefits source memory encoding through centrality change. *Scientific Reports, 9,* 3704. https://doi.org/10.1038/s41598-019-39999-1.

Ardah, J. (1982). *France in the 1980s: The Definitive Book.* Harmondsworth: Penguin.

Bathelt, H., Malmberg, A., & Maskell, P. (2004) Clusters and knowledge: Local buzz, global pipelines and the process of knowledge creation. *Progress in Human Geography, 28,* 31–56.

Braarud, P. O. (2001). Subjective task complexity and subjective workload: Criterion validity for complex team tasks. *International Journal of Cognitive Ergonomics, 5*(3), 261–273.

Brod, G., Werkle-Bergner, M., & Shing, Y. L. (2013). The influence of prior knowledge on memory: A developmental cognitive neuroscience perspective. *Frontiers in Behavioral Neuroscience, 7,* 139. doi: 10.3389/fnbeh.2013.00139. PMID: 24115923; PMCID: PMC3792618.

Chang, M. M., Zhang, Z., & Chiu, C. (2010). Adherence to perceived norms across cultural boundaries: The role of need for cognitive closure and ingroup identification. *Group Processes and Intergroup Relations, 13,* 69–89.

Cutting, J. E. (2016). The evolution of pace in popular movies. *Cutting Cognitive Research: Principles and Implications, 1,* 30. doi: 10.1186/s41235-016-0029-0.

Cutting, J. E., DeLong, J. E., & Brunick, K. L. (2018). Temporal fractals in movies and mind. *Cognitive Research: Principles and Implications, 3,* 8. https://doi.org/10.1186/s41235-018-0091.

Glaeser, E. L. (2003). Psychology and the market. Harvard Institute of Economic Research Discussion Paper Series, 20–23, 126–127.

Graf, A. (2004). Screening and training inter-cultural competencies: Evaluating the impact of national culture on inter-cultural competencies. *International Journal of Human Resource and Management, 15*, 1124–1148.

Hall, E. T. (1983). *Hidden Differences: Studies in International Communication*. Hamburg: Grunner & Jahr.

Hall, E. T., & Hall, M. R. (1990). *Understanding Cultural Differences*. Yarmouth, Maine: Intercultural Press Inc.

Hofstede, G. (1980). *Culture's Consequences*. Beverly Hills, CA: Sage.

Iandoli, L., Piantedosi, L., Salado, A., & Zollo, G. (2018). Elegance as complexity reduction in systems designs. *Complexity*, 1–10. https://doi.org/10.1155/2018/5987249.

Köhler, T., Cramton, C. D., & Hinds, P. J. (2012). The meeting genre across cultures: insights from three German–American collaborations. *Small Group Research, 43*(2), 159–185. https://doi.org/10.1177/1046496411429600.

Kopelman, S., & Rosette, A. S. (2008). Cultural variation in response to strategic emotions in negotiations. *Group Decision and Negotiation, 17*(1), 65–77.

Lehmann-Willenbrock, N., Allen, J. A., Meinecke, A. L. (2014). Observing culture: Differences in U.S.-American and German team meeting behaviors. *Group Processes & Intergroup Relations, 17*(2), 252–271.

Leung, K., Bhagat, N., Buchan, N., Erez, M., & Gibson, C. (2005). Culture and international business: Recent advances and their implications for future research. *Journal of International Business Studies, 36*, 357–378.

Ma, Z. (2010). The SINS in business negotiations: Explore the cross-cultural differences in business ethics between Canada and China. *Journal of Business Ethics, 91*, 123–135.

Mitchell, K. J., & Johnson, M. K. (2009). Source monitoring 15 years later: What have we learned from fMRI about the neural mechanisms of source memory? *Psychological Bulletin, 135*(4):638–677. doi: 10.1037/a0015849. PMID: 19586165; PMCID: PMC2859897.

Rosenbloom, B., & Larsen, T. (2003). Communication in international business-to-business marketing channels: Does culture matter?. *Industrial Marketing Management, 32*, 309–315.

Rudland, J. R., Golding, C., & Wilkinson, T. J. (2020). The stress paradox: How stress can be good for learning. *Medical Education 54*, 40–45. https://doi.org/10.1111/medu.13830.

Scupin, R. (1998). *Cultural Anthropology: A Global Perspective* (3rd ed.). Upper Saddle River, NJ: Prentice-Hall.

Spradley, J. P. (1972). *Culture and Cognition: Rules, Maps, and Plans*. San Francisco, CA: Chandler Publishing.

Street, N., Forsythe, A. M., Reilly, R., Taylor, R., & Helmy, M. S. (2016). A complex story: Universal preferences vs. individual differences shaping aesthetic response to fractal patterns. *Frontiers in Human Neuroscience*, 1–16. doi: 10.3389/fnhum.2016.00213.

Taylor, R., Spehar, B., Wise, J., Clifford, C., Newell, B., Hägerhäll, C., Purcell, T., & Martin, T. (2005). Perceptual and physiological responses to the visual complexity of fractal patterns. *Nonlinear Dynamics, Psychology, and Life Sciences, 9*, 89–114. doi: 10.1007/978-3-322-83487-4_4.

Whiting, S. B., Wass, S. V., Green, S., & Thomas, M. S. C. (2021). Stress and learning in pupils: Neuroscience evidence and its relevance for teachers. *Mind, Brain, and Education, 15*, 177–188. https://doi.org/10.1111/mbe.12282.

Wu, D., Kendrick, K. M., Levitin, D. J., Li, C., & Yao, D. (2015). Bach is the father of harmony: Revealed by a 1/f fluctuation analysis across musical genres. *PLoS ONE, 10*(11): e0142431. doi: 10.1371/journal.pone.0142431.

Chapter 12. The Risks and Rewards of Collective Attention

Allan, K., & Gabbert, F. (2008). I still think it was a banana: Memorable "lies" and forgettable "truths." *Acta Psychologica, 127*, 299–308.

Allan, K., Midjord, J. P., & Martin, D. (2012). Memory conformity and the perceived accuracy of self versus other. *Memory Cognition, 40*, 280–286.

Barde, A., Gumilar, A., Hayati, A. F., Dey, A., Lee, G., & Billinghurst, M. (2020). A review of hyperscanning and its use in virtual environments. *Informatics, 7*, 55. https://doi.org/10.3390/informatics7040055.

Crainer, S. (2002). *Business the Jack Welch Way* (2nd ed.). Bloomington, MN: Capstone.

Echterhoff, G., Hirst, W., & Hussy, W. (2005). How eyewitnesses resist misinformation: Social postwarnings and the monitoring of memory characteristics. *Memory & Cognition, 30*, 770–782.

French, L., Garry, M., & Mori, K. (2008). You say tomato? Collaborative remembering leads to more false memories for intimate couples than for strangers. *Memory, 16*, 262–273.

Gabbert, F., Memon, A., & Wright, D. B. (2007). I saw it for longer than you: The relationship between perceived encoding duration and memory conformity. *Acta Psychologica, 124*, 319–331.

Gabriel, M. T., Critelli, J. W., & Ee, J. S. (1994). Narcissistic illusions in self-evaluations of intelligence and attractiveness. *Journal of Personality, 62*, 143–155.

Gardner, W. L., Pickett, C. L., & Brewer, M. B. (2000). Social exclusion and selective memory: How the need to belong influences memory for social events. *PSPB, 26*(4), 486–496.

Hewitt, L. Y., Kane, R., & Garry, M. (2013). Speaking order predicts memory conformity after accounting for exposure to misinformation. *Psychology Bulletin Review, 20*, 558–565.

Horry, R., Palmer, M. A., Sexton, M. L., & Brewer, N. (2012). Memory conformity for confidently recognized items: The power of social influence on memory reports. *Journal of Experimental Social Psychology, 48*, 783–786.

Hu, Y., Hu, Y., Li, X, Pan, Y., & Cheng, X. (2017). Brain-to-brain synchronization across two persons predicts mutual prosociality. *Social Cognitive and Affective Neuroscience, 12*, 1835–1844. https://doi.org/10.1093/scan/nsx118.

John, O. P., & Robins, R. (1994). Accuracy and bias in self-perception: Individual differences in self-enhancement and the role of narcissism. *Journal of Personality and Social Psychology, 66*, 206–219.

Kernis, M. H., & Sun, C.-R. (1994). Narcissism and reactions to interpersonal feedback. *Journal of Research in Personality, 28*, 4–13.

Koriat, A., Goldsmith, M., & Pansky, A. (2003). Memory distortions and forgetting. In L. Nadel (Ed.), *Encyclopedia of Cognitive Science* (pp. 1076–1081). Nature Publishing Group (New York: Macmillan).

Legator, M., & Morris, D. L. (2003). What did Bradford Hill really say?. *Archives of Environmental Health, 58*, 718–720.

McFarland, C., & Ross, M. (1987). The relation between current impressions and memory of self and dating partners. *Personality and Social Psychology Bulletin, 13*, 228–238.

Meyer, M. L., Spunt, R. P., Berkman, E. T., Taylor, S. E., & Lieberman, M. D. (2001). Evidence for social working memory from a parametric functional MRI study. *PNAS, 109*(6), 1883–1888.

Muehling, D. D., & Sprott, D. E. (2004). The power of reflection: An empirical examination of nostalgia advertising effects. *Journal of Advertising, 33*(3), 25–36.

Naveh-Benjamin, M., Craik, F. I. M., Guez, J., & Kreuger, S. (2005). Divided attention in younger and older adults: Effects of strategy and relatedness on memory performance and secondary task costs. *Journal of Experimental Psychology: Learning, Memory and Cognition, 31*, 520–537.

Numbers, K. T., & Meade, M. L. (2014). The influences of partner accuracy and partner memory ability on social false memories. *Memory Cognition, 42*, 1225–1238.

Reysen, M. B. (2005). The effects of social pressure on group recall. *Memory & Cognition, 31*, 1163–1168.

Rhodewalt, F., & Eddings, S. K. (2002). Narcissus reflects: Memory distortion in response to ego-relevant feedback among high- and low-narcissistic men. *Journal of Research in Personality, 36*, 97–116.

Rowlinson, M., Booth, C., Clark, P., Delahaye, A., & Procter, S. (2010). Social remembering and organizational memory. *Organization Studies, 31*(01), 69–87.

Sanitioso, R., Kunda, Z., & Fong, G. T. (1990). Motivated recruitment of autobiographical memories. *Journal of Personality and Social Psychology, 59*, 229–241.

Stafford, L., & Daly, J. L. (1984). Conversational memory: The effects of recall mode and memory expectancies on remembrances of natural conversations. *Human Communication Research, 10*, 379–402.

Wheeler, R., Allan, K., Tsivilis, D., Martin, D., & Gabbert, F. (2013). Explicit mentalizing mechanisms and their adaptive role in memory conformity. *PLoS ONE, 8*(4), 1–7. https://doi.org/10.1371/journal.pone.0062031.

Ybarra, O. (1999). Misanthropic person memory when the need to self-enhance is absent. *Personality and Social Psychology Bulletin, 25*, 261–269.

INDEX

A

absorption, mind wandering and, 168–169

abstract concepts, 52

    metaphors linking concrete to, 149–150

abundant choices, attention-grabbing
    content and, 16–17

abusing metaphors, 157–160

Academic Boredom Scale, 102

"the Academy" *(Académie des Beaux- Arts)*,
    305

additive transitions, 209–211

Adidas, 70

adversative transitions, 211–213

affective priming
    creativity and, 38–39
    Eureka moments and, 41–42
    with negative and positive emotions, 43
    surprise and, 39–41

affective variables, in clichéd and fresh
    metaphors, 154

agenda slides, 10 percent message and, 222

aging, strategic monitoring and, 250

agreeable partners, conformity with, 288

AI (artificial intelligence)
    for attention-grabbing content, 4, 7
    consciousness and, 124–125
    design and, 79

Alda, Alan, 120

Alone (Byrd), 294

analyzing, 168

anecdotal evidence, 133–134

anticipation, for future perspective,
    201–202

"appear," 60

Apple, 218

approach/withdrawal, biometric sensors
    on, 12

AR (augmented reality), 54

Aristotle, 45

arousal
    definition of, 12, 100
    in emotional circumplex, 100–101
    fluctuation of, 103

art
    for attention-grabbing content, 4
    profluence and, 278
    rejection and, 305–309

artificial intelligence. *See* AI

associations, transitions building, 215

associative conditioning, 235

Atonement (McEwan), 144

attention. *See also* collective attention
    biometric sensors studying, 12
    conformity, 282
    credibility and confidence undermining,
        285
    defining, 7, 18
    ego and, 17
    elaboration and, 266, 268–270
    emotions and, 10

fatigue and, 16

in mind wandering, 169–170

narcissists and distortions of, 292–294

as social act, 281

solving problem of, 18–21

time and, 250

types of, 7, 18

variety for directing, 104

in virtual compared to face-to-face
    environment, 12, 13

attention-grabbing content. *See also*
    provocative content
    abundant choices and, 16–17
    AI-generated images for, 4, 7
    art for, 4
    audience baseline compared to stimulus
        in, 13
    excuses preventing, 301
    feedback for, 304
    neuroscience for, 10
    rejection and, 305–309
    rush slowly for, 303
    self-experimentation for, 309
    solitude and silence for, 310

audience(s)
    awareness for temporal transitions, 207
    baseline compared to stimulus of, 13
    in face-to-face compared to virtual
        environment, 12, 13
    participation for planning, 201

audience(s) *(con't)*
  sleep-deprived, 16
  technological tools for, 54
  virtual training sessions for, 54–55
augmented reality (AR), 54
Austen, Jane, 292
automatic triggers
  embodied cognition, 49–67
  guidelines for, 18, 19, 22, 95
  priming, 25–46
  provocative content, 69–93
awkward transitions, 227

B
backward referencing, 89
Bad Frog Brewery, 69
basic pleasures, 233
bazaar method, cathedral method
    compared to, 75, 76
behavior reinforcement, 236–238
"beige" content, perceptual priming for, 30,
    31
beliefs, cognitive flexibility and updating,
    160
belongingness, collective attention and,
    292
bias
  claim of value and, 130–132
  status quo, 16
biometric sensors, 11–12
Blahnik, Manolo, 309
bland ideas, 28, 29
borders, text and pictures with, 221
boredom
  challenge for fighting, 109–113
  choice for fighting, 113–116
  definition of, 102
  dispositional, 104
  EEG and ECG signals on, 100–103
  eye tracking for, 101–102
  habituation and, 106
  meaningful life and, 116
  mind wandering relieving, 172

neuroscience of, 99, 102–103
preventing, 104–116
questions for escaping, 116
scales of, 102
situational, 104
skydiving and, 99
variety fighting, 104–109
Boredom Proneness Scale, 102
BPI (Brand Power Index) score, 295
brain science. *See* neuroscience
Brains on Trial, 120
Brand Power Index (BPI) score, 295
Brandon, Kenneth, 109
Breaking Bad, 119
Brodsky, Joseph, 102, 116
Bublé, Michael, 155
business content. *See* corporate content
Byrd, Richard, 294

C
"calls to action," intention setting and,
    197–198
Carnegie, Dale, 45
cathedral method, bazaar method
    compared to, 75, 76
causative transitions, 214–215
cause, claim of, 126–130
cause-and-effect framing, 126–128
challenge
  absence of information for, 113
  complexity and, 111, 113
  in corporate content, 111–113
  pace of, 111
  Rubik's Cube example of, 109
  in test-taking, 109–111
Challenger dimension of value, 132
choice
  areas for, 116
  attention-grabbing content and
      abundant, 16–17
  collective attention and, 297
  control and, 115
  forced, 113–115

future perspective and, 192
for motivation, 115
Cirque du Soleil, 43
claims
  of cause, 126–130
  of definition, 124–125
  of fact, 125–126
  of policy, 132–133
  types of, 123
  of value, 130–132
clichéd metaphors, fresh metaphors
    compared to clichéd, 152–155
clickbait, 89
cloned sheep, 25
cocaine, 252
code-script, 151–152
cognition, emotions and, 182
cognitive closure
  benefits of, 224
  knowledge construction and, 224
  neuroscience on, 224–227
  10 percent message and, 222
  transitions for, 222–227
cognitive flexibility, for metaphors,
    160–161
cognitive variables, in clichéd and fresh
    metaphors, 154
cognitive workload. *See* working memory
coherence, claim of cause and, 130
collected attention, collective attention
    compared to, 282
collective attention
  belongingness and, 292
  choice and, 297
  collected attention compared to, 282
  conformity and, 282, 287–288, 294–295
  credibility and confidence undermining,
      285
  interbrain synchrony and, 282–283
  meaning through, 282
  memory and, 281–282
  narcissists and, 292–294
  nostalgia and, 295–297

reliance on, 281
social brain hypothesis and, 291
social contagion and, 288–292
time and, 287–288
complexity
challenge and, 111, 113
cultural preferences for, 260–262
definition of, 258
design and, 265
elaboration and, 266–270
fractals and, 270–276
management of, 262–265
metaphors managing, 151
minimalism and, 276
of movie shots, 276
profluence and, 278
randomness compared to, 258
simplicity and, 257–258
visual search harnessing, 257–278
components, treated equally, 28
concentration meditation, 169
concrete concepts, metaphors linking
        abstract to, 149–150
confidence, collective attention and, 285
conflict, in design, 84
conformity
with agreeable partners, 288
collective attention and, 282, 287–288,
        294–295
nostalgia and, 295–297
personal experience counteracting,
        294–295
social contagion and, 288–292
social loafing and, 287
Connery, Sean, 189
conscientiousness, mind wandering and, 176
conscious fantasy, 168
consciousness, AI and, 124–125
consequences, for future perspective, 189
consistency
claim of cause and, 130
metaphor abuse compared to, 157–160
for planning, 200

context
in framing, 90
truth changing with, 120–122
continuous reinforcement, 236
contradiction, in provocative content, 85
contrast
adversative transitions and, 212
in design, 75
metaphors and, 148
texture and, 36
control, choice and, 115
convenience, content based on, 123
conventional metaphors, generating,
        159–160
Cope, David, 214
"copy and paste" technique, for corporate
        content, 28
corporate content. See also attention-
        grabbing content
challenge in, 111–113
convenience-based, 123
disembodied concepts in, 52
embodied cognition for, 51–54
forward referencing in, 89
frequency of movement and, 65–67
incentive salience for, 242
metaphors in, 139–141
mistakes in, 28
movement types for, 60–65
movie elements for, 63–65
neuroscience on metaphors in,
        152–161
perception of movement in, 59–60
perspective-taking for, 93
physical movement for, 54–59
priming ignored by, 28–29
repetition priming concerns for, 45
simplistic, 258
text and pictures in, 217–218
validation-based, 123
"corporate museums," 297
"correlation is not causation," 128
cravings, 235

creativity
affective priming and, 38–39
mind wandering and, 172, 175
credibility, collective attention and, 285
critical thinking
claims for, 123–133
evidence and, 123, 133–136
importance of, 119
scientific method and, 120
truth and, 120–123, 133
cultural preferences, for complexity, 260–262

D

daydreaming, mind wandering and, 168
decision-making, memory and, 7
default layouts, in PowerPoint, 218
definition, claim of, 124–125
Le Dejeuner sur l'herbe ("The Luncheon on
        the Grass"), 305
delivery, unusual, 72
design
AI-generated images and, 79
bazaar method compared to cathedral
        method in, 75, 76
"beige," 30, 31
complexity and, 265
conflict in, 84
contrast in, 75
empathy triggered by, 78
for future perspective, 192–193
hand-drawn illustrations in, 75–79
intensity levels of, 86–88
journey through, 79
provocative content with, 75–80
range of ideas in, 78
safe and unsafe options for, 80
straight edges eliminated in, 79–80
detailed thinking, 265
Deventer, Oskar van, 109
disembodied concepts, in corporate
        content, 52
dispositional boredom, 104
divided attention, 7

Dolly (cloned sheep), 25

domain knowledge, cognitive flexibility building, 161

dopamine, 104, 235, 241, 250, 252

dose-response relationships, claim of cause and, 128, 130

Duijf, Suna, 247

E

Eagles, 139

ECG (electrocardiogram) signals, 10, 11
  on boredom, 100–103
  on emotional circumplex, 100–101
  on engagement, 100–102
  eye tracking paired with, 101–102
  handwriting and, 56

EEG (electroencephalogram) signals, 11
  on boredom, 100–103
  on emotional circumplex, 100–101
  on engagement, 100–102
  eye tracking paired with, 101–102
  features of using, 10
  fractal properties of, 271–276
  handwriting and, 56
  ISC score and, 102
  variables studied with, 12

ego
  attention and, 17
  narcissists and, 292–294

elaborated metaphors, 150

elaboration, complexity and, 266–270

electrocardiogram signals. *See* ECG signals

electroencephalogram signals. *See* EEG signals

embodied cognition
  concept of, 49, 51
  for corporate content, 51–54
  frequency of movement and, 65–67
  handwriting and, 55–59
  movement types in corporate content and, 60–65
  perception of movement and, 59–60

physical movement and, 54–59
  rules and, 49, 51
  time and, 254
  virtual training sessions and, 54–55

emotional circumplex, 100–101

emotions
  affective priming and, 38–43
  attention and, 10
  cognition and, 182
  mood management and, 182–185
  movies and, 254
  negative and positive, 43
  nostalgia and, 297
  provocative content targeting, 74
  in test-taking, 109–111
  time and, 254

empathy, design triggering, 78

engagement
  brain synchronization and, 102
  challenge for, 109–113
  choice for, 113–116
  creating, 104–116
  defining, 100
  EEG and ECG signals on, 100–102
  eye tracking for, 101–102
  ISC score and, 102
  neuroscience of, 100–102
  variety for, 104–109

Entrapment, 189

environment, choice for, 116

environmental cues, habit and, 132

Epstein, Joseph, 104

Eureka moments, affective priming and, 41–42

everyday experience, metaphors for interpretation of, 145–147

"Everything" (Bublé), 155

evidence
  amount of, 134
  humility and, 136
  meaning attached to, 134–136
  from multiple sources, 134
  transparency and, 136

for truth, 123, 133
  types of, 133–134

exaggeration
  conflict and, 84
  contradiction and, 85
  examples of, 82–84
  in fashion, 80
  intensity levels of, 86–88
  literal interpretation for, 85

"Exhibition of Rejected Art" (*Salon des Refusés*), 305–309

expectancy disconfirmation, 70

experience. *See* personal experience

extended reality (XR), 54

extrapersonal motivation, 241

eye tracking, 10, 11
  for boredom and engagement, 101–102
  handwriting and, 56
  variables studied with, 12

F

face-to-face environment, attention in virtual environment compared to, 12, 13

facial coding, 11

fact, claim of, 125–126

"fade in," 60

fantasizing, 168

fashion, exaggeration in, 80

fatigue
  attention and, 16
  biometric sensors studying, 12
  Zoom, 65

F.C.U.K., 69

FD (fractal dimension), 271, 273

fear appeal, 87

feature integration, 7

feedback, for attention-grabbing content, 304

field of vision, 7, 10

filler words, transitions eliminating, 227

Fischer, Bobby, 69

fixation-related parameters, mind wandering and, 177–178

fixed interval schedule, 236

fixed ratio schedule, 236

focused attention, 7

forced choice, 113–115

forward referencing, 89

fractal dimension (FD), 271, 273

fractals
  complexity and, 270–276
  definition of, 270–271
  in EEG signals, 271–276
  examples of, 271
  movie shot complexity and, 276

framing
  cause-and-effect, 126–128
  for mood management, 182, 184, 185
  perspective-taking and, 90

frequency of change, variety and, 109

frequency of movement, 65–67

fresh metaphors, clichéd metaphors compared to clichéd, 152–155

Freud, Sigmund, 291

Frey, Glenn, 139

frontoparietal network, 160

future perspective
  anticipation for, 201–202
  consequences for, 189
  design for, 192–193
  intention setting for, 197–199
  metaphors and, 191–192
  past-oriented thinking compared to, 189–190
  planning for, 199–201
  prediction for, 193–197
  simulation for, 190–193
  strategies for, 190

futurism, 190

G

galvanic skin response. *See* GSR

Gauguin, Paul, 305

Gen Xers, sex appeal and, 244–245

goal setting
  intention setting compared to, 198
  mind wandering and, 180–182

goal-centered attention, 7

grabbing attention. *See* attention-grabbing content

GSR (galvanic skin response), 10, 11
  handwriting and, 56

guided action
  boredom and, 99–116
  critical thinking, 119–136
  guidelines for, 18, 19, 96, 163
  metaphors and, 139–161

guided tours, for temporal transitions, 207, 208

H

habit
  boredom and, 106
  claim of policy and, 132–133
  components of, 132

Hallmark Cards, 99

hand-drawn illustrations, in design, 75–79

handwriting, embodied cognition and, 55–59

Hangover, 93

hedonic adaptation, 240

Her, 211

HFD (Higuchi's fractal dimension), 273, 275

higher-order pleasures, 233, 246

Higuchi's fractal dimension (HFD), 273, 275

Hollywood movies. *See* movies

home improvement shows, 201

"Hotel California" (Eagles), 139

Huber, Max, 3

humility, evidence and, 136

humor, in framing, 90

Hyneman, Jamie, 119, 120

hyperbole, 80. *See also* exaggeration

hyperscanning, 252

I

Imagine Dragons, 294–295

imagined texture, 33

Impossible to Ignore (Simon), 7

incentive salience, 235
  for corporate content, 242
  features of, 242–244
  for rewards, 241–246
  sex appeal and, 244–246

incongruity, 70

information appeal, 87

inspirational keynotes, 198

intention setting, for future perspective, 197–199

interbrain synchrony, 282–283

intermittent reinforcement, 238

intermittent reward schedules, 236–240

Internet of Things (IoT), 29

intersubject correlation (ISC) score, 58, 102

introductory sales presentations, variety for, 106–109

introspection
  future perspective and, 189–202
  guidelines for, 18, 19, 164, 229
  mind wandering and, 167–186
  transitions and, 205–227

IoT (Internet of Things), 29

ISC (intersubject correlation) score, 58, 102

J

Jack Daniels, 295

Jeong, Ken, 93

Job Boredom Scale, 102

jokes, reframing and, 90

K

Kaku, Michio, 124–125

Kaplan, Sam, 2, 3

Kierkegaard, Søren, 102

Klee, Paul, 51, 79

knowledge construction, cognitive closure and, 224

Krasner, Lee, 278
Kurzweil, Ray, 211

L

language control, 51
Leader dimension of value, 132
learning, in rewards, 235–236
"less is more," 258
liking, in rewards, 235
Lodge, David, 150
"The Luncheon on the Grass" *(Le Dejeuner sur l'herbe)*, 305
Lynas, Mark, 25

M

MacKenzie, Gordon, 99
Malaysia, 189
Manet, Édouard, 305
Marshall, Barry, 309
The Masked Singer, 93
Matisse, Henri, 305
McEwan, Ian, 144
meaning
    causative transitions and, 214
    through collective attention, 282
    evidence and, 134–136
    in framing, 90
    metaphors for, 161
meaningful life, boredom and, 116
mechanoreceptors, 32
meditation, mind wandering and, 169
memory
    belongingness and, 292
    collective attention and, 281–282
    conformity, 282
    credibility and confidence undermining, 285
    decision-making and, 7
    elaboration and, 266, 268–270
    handwriting and, 56–59
    movement and, 61
    narcissists and distortions of, 292–294
    nostalgia and, 295–297

semantic priming and, 37–38
surprise building, 41
time and, 250
working, 12, 175, 178–180, 291
Le Mer moisturizing cream, 3
metaphors, 142–143
    for abstract concepts made concrete, 149–150
    cognitive flexibility for, 160–161
    complexity managed with, 151
    confusion from, 151–152
    consistency compared to abuse of, 157–160
    contrast and, 148
    in corporate content, 139–141
    definition of, 139
    elaborated, 150
    fresh compared to clichéd, 152–155
    future perspective and, 191–192
    generating novel and conventional, 159–160
    for meaning, 161
    mixed, 152, 155–157
    multiple original, 154
    neuroscience on corporate content and, 152–161
    perceived similarities and, 146–147
    sources in, 141
    specific concepts emphasized with, 148
    as stories, 144–145
    targets in, 141
    twists added to, 161
    for unique interpretation of everyday experience, 145–147
    for universal understanding of subjective experience, 144–145
millennials, sex appeal and, 244–245
mind wandering
    absorption and, 168–169
    allowances for, 186
    attention in, 169–170
    boredom relieved through, 172
    bring brain back from, 176–186

    conscientiousness and, 176
    creativity and, 172, 175
    dark side of, 175–176
    daydreaming and, 168
    defining, 168–170
    fixation-related parameters and, 177–178
    goal setting and, 180–182
    importance of addressing, 167
    measuring, 170–172
    meditation and, 169
    mood management and, 182–185
    neuroscience on, 170
    neuroticism and, 176
    openness and, 176–177
    perceptual load and, 177–180
    phubbing and, 167
    planning and, 168
    for problem-solving, 186
    rumination and, 168–169, 175
    stimulus-independent thoughts and, 168, 170
    task-unrelated thoughts and, 168, 169
    thought sampling method for, 172
    time perception and, 172
    transitions and, 205
    as ubiquitous, 168
    unintentional, 170
    upside of, 172–175
    working memory and, 175
    Zoom and, 177
mindfulness meditation, 169
Mini Cooper, 295
minimalism, complexity and, 276
mixed metaphors, 152, 155–157
Mohamad, Mahathir, 189
mood management, mind wandering and, 182–185
motivation
    biometric sensors studying, 12
    choice for, 115
    extrapersonal, 241
    incentive salience and, 235, 241–246
    peripersonal, 241

social rewards and, 250
in test-taking, 109–111
movement
control of, 51
corporate content and physical, 54–59
corporate content and types of, 60–65
frequency of, 65–67
in handwriting, 55–59
memory and, 61
in movie shots, 61–63
neuroscience and, 49
perception of, 59–60
perceptual priming and, 67
movies
complex shots in, 276
corporate content and elements of, 63–65
emotions and, 254
movement in, 61–63
shot duration in, 61, 63
story components in, 63
multiple dimensions, cognitive flexibility
and observing, 160–161
MythBusters, 119

N

narcissists, 292–294
negative emotions, affective priming with,
43
nerve receptors, 32
neuroleptics, 252
neuroscience
for attention-grabbing content, 10
of boredom, 99, 102–103
on cognitive closure, 224–227
on cultural preferences for complexity,
260–262
of engagement, 100–102
handwriting and, 56–59
interbrain synchrony and, 282–283
on metaphors in corporate content,
152–161
on mind wandering, 170
movement and, 49

on provocative content, 70
on repetition priming, 44–45
social load and, 291
synchronization and, 58, 102
on unstimulated state, 310
neuroticism, mind wandering and, 176
Niche Player dimension of value, 132
Nistor, Irina, 113
No. 5, 1948, 278
nociceptors, 32
nonconventional thinking, 265
norm violations, provocative content and,
69
nostalgia, collective attention and, 295–297
novel metaphors, generating, 159–160
novelty, surprise compared to, 39

O

observing multiple dimensions, cognitive
flexibility and, 160–161
off-task thinking, 167. *See also* mind
wandering
openness, mind wandering and, 176–177
opinions, claim of fact and, 125–126
opposite perspectives, in framing, 90
oral presentation transitions, 206
organized steps, for planning, 200
Ortega, Amancio, 200
outsourcing, corporate content, 28
over-the-top aesthetics, 72

P

Pascal, Blaise, 212
past-oriented thinking, future perspective
compared to, 189–190
Pen function, in PowerPoint, 60
perceived similarities, metaphors and,
146–147
perceived texture, 34
perception of movement, 59–60
perceptual load, mind wandering and,
177–180
perceptual load theory, 177

perceptual priming
for "beige" content, 30, 31
contrast and, 36
examples of, 34–36
movement and, 67
semantic priming compared to, 36
texture for, 30, 32–36
peripersonal motivation, 241
permanence, cognitive closure and, 224
personal experience
conformity counteracted with, 294–295
for planning, 200
perspective-taking
for corporate content, 93
definition of, 90
examples of, 91–92
framing, reframing and, 90
questions for, 93
phubbing, 167
physical movement
for corporate content, 54–59
handwriting and, 55–59
virtual training sessions and, 54–55
physical texture, 33
Physics of the Future (Kaku), 124–125
pictures and text, in transitions, 217–221
planning
audience participation for, 201
consistency for, 200
for future perspective, 199–201
mind wandering and, 168
organized steps for, 200
personal experience used in, 200
PlayStation, 69–70
pleasure. *See also* rewards
basic, 233
generating, 234–236
higher-order, 233, 246
points of view, in framing, 90
policy, claim of, 132–133
Pollock, Jackson, 271, 278
positive emotions, affective priming with,
43

positive words and images, priming with, 182

PowerPoint, 18, 20, 56–60
  default layouts in, 218
  frequency of movement and, 65–67
  movie elements for, 63–65
  Pen function in, 60
  straight edges eliminated in, 79–80

predictable behavior, prediction compared to, 197

prediction
  for future perspective, 193–197
  improving, 194
  predictable behavior compared to, 197
  process of, 193–194

present focus, for mood management, 185

Presley, Elvis, 295

previous/next, for temporal transitions, 207, 208

priming
  affective, 38–43
  benefits of, 46
  corporate content ignoring, 28–29
  definition of, 26
  for detecting differences, 25–26
  perceptual, 30–36, 67
  with positive words and images, 182
  repetition, 43–46
  semantic, 36–38
  steps for, 26, 27
  types of, 30–46

probabilities, truth and, 122

problem-solving, mind wandering for, 186

process, choice for, 116

profluence, complexity and, 278

Property Brothers, 201–202

provocative content
  aims of, 72
  clickbait and, 89
  conflict in, 84
  contradiction in, 85
  defining, 69
  with design, 75–80, 84

"don'ts" for, 74–75
  effectiveness of, 70–72
  elements of, 72
  emotional reactions and, 74
  exaggeration for, 80–88
  expectancy disconfirmation and, 70
  famous examples of, 69–70
  intensity levels of, 86–88
  neuroscience on, 70
  norm violations and, 69
  perspective-taking in, 90–93
  "punching down" and, 74
  referencing in, 89
  superficiality and, 74

"punching down," provocative content and, 74

R

randomness, complexity compared to, 258

range of ideas, in design, 78

Reagan, Ronald, 285

referencing, 89

reflection-worthy messages, claim of cause and, 126

reframing, 90

reinforcement theory, 236

rejection, attention-grabbing content and, 305–309

repetition priming
  Cirque du Soleil and, 43
  corporate content concerns with, 45
  neuroscience on, 44–45
  T3 principle and, 45–46

resistance to extinction, 238

retrospective focus, 185

return on attention (ROA), 18

reversible association, claim of cause and, 130

reward-behavior cycle, 236

rewards
  components of, 234–236
  habit and, 132
  incentive salience for, 241–246

intermittent schedules of, 236–240
  learning in, 235–236
  liking in, 235
  pleasure and, 233–236, 246
  social, 247–250
  time and, 250–254
  unpredictable, 238
  wanting in, 235

Reynolds, Dan, 294–295

rhetorical questions, for temporal transitions, 207

ROA (return on attention), 18

Romania, 281–282

Rosenthal, Barry, 4, 21

routines, habit and, 132

Rubik's Cube, 109

rumination, mind wandering and, 168–169, 175

rush slowly, for attention-grabbing content, 303

S

Saatchi & Saatchi, 218

salience network, 160

Salon des Refusés ("Exhibition of Rejected Art"), 305–309

Savage, Adam, 119, 120

Schitt's Creek, 70, 72

schizophrenia, 252

Schrödinger, Erwin, 151–152

scientific method, critical thinking and, 120

Sealife, 4

selective attention, 7

self-esteem, social acceptance and, 291

self-experimentation, for attention-grabbing content, 309

self-importance, 292

self-reports, bypassing, 10

semantic priming
  concept of, 36–37
  example of, 37–38
  memory and, 37–38
  perceptual priming compared to, 36

Sensation Seeking Scale, 102

sex appeal, incentive salience and, 244–246

Sexual Boredom Scale, 102

shock appeal, 87

Siffre, Michel, 309

silence, for attention-grabbing content, 310

silver lining, in framing, 90

similarities, metaphors and perceived, 146–147

simplicity, complexity and, 257–258

simplistic content, 258

simulation, for future perspective, 190–193

Sinatra, Frank, 295

"singularity," 211

sitting presentation, standing compared to, 67

situational boredom, 104

skydiving, boredom and, 99

sleep-deprived audiences, 16

social acceptance, self-esteem and, 291

social brain hypothesis, 291

social contagion, collective attention and, 288–292

social load, 291

social loafing, 287

social rewards, 247–250

solitude, for attention-grabbing content, 310

somatosensory system, texture and, 32

sources, in metaphors, 141

spatial attention, 7

speeding up perception of time, 252

standing presentation, sitting compared to, 67

State Farm Insurance, 295

statistical evidence, 133–134

status quo bias, 16

stimulus-independent thoughts, mind wandering and, 168, 170

stories
  causative transitions with, 214
  metaphors as, 144–145
  movies and components of, 63

storyboards, transitions and, 215–217

Stötter, Johannes, 4

straight edges, design eliminating, 79–80

strategic monitoring, aging and, 250

subjective experience, metaphors and, 144–145

superficiality, provocative content and, 74

surprise
  affective priming and, 39–41
  expectancy disconfirmation and, 70
  memories built from, 41
  novelty compared to, 39

sustained attention, 7

switching frames, 90

synchronization, neuroscience and, 58, 102

T

T3 principle, repetition priming and, 45–46

targets, in metaphors, 141

task-unrelated thoughts, mind wandering and, 168, 169

temporal relationships, claim of cause and, 128

temporal transitions, 207–208

10 percent message, transitions and, 222

testimonial evidence, 133–134

test-taking, challenge in, 109–111

text and pictures, in transitions, 217–221

texture
  contrast and, 36
  definition of, 32
  examples of, 34–36
  imagined, 33
  implementing, 34
  perceived, 34
  perceptual priming using, 30, 32–36
  physical, 33
  somatosensory experience of, 32

thermoreceptors, 32

Thinks (Lodge), 150

thought sampling method, for mind wandering, 172

time
  attention and, 250
  collective attention and, 287–288
  embodied cognition and, 254
  emotions and, 254
  memory and, 250
  mind wandering and perception of, 172
  rewards and, 250–254
  speeding up perception of, 252
  truth changing with, 120–122

Tinnitus Association, 218

transitions
  additive, 209–211
  adversative, 211–213
  associations built through, 215
  awkward, 227
  benefits of, 206
  causative, 214–215
  for cognitive closure, 222–227
  cognitive flexibility and, 160
  filler words eliminated for, 227
  mind wandering and, 205
  in oral presentations, 206
  practicing, 227
  storyboards and, 215–217
  temporal, 207–208
  text and pictures in, 217–221
  types of, 206–215
  in written presentations, 206

transitivity, in framing, 90

transparency, evidence and, 136

truth. See also claims
  definition of, 120
  evidence for, 123, 133
  probabilities and, 122
  time and context changing, 120–122

Turner, Ike and Tina, 297

The Twilight Zone, 139

U

unexpected vocabulary, 72

unintentional mind wandering, 170

universal understanding, metaphors for, 144–145

unpredictable rewards, 238

unstimulated state, neuroscience on, 310

unusual delivery, 72

Unusual Uses Test (UUT), 172

updating beliefs, cognitive flexibility and, 160

urgency, cognitive closure and, 224

UUT (Unusual Uses Test), 172

V

valence
    definition of, 12, 100
    in emotional circumplex, 100–101
    fluctuation of, 103

validation, content based on, 123

value, claim of, 130–132

van Gogh, Vincent, 305

variable ratio schedule, 238

variety
    for directing attention, 104
    examples of utilizing, 104–106
    frequency of change and, 109
    habituation fought with, 106
    for introductory sales presentations, 106–109
    of message types, 109

virtual environment.
        See also Zoom
    attention in face-to-face environment
        compared to, 12, 13
    movement in, 67
    sitting compared to standing
        presentation in, 67

virtual reality (VR), 54

virtual training sessions, 54–55

vision, field of, 7, 10

Visionary dimension of value, 132

visual search
    collective attention and, 281–297
    complexity and, 257–278
    definition of, 7
    guidelines for, 18, 19, 230, 299
    rewards and, 233–254

Vogue, 309

VR (virtual reality), 54

W

wanting, in rewards, 235

Warwick, Kevin, 309

working memory (cognitive workload)
    biometric sensors studying, 12
    mind wandering and, 175
    perceptual load and, 178–180
    social load and, 291

written presentation transitions, 206

X

XR (extended reality), 54

Z

Zagat, 132

Zappa, Frank, 194

Zara, 200

zoning out, 168

Zoom, 56, 60
    fatigue, 65
    frequency of movement and, 65–67
    mind wandering and, 177
    movie elements for, 63–65
    sitting compared to standing for, 67

ABOUT THE AUTHOR

Carmen Simon, PhD, Chief Science Officer at Corporate Visions, is a Silicon Valley entrepreneur and cognitive neuroscientist, addressing a groundbreaking approach to creating attention-grabbing, memorable, and actionable messages—using the latest in brain science. Dr. Simon also teaches at Stanford University and speaks frequently on the importance of using neuroscience to understand the buyer's brain when crafting corporate communication. Her practical principles have been instrumental in empowering some of America's most renowned brands, including UPS, Deloitte, Amazon, ADP, Microsoft, AT&T, Boston Scientific, Cisco, ESPN, SAP, Salesforce, and more.

Getting attention is an everyday challenge for business professionals, especially when distractions abound, pulling eyes and ears away just as your message tries to gain focus. It's like trying to recite poetry in the midst of a rock concert. Your voice needs to rise above—but how? How do you craft a message so magnetic that it prompts the viewer to look, to stay, and to remember?

In *Made You Look*, Dr. Carmen Simon does not just present a collection of facts and figures. She offers practical guidelines that enable you to capture your audience's gaze and hold it long enough to leave an indelible mark. After all, in the age of fleeting glances, a prolonged look is the most profound compliment.